Attachment-Focused Treatment for Child Adolescents

Attachment-Focused Trauma Treatment for Children and Adolescents brings together two powerful treatment directions that exponentially expand the knowledge and skills available to child and adolescent trauma therapists. The book provides theoretical knowledge, clinical approaches, and specific, detailed techniques that clinicians will find indispensable in the treatment of the most challenging and high-risk young trauma victims. Also included are case studies, developed from over three decades of experience, that show the reader how to use the techniques in real-life settings. The treatment approach described here is flexible enough to adapt to real clients in the real world, regardless of trauma and attachment histories, family and living situations, or difficulties engaging in supportive therapeutic relationships. Clear and cohesive, the model presented here allows room for the individuality and approach of each therapist so that the therapeutic relationship can evolve in a genuine and unique way. An appendix of photocopiable worksheets gives interactive tools for therapists to immediately use with clients.

Niki Gomez-Perales, MSW, RSW, has over twenty-five years' experience working with children and adolescents impacted by complex trauma and attachment. She is a child and adolescent therapist in Hamilton, Ontario, and is an active member of the International Society for the Study of Trauma and Dissociation (ISST-D).

Attachment-Focused Trauma Treatment for Children and Adolescents

Phase-Oriented Strategies for Addressing Complex Trauma Disorders

Niki Gomez-Perales

Routledge
Taylor & Francis Group
NEW YORK AND LONDON

First published 2015
by Routledge
711 Third Avenue, New York, NY 10017

and by Routledge
27 Church Road, Hove, East Sussex BN3 2FA

Routledge is an imprint of the Taylor & Francis Group, an informa business

Library of Congress Cataloging-in-Publication Data
Gomez-Perales, Niki.
Attachment-focused trauma treatment for children and adolescents : phase-oriented strategies for addressing complex trauma disorders / by Niki Gomez-Perales.—1 Edition.
pages cm
Includes bibliographical references and index.
1. Attachment behavior in children. 2. Attachment behavior in adolescence. I. Title.
RJ507.A77G66 2016
618.92'89—dc23
2014049067

ISBN: 978-1-138-80005-2 (hbk)
ISBN: 978-1-138-80008-3 (pbk)
ISBN: 978-1-315-75565-6 (ebk)

Typeset in Baskerville
by Apex CoVantage, LLC

Printed and bound by CPI Group (UK) Ltd, Croydon, CR0 4YY

Contents

Acknowledgments

I first want to thank my family for their endless patience as I sacrificed so much of my time and energy during the long process of writing this book. We had no idea at the beginning what this last year was going to bring, or just how difficult it would be to keep this going. Brian and Liam, you have been incredibly generous with my time and with your own, and I am so grateful to have you both in my life. I want to thank my sister Lia for picking up so many burdens and responsibilities. You made this possible. My mother, Helen Gomez-Perales, provided boundless enthusiasm, excitement and support, not just this year, but always. I want to thank my late father for passing on his determined beliefs in social justice and encouraging me to follow in his footsteps. I want to thank Juan for believing in me and encouraging me, and my late grandmother, Natalia Kohuska, for teaching me that anything can be accomplished and nothing is out of reach if you are stubborn enough. Lisa, you have taught me more about parenting, attachment and relationships than you can ever know. I am lucky to have you in my life.

I have been lucky to be surrounded by supportive, caring colleagues who have alternately cheered me on and challenged me to learn more. Hillary Meggison, Jennifer Boshis, Karen Timmerman, Van Vu, Margarita Rabinovitch, Danielle Clement, Louise Oke, Dina Bednar and Geri VanEngen have contributed by teaching me, questioning me, challenging me and encouraging me. I want to thank Gord Greenway for believing in me when others didn't, and Kathy de Jong for standing up for me and putting up with me. I particularly want to thank Diane Ribbins for being who she is and doing all the things she has done to support and sometimes save me over the past twenty years. This book would not exist without any of you.

I owe a debt of gratitude to the members of the Hamilton Dissociative Disorders Discussion Group, particularly Marilyn Korzekwa, David Cree, Susan Wortman and Debbie Davis. I have learned so much from the International Society for the Study of Trauma and Dissociation, particularly the wonderful members of the Child and Adolescent Committee. Dr. David Benner was my first teacher on dissociative disorders, and introduced me to the ISST-D.

There are numerous other personal supports and inspirations that deserve credit. Heather Woods, Monica Stec, Tim Gordon and Stan Donovan stand out as friends and supporters. Stan, I wish you were here for this! I will always be grateful to Ailish, Brittany and Nick for everything you have given me and everything you have done to support me. Finally I want to thank all of my young clients and the adults who have worked to support them. You have been my true teachers, and you are a constant source of inspiration and hope. It is impossible not to believe in a better world when privileged to witness and be part of such amazing stories.

The cases written about in this book are a compilation of thirty years of experience. Most are fictionalised accounts in order to respect the stories and protect the privacy of the many children, adolescents and adults I have worked with over the past three decades.

Introduction

Looking back over thirty years in the fields of child welfare and children's mental health, I am astounded by how much I've learned. It would be an easy mistake to assume that through those years of learning and exploring, I had been absorbing knowledge that was already there. It's a bit of a shock to look back and realise that I entered the cusp of a new and changing world. As a student I assumed that my teachers knew things; that I would learn the things that they knew, and then I would also know things. Of course, it hasn't been like that at all, and that has made this process of learning so much more dynamic and exciting, and also scary. I entered into a world where sexual abuse was considered rare and physical abuse was almost always considered to be well-meaning discipline gone wrong. As professionals, we knew that there were "extreme" situations out there, but we didn't expect to see them. A judge once asked me to leave his courtroom for spouting "unthinkable conspiracy theories" while presenting evidence. I had suggested that the child had been abused by her father and grandfather, and that her grandmother had been aware of it. When I first started in child welfare, the intake unit I was part of had eight staff members. The current intake department in the same agency is now larger than the agency itself was at the time.

I suppose the point of these ramblings is that it feels almost like we have been making this up as we go along. I suspect that this is what most innovation feels like. Yes, there are many brilliant teachers out there who have a lot of knowledge, and from whom I have learned an incredible amount. They are to be applauded for their courage in creating responses as they have found what so many people considered to be unthinkable. I am in no way minimising the incredible body of knowledge that exists in this field. It is new knowledge, forged of necessity, researched out of a need to have solutions, and worked out in collaboration with trauma survivors who were determined to be heard, understood and helped. I suspect that this was much more challenging than mastering what others know. We owe these teachers a great debt.

It seems to me that as we have struggled to figure out what we know and to create what we don't, a divide has developed between trauma therapy and children's trauma therapy. We come from two different directions, each with its own histories and traditions—children's therapists who have discovered trauma work, and trauma therapists who have begun working with children. We've met in the middle, but haven't gotten to know each other very well. Coming from a child welfare and children's mental health background, the training and practices I have been most exposed to arise from developmental models and child welfare models. More recently, attachment work has entered the picture, providing more of a psychodynamic framework. Overall, the focus is either on treating children who happen to have been traumatised, or on treating discrete traumatic events and relationships. We do individual therapy, family therapy, dyadic treatment, trauma impact work and trauma-focused cognitive behavioral therapy (CBT). We treat the active symptoms, the behaviour and the immediate impact. The concept of complex trauma disorders, dissociative trauma disorders and phase-oriented psychotherapy is often unknown or undiscussed. Most of what we do is phase one psychotherapy. On the other hand, many therapists who are treating children using a complex trauma model, or a phase-oriented model, seem to be treating children as individuals, without directly and purposefully working within the systemic, the dyadic, the attachment relationships and the here and now. They are treating the internal impact of trauma on the child without working with the child's context.

As the field of trauma therapy develops we are privileged with new research and knowledge about the developmental and neurological impact of both trauma and disrupted attachment relationships. This new knowledge provides us with insights into the treatment needs of both traumatised children and traumatised adults. It's an opportunity to bring together the knowledge from both areas, in a way that can help us apply decades of knowledge about treating adults with complex trauma issues in developing a synthesised and unified model for treating children.

It is my hope in this book to begin the combining of two very important models: phase-oriented psychotherapy, which has been the predominant approach taken in the treatment of complex trauma in adult survivors of childhood abuse, and attachment-informed psychotherapy, which is rapidly becoming the predominant approach in the treatment of children with complex trauma histories. There are many skilled therapists in both fields, and we have been informed by one another's knowledge, research and experience for many years. We use many of the same techniques, and base our work on much of the same research. How can we bring both models together in a way that works, in the therapy room, in the real world, with real children and their families? It will take insight and flexibility, but the results so far seem to be worth the effort.

1 Complex Trauma and Dissociation in Children and Adolescents

I first met Terra when she was nine. A mature and well-spoken girl, she was brought by her paternal grandmother, Janet, a witty, straight-spoken woman in her sixties. There was an evident closeness between them, broken at times by bickering that ranged from playful teasing to sarcastic anger. At its worst Terra became physically aggressive and Janet would be hurt, angry and critical. Terra had been abused and neglected by her drug-addicted mother. Her father lived with his parents, who gained custody of her when she was three. When Terra was six, her father was shot and killed. A month later, her grandfather died of a heart attack in front of her. Janet put her own grief for her husband and son aside, and focused on caring for her young granddaughter. The two of them managed well, until two years later, when Terra was kidnapped by her mother on an access visit. She was returned by the police, unharmed, but terrified that her mother would come back for her. Shortly after that Terra came for therapy. She and her grandmother had moved to our city hoping that Terra would feel safe, but she remained terrified and angry. She refused to go to school, and had missed several months of grade four. Her grandmother was doing her best to homeschool her, but Terra was angry, oppositional and aggressive. When angry, she would "turn into" a cat—backing into a corner, arching her back and hissing and scratching at anyone who approached her. She had frequent nightmares and refused to sleep by herself. She was alternately dependent on the family pets, and rejecting and mean to them.

I have been part of a "complex trauma" team since its inception eight years ago, and since then we have struggled with what defines "complex trauma." We have arrived at an understanding that a situation of complex trauma is one in which the child or adolescent has experienced either chronic or multiple traumas combined with disrupted attachment relationships, with or without dissociative features. What this looks like in the room varies from child to child and family to family. Many of these children, like Terra, are living with a grandparent or extended family member. This often means that, as for Janet, the trauma that has impacted the child has been close to home for the caregiver. We work with a lot of children in care, generally either Crown Wards (wards of the state in the Canadian system) or on their way to becoming Crown Wards. These are children who have come into and remained in care due to chronic and unresolved child protection issues. Sometimes they have been removed from and returned to their family of origin repeatedly over several years. Many of them have a history of neglect, abandonment, exposure to addictions and violence, and physical, sexual and emotional abuse. Some of these young people are in long-term foster placements, and others have had multiple placements in foster homes and group homes. There is sometimes institutional trauma, with multiple placement breakdowns, moves, instability, and sometimes abuse and rejection within foster or group homes. Sometimes separation from family is permanent, and sometimes there are attempts being made to reintegrate these children into families where there has been trauma in the past. We work with many children who are struggling in adoptive placements, both local and international adoptions. Sometimes adolescents self-refer after the age of sixteen, when we are no longer mandated to report if they have been abused. These children may be living in the home in which they were abused, or with relatives, friends or on their own. They often have limited support and unstable living situations. Some of the children and adolescents we see have had a long history of chronic physical and sexual abuse; some have complicated, frightening and painful medical histories; some come with supportive foster parents, adoptive parents or family members; some come with families in crisis, and some come on their own. In other words, each child, family and situation is different.

Complex trauma disorders include but are not limited to the dissociative disorders. They also include those referred to as developmental trauma disorders,[1] attachment disorders and some forms of post-traumatic stress disorder (PTSD). Many of the young people I see are not referred for treatment of trauma. They are referred for behavioural and emotional concerns that haven't been connected by the child or family to the trauma history. Many children who present for anxiety, depression, self-harm, suicidality, anger, school refusal and oppositional behaviours are soon found to have complex trauma histories and related symptoms.

What does this mean for the child? If we each think about who we are and how we became who we are, we get a sense of how much of our identity and worldview is impacted by our lives and relationships. Through the next several chapters, this book will look at research, literature, theory and cases to shed light on the known and suspected impact of early childhood trauma and disrupted attachment. Formal knowledge aside, it is empathic connection to their internal reality that allows for therapeutic relationships and the negotiation of the minefield of attachment and trauma treatment when working with children who have no reason to trust us or to believe in a positive future. Sometimes they are therapy veterans. When they engage well and grow and learn from the experience, children often say that the difference is having found a therapist who "got them." I hope these next chapters are mostly about how we become therapists who "get" them.

Like Terra, many of the children that come to my office have been taught, fairly consistently through their earliest years, that adults are dangerous, that authority is selfish and that rules are in place not for the good or safety of children or the powerless, but for the convenience and ease of adults and the powerful. They learn that their own needs for food, safety, care and attention are at best unimportant and likely to be ignored, and at worse, are selfish, greedy, and make them worthy of abuse and rejection. Rather than learning that they are wonderful, lovable and delightful, they learn to experience themselves as bad, greedy and selfish. The act of crying when frightened, hungry or wet may at times bring care, but other times rejection, anger or abuse. Responses are unpredictable, although they might learn that responses depend on how good they are at pleasing the adults around them. Older children may show a good understanding of rules and expectations. Their understanding and surface compliance with rules, along with their secretive noncompliance, their covering up their misdeeds and lying about them, is interpreted by well-meaning adults as badness and manipulation. What gets missed is the deep knowing that these children have that these rules are not there for their protection or safety, they are there for their oppression and control. They have an internalised view of "every man for himself." When these children are placed in safer homes, whether as young children or as older ones, they maintain this sense of themselves and the world. They may come to know and understand the rules, but unless their internal experience is directly addressed, they will not come to realise or believe that these rules are for their protection and safety. They experience themselves as "other" to the group. I refer to "safer" rather than "safe" homes. There is no home that is completely safe, and all adults are human and capable of mistakes, anger and negative responses. As children generally see things in black and white, and as these children absolutely see the world this way, they interpret every angry word, every consequence and every punishment as proof that they don't belong and that they are bad and not deserving of love. They experience every positive interaction as an attempt to trick them or to get them to comply. When they have dissociated parts, this adds to the confusion even more, as different parts may understand and internalise different realities. A child who seems to make a good and secure transition to a new home or family may have parts that do not know or recognise the new parents.[2] As these children have difficulty understanding grey areas, they may be unable to tolerate the negatives, and need to compartmentalise normal negative experiences. This can lead to there being a part of the child who feels safe and connected to their new parents, who idealises them and has no awareness of ever having been consequenced, grounded or in trouble, and another part whose only experience of the parent is consequence, grounding and being in trouble.

A challenge to dyadic work with these children is the need to form a solid alliance with both the child and the adult, even though they may experience their sides as opposing at the beginning of treatment. This problem will be discussed in detail in the chapters on phase one work. It's important to note that many of the adults who are caring for these children may also have trauma and trust issues. This is not only the case with biologically related caregivers. We can't assume that adoptive parents, foster parents and even group home staff don't have difficulties with trust and relationships. Everyone has a history, and caring for a traumatised child can be traumatic in itself. We need to assume that the challenges of caring for a child who presents as confusing, defiant, explosive, unresponsive or unpredictably alternating between loving and rejecting take their toll on even the most committed and confident adult.

Trauma, Attachment and Dissociation

There are many terms used to describe the experiences that affect the children we work with. Some are used either interchangeably or to refer to very slightly different situations. Some are used differently by different authors or groups. I will briefly define how I will use these terms in this book.

Trauma—The DSM V defines "a traumatic stressor" as:

> Exposure to actual or threatened death, serious injury, or sexual violence . . . either through directly experiencing, witnessing in person, or learning that the traumatic events happened to a close family member or close friend. Experiencing repeated or extreme exposure to aversive details of the traumatic events (e.g. for first responders or police).[3]

As this book is clinical in nature, and as the experiences in question are frequently ones which occurred early in the children's experience, it makes more sense to use a definition which fits within the child's experiences. For this reason I use trauma to refer to extreme stressors which have overwhelmed the child or adolescent's ability to cope. The experiences which may have very significant traumatic impact on children may not meet the definition as laid out in the DSM V. It is possible for a young child to experience extreme, overwhelming terror in situations in which the child is not in immediate danger or their life is not actually threatened. It is also possible for a young child to experience events which we would consider traumatic, but the child is not aware of the danger and so the child's resources are not overwhelmed. It is often the case that we do not know the nature or details of the trauma which has impacted the child.

Complex Trauma—A combination of chronic or multiple traumas combined with disruption of or trauma within the primary attachment relationship or relationships. Lanius et al.[4] describes complex trauma as "repeated interpersonal trauma occurring during crucial developmental periods."

Relational Trauma—Trauma which occurs within a close relationship which disrupts the victim's experience of trust and attachment relationships. Children are dependent on their caregivers for survival. This means that a caregiver does not need to be abusive or dangerous for a child to experience trauma. A caregiver's sudden absence, loss or sudden or ongoing emotional unavailability can result in real terror for a child.[5,6]

Betrayal Trauma—Trauma which includes the betrayal or experienced betrayal by a person in a position of trust or expected trust.

Attachment Trauma—Similar to relational trauma.

Disrupted Attachment—An interruption in the development of primary attachment relationships, either by separation of the child from their primary attachment figure or by some form of emotional unavailability of the attachment figure resulting in their inability to form an attachment with the child.

Dissociation—According to the International Society for the Study of Trauma and Dissociation,[7] "Dissociation is a word that is used to describe the disconnection or lack of connection between things usually associated with each other. Dissociated experiences are not integrated into the usual sense of self, resulting in discontinuities in conscious awareness."[8,9,10,11,12,13,14,15,16,17]

> In severe forms of dissociation, disconnection occurs in the usually integrated functions of consciousness, memory, identity or perception. For example, someone may think about an event that was tremendously upsetting yet have no feelings about it. Clinically, this is termed emotional numbing, one of the hallmarks of post-traumatic stress disorder. Dissociation is a psychological process commonly found in persons seeking mental health treatment.[18]

Dissociative Symptoms—The term "dissociative symptoms" refers to nonintentional or nonconsciously intentional dissociation, often resulting from traumatic experience. There are different types of dissociative symptoms, each involving some form of experiential disconnection. These symptoms range from mild to severe. The following definitions are taken from the International Society for the Study of Trauma and Dissociation website and used with permission.[19]

Depersonalisation—The sense of being detached from, or "not in" one's body. This is what is often referred to as an "out-of-body" experience. However, some people report rather profound alienation from their bodies, a sense that they do not recognize themselves in the mirror, recognize their face, or simply feel not "connected" to their bodies in ways which are challenging to articulate.[20,21,22,23,24,25]

Derealisation—The sense of the world not being real. Some people say the world looks phony, foggy, far away, or as if seen through a veil. Some people describe seeing the world as if they are detached, or as if they were watching a movie.[26]

Dissociative Amnesia—Amnesia refers to the inability to recall important personal information that is so extensive that it is not due to ordinary forgetfulness. Most of the amnesias typical of dissociative disorders are not of the classic fugue variety, where people travel long distances, and suddenly become alert, disoriented as to where they are and how they got there. Rather, the amnesias are often an important event that is forgotten, such as abuse, a troubling incident, or a block of time, from minutes to years. More typically, there are micro-amnesias where the discussion engaged in is not remembered, or the content of a conversation is forgotten from one moment to the next. Some people report that these kinds of experiences often leave them scrambling to figure out what was being discussed. Meanwhile, they try not to let the person with whom they are talking realize they haven't a clue as to what was just said.[27,28,29]

Identity Alteration and Identity Confusion—Identity confusion is a sense of confusion about who a person is. An example of identity confusion is when a person sometimes feels a thrill while engaged in an activity (e.g., reckless driving, drug use) which at other times would be repugnant. Identity alteration is the sense of being markedly different from another part of oneself. This can be unnerving to clinicians. A person may shift into an alternate personality, become confused, and demand of the clinician, "Who the dickens are you, and what am I doing here?" In addition to these observable changes, the person may experience distortions in time, place and situation. For example, in the course of an initial discovery of the experience of identity alteration, a person might incorrectly believe they were five years old, in their childhood home and not the therapist's office, and expecting a deceased person whom they fear to appear at any moment.

More frequently, subtler forms of identity alteration can be observed when a person uses different voice tones, range of language, or facial expressions. These may be associated with a change in the patient's world view. For example, during a discussion about fear, a client may initially feel young, vulnerable and frightened, followed by a sudden shift to feeling hostile and callous. The person may express confusion about their feelings and perceptions, or may have difficulty remembering what they have just said, even though they do not claim to be a different person or have a different name. The patient may be able to confirm the experience of identity alteration, but often the part of the self that presents for therapy is not aware of the existence of dissociated self-states. If identity alteration is suspected, it may be confirmed by observation of amnesia for behavior and distinct changes in affect, speech patterns, demeanor and body language, and relationship to the therapist. The therapist can gently help the patient become aware of these changes.[30,31,32,33]

Impacts of Complex Trauma on the Child Victim

As complex trauma most often occurs within the child's primary attachment relationship, it generally has a very early onset. Although not always the case, it isn't unusual for the children we are working with to have never experienced safe attachment and security. Children who have been born into chaotic, dysfunctional or abusive homes may have experienced trauma and neglect rather than safety, security and nurturing. Other children may have experienced significant stability and safety early, before they and their family experienced some sudden loss, illness, disaster or change which precipitated a change in the environment. When assessing complex trauma, it's important, when possible, to explore the onset of the trauma and the point at which attachment was disrupted.

The impact of complex trauma on children is pervasive. It is not a matter of symptoms of the trauma itself; trauma has impact, but when we are talking about young children traumatised within their attachment system, we also consider the disruption of the elements of normal, healthy development. Cook et al.[34] identify seven developmental domains which can be impacted by complex trauma in children. These are attachment, biology, affect regulation, dissociation, behavioural control, cognition and self-concept. These areas are interrelated, being both impacted by and impacting on each other. To these seven domains, I would add two more—worldview and social development. These nine domains of development are not discrete. They are interdependent on each other and there is no defining boundary between them. Each impacts on and is impacted by the others.

Dissociation is a complex cluster of symptoms which when present is involved in all domains. Dissociation and its presentation can be subtle or blatant. It can be evident in terms of a child's experiences, behaviours and communications, or it can be hidden. Some child therapists view dissociation as inevitable in childhood trauma, as something which must always be addressed specifically and intentionally. Others view dissociation as a group of possible symptoms or coping styles that will resolve through the course of good trauma treatment. I don't feel I can comment on whether or not dissociation is always present, or always a major factor, but my experience is that when significant dissociation is present and not identified and addressed, treatment is less effective, and the child will continue to struggle. These findings seem to be borne out by current research.

Attachment

Children whose early relationships are disrupted experience a number of difficulties relating to attachment. Some may find it difficult to rely on adults for help, or to recognise adults as having valid authority or guidance. Others may look to have security and nurturing needs met elsewhere, which can lead to their being socially inappropriate and vulnerable to exploitation. Some may be less able to explore their world, and more likely to see the world as unsafe and unpredictable. As these children grow older they experience more social difficulties, they find it harder to experience empathy and they react to others with mistrust.

Amie was referred for counselling as a result of "an obsessive" relationship with an educational assistant at her school. Amie had few friends and was socially isolated. She engaged in frequent self-harm. This assistant became involved by offering Amie extra support and assistance. Amie became dependent on her. She began writing her daily letters about sad and lonely feelings, and eventually about her suicidal thoughts. Amie asked the aid if she would be her mother. This precipitated the therapy referral. Following the referral, Amie came for family counselling with her father and older sister, who were most concerned about her anger outbursts. Her parents had separated and she lived with her father and three sisters. Amie presented as closed and uninterested during family sessions. The family stopped coming. Amie told the male family therapist that she would be willing to see a female therapist individually, and he asked if I would work with her. I first met with Amie shortly before her sixteenth birthday. After reviewing rules around confidentiality, which specified that any child protection concerns involving children under the age of sixteen were required by law to be reported to child welfare, she left, announcing she would return when she was sixteen. She did return, a few days after her sixteenth birthday. During her first appointment after turning sixteen she began to disclose a history involving profound neglect, emotional abuse and sexual exploitation by her mother. Over her course of therapy Amie struggled with alternating feelings of desperately needing connection and difficulties in trusting others. She saw her need for connection as shameful and weak.

Dissociation can add complication to the picture of an attachment-disordered child. It is not unusual for a child to have some parts that want attachment, some that will achieve attachment with new caregivers, and others that are mistrustful and dismissive of attachment needs. In situations involving caregiver abuse it is common to have one or more parts that are aligned with the abusive caregiver and may not be aware of the abuse, and another part that is terrified of the caregiver and remembers only abuse. There may also be parts that identify with the abusive caregiver and look for strength in abusive or violent behaviours. These conflicting loyalties can lead to complications in building treatment relationships. It is necessary to assume that whether or not a young person is displaying dissociative symptoms, their alliances with their family are likely to be conflicted, multilayered and unclear.

Biology

Biological development can be compromised in many ways. Medical issues can arise directly from neglect or physical and sexual injury. Beth, twenty-one, has a chronic and painful tendon condition believed to be caused by repeated trauma combined with a lack of exercise from spending long periods of time confined to her room; back, hip and jaw pain resulting from multiple early injuries; and cervical cancer stemming from human papillomavirus (a sexually transmitted disease) diagnosed at age twelve.

Prenatal and neonatal environmental impacts can lead to long-term developmental issues. Many of the children we work with have had in-utero exposure to drugs, alcohol and tobacco, poor prenatal care and nutrition, and exposure to high levels of maternal stress hormones during incidences of domestic violence. Early malnutrition and poor early medical and dental care also impact on development.

Some of the children we work with are small, and stay well below the growth curve for their age even when their nutritional needs are being met. In my early days in child welfare "nonmedical failure to thrive" was considered a possible marker that a child was being maltreated. Sophie, discussed in some detail in later chapters, looks much younger than her thirteen years. Adopted at age three, she has been in her home for ten years. She is chronically hyperaroused. During the first three months that Sophie engaged in attachment-focused therapy, with a specific goal of increasing feelings of safety and helping her to rely on her adoptive parents to help regulate her chronically hyperaroused affective states, she gained ten pounds. This growth has continued as her hyperarousal has decreased.

Child maltreatment is now understood to affect development in less direct ways as well. There is increasing evidence that childhood trauma impacts long-term health outcomes. The Adverse Childhood Experiences Study, conducted at Kaiser Permanente between 1995 and 1997, explores links between early childhood trauma and long-term health. This study has found "a strong graded relationship between the breadth of exposure to abuse or household dysfunction during childhood and multiple risk factors for several of the leading causes of death in adults."[35] This study has identified strong correlations between childhood exposure to trauma and many different types of adult illness. Some of these are connected to lifestyle issues which are sequelae of early trauma, and others may be related to the chronic stress.

There is a growing body of research connecting childhood experience to neurological development and early trauma to impairments in neurological development. The impact of early trauma and disrupted attachment on neurobiological development is explored in more detail in Chapter 2. There are a number of neurologically based conditions which are seen often in children with early trauma histories. Attention deficit hyperactivity disorder (ADHD) is a diagnosis based on symptoms. ADHD is a genetic predisposition, and many children who have ADHD have no trauma history. The symptoms of ADHD, however—short attention span, difficulty focusing, and poor impulse control—are symptoms seen frequently in children who have been exposed to trauma or who have not had secure attachment relationships. Sensory processing disorders are known to affect five to sixteen percent of school-age children.[36] Many children with complex trauma histories have difficulties with managing and integrating sensory experiences. Learning disabilities, language disorders,[37] depression, anxiety disorders and other difficulties with their roots in neurological functioning are all common in traumatised children. This is not to say that all or even most childhood disorders are caused by early trauma. Many children experience neurological and mental health difficulties without having experienced trauma. Given, however, how widespread the impact of early experience is on neurological development, it seems credible to say that complex trauma could be one pathway to the development of many common children's disorders.

Dissociation may be connected to the biological impacts of complex trauma. Current neurological theory suggests that early trauma and lack of secure attachment affect integration within the brain itself, leading to difficulty in integrating sensory, cognitive and affective material, and decreased communication between the left and right hemisphere.[38,39,40,41] This lack of neurological integration seems to mirror the lack of experiential integration in children with dissociative disorders. Dissociation also negatively impacts on a child's ability to have adequate sensory awareness or body connectivity. I have met many children who struggle to know when they are hungry, and who have difficulties with incontinence because they are not aware of their body signals. Children with dissociative disorders often suffer from somatic complaints including headaches, stomach aches, and aches and pains. They feel physically ill more often, and struggle with self-care and regular medical and dental care.

Affect Regulation

Affect regulation is a complex process impacted by the neurological, emotional and behavioural development of the child. Difficulties with affect regulation are at the core of many referrals to children's mental health programs. Affect regulation is the ability to experience, identify and manage one's own affective experiences. The earliest lessons in affect regulation occur when an infant, upset, hungry or frightened, cries. In a good enough attachment setting a caring adult responds to the infant, fixes what is upsetting by providing safety, food or a clean diaper, and then soothes the child's fears or loneliness. This combination of responding and soothing provides the infant with the first experience of coregulation. As this experience is repeated, the child begins to be confident of the response of the caregiver and learns to regulate some of their own internal responses.[42,43,44,45] It is suggested that these early interactions set the stage not just for the development of affect regulation skills, but also for the child's development of their sense of self and other, their experience of themselves within the world, their experience of caregivers as safe and nurturing, and their experience of the world as a safe place in which their actions have impact.[46,47] An infant's dependence on its caregiver is so complete that their inability to illicit a caring response from their caregiver is experienced as a life-threatening and overwhelming trauma. When children are not responded too, or when they are responded to in inconsistent, frightening or painful ways, their resources are overwhelmed and they do not learn to be soothed, and then to soothe themselves. This leads to an inability to experience, understand and manage their affective experiences. These children present as either having little or no emotion, little or no emotional awareness, or little or no emotional control. Many of these children learn to dissociate early in order to shut down the overwhelming and terrifying emotional stimulation. Once children have developed dissociative strategies for coping with overwhelming experiences, different affective states can become compartmentalised so as to be operating outside of the child's awareness, making them more difficult to access and soothe.

Behavioural Regulation

Behavioural regulation is the ability to make choices and be in control of one's own behaviour. Like affect regulation, behavioural regulation is behind many referrals to children's mental health centres. There are a number of ways in which behaviour can become disregulated as a result of trauma. Difficulties with affect regulation lead children to respond with anger or fear to triggering experiences, resulting in behaviours which are inappropriate or out of proportion. Dissociated affect states can be even more confusing and difficult for a child to manage, in that they may be operating outside the child's experienced awareness. Difficulties in reading and understanding social cues can lead to children behaving in ways which are unusual or inappropriate to the situation. Often, children who have come to experience adults not as protective allies, but rather as selfish and dangerous, do not have the same motivation to accept adults' rules about right and wrong. Children who see adults as safe and protective are able to understand that rules exist for their safety and development, and that following the rules can help them gain approval from caregivers, contributing to their self-worth. Children who experience adults as selfish and dangerous may still want approval in order to increase their chances of safety, but they are unlikely to trust or rely on that approval. They see themselves as operating in their own best interests, taking care of their own needs. Manipulation and dishonesty is not experienced as bad, but as necessary for survival. Dissociation complicates this picture in that it is common to have some self-states who have adjusted to a safe environment and others which continue to exist in a state of mistrust and alienation. When these parts are operating out of each other's knowledge and awareness, it can create an all too familiar picture clinically: a child who looks motivated, caring and connected, who is frequently caught breaking rules, and then seems devastatingly sincere when blatantly lying about behaviours they were witnessed doing. These children develop reputations for being cold, calculating dishonest manipulators. The alliances that their more engaged and connected parts have begun to build become fragile and break down when they feel betrayed by adults who don't believe them. It is critical to remember when working with these children that every behaviour, no matter how baffling, serves an important purpose experienced as necessary for survival.[48] When children are repeatedly lying, even when their actions are witnessed, and they seem devastated by not being believed, there may be other answers. It is possible that the child either does not remember the incident, or does not experience themselves as having been the one involved.

Cognition

Early trauma and poor early attachment experiences affect both direct cognitive development and children's ability to learn. The impact of trauma on neurological development directly affects cognitive development.[49,50] Children with early complex trauma histories are found to have less developed brains with less electrical activity. Prenatal exposure to drugs, alcohol, tobacco and maternal stress hormones as well as early malnutrition and lack of cognitive stimulation all lead to difficulties with cognitive development. Difficulties focusing attention, integrating experiences and processing memories decrease a child's ability to learn. Difficulties with affective and behavioural regulation and the ability to experience adults as allies negatively affect children's success within the classroom and their ability to gain from educational opportunities. Lack of parental support and assistance with academics, missed school and lack of stimulation in the home environment create further deficits in learning experienced by children living in traumatic, nonsupportive environments. Dissociation complicates both cognitive functioning and learning by creating gaps in experience and knowledge. Children who have long-standing dissociative symptoms sometimes have major learning gaps and histories of academic failure while presenting as being cognitively sophisticated. Often by the time children present for therapy they have a history of academic failure, a diagnosis of one or more learning disabilities, and are viewed by themselves and others as having cognitive impairments. Sometimes it is difficult to tell whether these children are cognitively impaired, affected by highly intrusive trauma symptoms and dissociation, or a combination of the above. Many of them, once effectively treated, become much more academically successful then was initially believed possible. In spite of this hopeful experience, many of these children have deficits, delays and disabilities caused by direct impact on their neurological development.

Self-Concept

A child's first understanding of themselves as a person is acquired through their early attachment experiences.[51,52,53,54] Their first experience of having an effect on their environment is when their caregiver responds to their cries. Their first view of themselves is through the eyes of the caregiver who responds. As children get older, if they have a safe, supportive relationship, they begin to explore their world, developing a sense of effectiveness as they take on challenges, master new tasks, and receive positive, enthusiastic responses from those around them. When an infant's cries get no response, they learn they have no effect on others. When the adults who look at them are bored, uninterested or hostile, they begin to experience themselves as having no self-worth. If rather than being encouraged, their explorations of their world are restricted or punished, this experience of ineffectiveness and worthlessness are reinforced. In this way, neglect in infancy is enough to create a negative experience of self in a child. Experiences of emotional, physical and/or sexual abuse create identities of being bad, deserving of harm or useful only for the satisfaction of adults. Inconsistency and the need to feel connected to powerful caregivers can lead to children developing multiple, incompatible experiences of themselves. This in turn can lead to children with dissociative symptoms, including dissociative identity disorders.[55,56,57,58,59] When a child presents with dissociative identity disorder it is common to find parts that see themselves as good, and others that see themselves as bad; some that ally with adults and work to gain their favour, and parts that distrust adults and actively work against them; sexualised parts who use sexualised behaviour either to gain affection and connection, or to control situations; child parts who experience themselves as very young and helpless, and older parts who see themselves as able to manage and control life situations and environments in a pseudomature and responsible manner. The degree of separation and awareness between parts can vary depending on the child and the situation.

Worldview

Worldview is inextricably linked to self-concept. As a child develops their idea of self, they are developing their idea of themselves in relation to others and of others in relation to themselves. If a loving, nurturing response to an infant's cries is the beginning of their sense of themselves as effective and lovable, it is also the beginning of their sense of the world as safe and responsive. If there is no response or if that response is cold, dismissive or frightening, then their experience of the world is that it is dismissing and dangerous. Porgess[60] describes how mammals have developed a second vagal system in order to facilitate our dependence on a social environment. This is described in more detail in the next chapter. When we don't have safe early attachment relationships we don't internalise the experience of safe others, and so we respond to the world as threatening. As the child grows, their experiences continue to help them adapt to the world in which they live. If the world in which they live is dangerous, unpredictable and violent, this is what they will internalise and adapt to. Their ability to rely on others, build trusting relationships and experience themselves as an interdependent part of a social group is compromised. They view others as individually and selfishly motivated and the world as unpredictable. Although there are ways and times in which this may be an accurate view of the world, research supports the view that those who grow up with an experience of a safe and supportive world are overall healthier, more successful and more adaptive.[61]

Social Development

Man is a social animal. Our success as a species has been determined by our ability to work in mutually supportive social groups. Human infants are helpless and dependent on their caregivers. According to Porgess,[62] our vagal system has adapted to facilitate our recognising safe people and situations in order to allow for social and physical interdependence. From the beginning, children who don't have safe early experiences develop a different worldview (see above). As they grow, the many different ways in which they have been impacted by trauma work together to undermine their ability to engage socially and build satisfying, mutual relationships. A limited ability to trust creates an individual focus, where children do not see others as allies. Poorly developed affective and behavioural regulation skills lead them to be different from other children, sometimes threatening, and often odd. The impacts on their neurological development and cognitive abilities leave them less able to read and respond to social cues. Their experience of themselves as bad and others as potentially hostile continues to reinforce itself as they fail socially and academically and are responded to as bad, negative and different. These children often crave connection and try different ways to make friends, but without basic trust or social skills their attempts leave them vulnerable to exploitation or bullying, increasing their likelihood of becoming aggressive and bullying themselves. Others may identify socially inappropriate ways of making connections through theft, attention-seeking activities, sexualised behaviours or antisocial actions. They are most likely to find social success with others with similar experiences, and so often become part of a negative peer group. Very few of the children we see for complex trauma treatment are socially successful.

Dissociation can impact on social development in different ways. Some children may have parts that are able to, on the surface, appear socially well adjusted and have friendships. These friendships tend to be shallow and unsatisfying, as they have such an internalised sense of shame and difference that they find it hard to let their friends close or to get to know them well. Children who dissociate are rarely completely in control of their responses. These young people find themselves in the situation of having alienated friends through odd, angry or inappropriate behaviour without remembering what happened or what went wrong. As age regression is a common dissociative symptom children with dissociative disorders sometimes gravitate to younger children, or have interests in activities that are more appropriate to children younger than their peers. This can be a consistent issue, or it can be one that shifts back and forth, again leading to confusion, rejection and shame.

The impact of complex trauma is pervasive. The young clients we work with have had the trajectories of their development altered to adapt to a hostile, dangerous environment. This leaves them poorly equipped to manage in a society dependent on connection and relationships.

Notes

1. van der Kolk, B. A. (2005). Developmental trauma disorder: Towards a rational diagnosis for children with complex trauma histories. *Psychiatric Annals, 35*(5), 401–408.
2. Silberg, Joyanna. (2013). *The Child Survivor: Healing Developmental Trauma and Dissociation*. Routledge. New York. p 163.
3. American Psychiatric Association. (2013). *Diagnostic and Statistical Manual of Mental Disorders* (5th ed.). Arlington, VA. p 271.
4. Lanius, R. A., Bluhm, R. L., & Frewen, P. A. (2011). How understanding the neurobiology of complex post-traumatic stress disorder can inform clinical practice: A social cognitive and affective neuroscience approach. *Acta Psychiatrica Scandinavica, 124*(5), 331–348. p 875.
5. Alexander, Pamela C. (2013). Relational trauma and disorganized attachment. In J. Ford and C. Courtois (Eds.), *Treating Complex Traumatic Stress Disorders in Children and Adolescents Scientific Foundations and Therapeutic Models*. Guilford. New York.

6. Henninghausen, Bureau, David, Holmes, & Lyons, Ruth. (2011). Disorganized attachment behaviour observed in adolescence: Validation in relation to adult attachment interview classifications at age 25. In J. Solomon & C. George (Eds.), *Disorganized Attachment and Caregiving*. Guilford. New York.
7. International Society for the Study of Trauma and Dissociation Website. (2004–2014). *Frequently Asked Questions*. McLean, VA. Retrieved from: http://www.isst-d.org
8. Anderson, C. L., & Alexander, P. C. (1996). The relationship between attachment and dissociation in adult survivors of incest. *Psychiatry: Interpersonal & Biological Processes, 59*(3), 240–254.
9. Frey, R. J. (2001). Dissociative disorders. In Jacqueline L. Longe (Ed.), *The Gale Encyclopedia of Medicine* (2nd ed., Vol. 5). Gale Group. Farmington Hills, MI.
10. International Society for the Study of Dissociation (now ISSTD) (2002). *Understanding dissociation: A videofilm.*
11. Maldonado, J. R., Butler, L. D., & Spiegel, D. (2002). Treatments for dissociative disorders. In Peter E. Nathan & Jack M. Gorman (Eds.), *A Guide to Treatments That Work* (2nd ed.). Oxford University Press. New York.
12. Pascuzzi, R. M., & Weber, M. C. (1997). Conversion disorders, malingering, and dissociative disorders. In Rex B. Conn, William Z. Borer, & Jack W. Snyder (Eds.), *Current Diagnosis* (Vol. 9). W. B. Saunders Co. Philadelphia, PA.
13. Rauschenberger, S. L., & Lynn, S. J. (1995). Fantasy proneness, DSM-III-R axis I psychopathology, and dissociation. *Journal of Abnormal Psychology, 104*, 373–380.
14. Simeon, D., Guralnik, O., & Schmeidler, J. (2001). Development of a depersonalization severity scale. *Journal of Traumatic Stress, 14*(2), 341–349.
15. Spiegel, D., & Cardeña, E. (1991). Disintegrated experience: The dissociative disorders revisited. *Journal of Abnormal Psychology, 100*, 366–378.
16. Steinberg, M., Rounsaville, B., & Cicchetti, D. V. (1990). The structured clinical interview for DSM-III-R dissociative disorders: Preliminary report on a new diagnostic instrument. *American Journal of Psychiatry, 147*(1), 76–82.
17. Steinberg, M., Cicchetti, D., Buchanan, J., Hall, P., & Rounsaville, B. (1993). Clinical assessment of dissociative symptoms and disorders: The structured interview for DSM-IV dissociative disorders (SCID-D). *Dissociation: Progress in the Dissociative Disorders, 61*(1), 108–120.
18. Maldonado, J. R., Butler, L. D., & Spiegel, D. (2002). Treatments for dissociative disorders. In Peter E. Nathan & Jack M. Gorman (Eds.), *A Guide to Treatments That Work* (2nd ed.). Oxford University Press. New York.
19. International Society for the Study of Trauma and Dissociation Website. Frequently Asked Questions. McLean, VA 22102. Copyright © 2004–2014 by ISSTD.
20. Frey, R. J. (2001). Dissociative disorders. In *The Gale Encyclopedia of Medicine* (2nd ed., Vol. 5). Gale Group. Farmington Hills, MI.
21. Guralnik, O., Schmeidler, J., & Simeon, D. (2000). Feeling unreal: Cognitive processes in depersonalization. *American Journal of Psychiatry, 157*(1), 103–109.
22. Maldonado, J. R., Butler, L. D., & Spiegel, D. (2002). Treatments for dissociative disorders. In Peter E. Nathan & Jack M. Gorman (Eds.), *A Guide to Treatments That Work* (2nd ed.). Oxford University Press. New York.
23. Simeon, D., Guralnik, O., & Schmeidler, J. (2001). Development of a depersonalization severity scale. *Journal of Traumatic Stress, 14*(2), 341–349.
24. Spiegel, D., & Cardeña, E. (1991). Disintegrated experience: The dissociative disorders revisited. *Journal of Abnormal Psychology, 100*, 366–378.
25. Steinberg, M., & Steinberg, A. (1995). Using the SCID-D to assess dissociative identity disorder in adolescents: Three case studies. *Bulletin of the Menninger Clinic, 59*(2), 221–231.
26. Steinberg, M., & Steinberg, A. (1995). Using the SCID-D to assess dissociative identity disorder in adolescents: Three case studies. *Bulletin of the Menninger Clinic, 59*(2), 221–231.

27. Maldonado, J. R., Butler, L. D., & Spiegel, D. (2002). Treatments for dissociative disorders. In Peter E. Nathan & Jack M. Gorman (Eds.), *A Guide to Treatments That Work* (2nd ed.). Oxford University Press. New York.
28. Steinberg, M., Cicchetti, D., Buchanan, J., Hall, P., & Rounsaville, B. (1993). Clinical assessment of dissociative symptoms and disorders: The structured interview for DSM-IV dissociative disorders (SCID-D). *Dissociation: Progress in the Dissociative Disorders, 61*(1), 108–120.
29. Steinberg, M., & Steinberg, A. (1995). Using the SCID-D to assess dissociative identity disorder in adolescents: Three case studies. *Bulletin of the Menninger Clinic, 59*(2), 221–231.
30. Fine, C. G. (1999). The tactical-integration model for the treatment of dissociative identity disorder and allied dissociative disorders. *American Journal of Psychotherapy, 53*(3), 361–376.
31. Maldonado, J. R., Butler, L. D., & Spiegel, D. (2002). Treatments for dissociative disorders. In Peter E. Nathan & Jack M. Gorman (Eds.), *A Guide to Treatments That Work* (2nd ed.). Oxford University Press. New York.
32. Spiegel, D., & Cardeña, E. (1991). Disintegrated experience: The dissociative disorders revisited. *Journal of Abnormal Psychology, 100*, 366–378.
33. Steinberg, M., & Steinberg, A. (1995). Using the SCID-D to assess dissociative identity disorder in adolescents: Three case studies. *Bulletin of the Menninger Clinic, 59*(2), 221–231.
34. Cook, A., Blaustein, M., Spinazzola, J., & van der Kolk, B. (2003). *Complex trauma in children and adolescents* [White paper]. National Child Traumatic Stress Network Complex Trauma Task Force. National Centre for Child Traumatic Stress. Los Angeles, CA. Retrieved from: http://www.nctsnet.org/nctsn_assets/pdfs/edu_materials/ComplexTrauma_All.pdf
35. Felitti, V. J., Anda, R. F., Nordenberg, D., Williamson, D. F., Spitz, A. M., Edwards, V., Koss, M. P., & Marks, J. S. (1998). Relationship of childhood abuse and household dysfunction to many of the leading causes of death in adults: The Adverse Childhood Experiences (ACE) Study. *American Journal of Preventive Medicine, 14*, 245–258.
36. Owen, J. P., Marco, E. J., Desai, S., Fourie, E., Harris, J., Hill, S. S., Arnett, A. B., & Mukherjee, P. (2013). Abnormal white matter microstructure in children with sensory processing disorders. *Neuroimage Clinical, 2*, 844–853.
37. Yehuda, Na'ama. (2011). Leroy (seven years old)—"It is almost like he is two children" Working with a dissociative child in a school setting. In S. Wieland (Ed.), *Dissociation in Traumatized Children and Adolescents*. Routledge. New York.
38. Kackowski, A. P., de Araujo, D. M., de Lacerda, A.L.T., Mari, M.D.J., & Kaufman, J. (2009). Neurostructural imaging findings in children with post-traumatic stress disorder: Brief review. *Psychiatry of Clinical Neurosciences, 63*(1), 1–8.
39. Teicher, M. H., Tomoda, A., & Anderson, S. L. (2006). Neurobiological consequences of early stress and childhood maltreatment: Are results from human and animal studies comparable. *Annals of the New York Academy of Sciences, 1071*, 313–323.
40. Siegel, Daniel J. (2013). *The Developing Mind: How Relationships and the Brain Interact to Shape Who We Are.* Guilford. New York.
41. Schore, Allan. (2009). Relational trauma and the developing right brain. *Annals of the New York Academy of Sciences, 1159*, 189–203.
42. Hughes, Daniel A. (2007). *Attachment Focused Family Therapy.* W. W. Norton & Company. New York. pp 20–28.
43. Sroufe, L. A. (1995). *Emotional Development: The Organization of Emotional Life in the Early Years*. Cambridge University Press. New York.
44. Stern, D. (1985). *The Interpersonal World of the Infant.* Basic Books. New York.
45. Schore, Allan. (1994). *Affect Regulation and the Origin of the Self.* Erlbaum. Hillsdale, NJ.

46. Siegel, Daniel J. (2013). *The Developing Mind: How Relationships and the Brain Interact to Shape Who We Are.* Guilford. New York.
47. Porgess, Stephen W. (2011). *The Polyvagal Theory: Neurophysiological Foundations of Emotions, Attachment, Communication, Self-Regulation.* W. W. Norton & Company. New York.
48. Silberg, Joyanna. (2013). *The Child Survivor: Healing Developmental Trauma and Dissociation.* Routledge. New York.
49. Cook, A., Spinazzola, J., Ford, J., Lanktree, C., Blaustein, M., Cloitre, M., DeRosa, R., Hubbard, R., Kagan R., Liautaud, J., Mallah, K., Olafson, E., & van der Kolk, B. (2005). Complex trauma in children and adolescents. *Psychiatric Annals, 35,* 390–398.
50. Cook, A., Blaustein, M., Spinazzola, J. & van der Kolk, B. (Eds.). (2003). *Complex trauma in children and adolescents* [White paper]. National Child Traumatic Stress Network Complex Trauma Task Force. National Centre for Child Traumatic Stress. Los Angeles, CA. Retrieved from: http://www.nctsnet.org/nctsn_assets/pdfs/edu_materials/ComplexTrauma_All.pdf
51. Bowlby, John. (1990). *A Secure Base: Parent-Child Attachment and Healthy Human Development.* Basic Books. New York.
52. Bowlby, John. (1983). *Attachment.* Basic Books. New York.
53. Siegel, Daniel J. (2013). *The Developing Mind: How Relationships and the Brain Interact to Shape Who We Are.* Guilford. New York.
54. Hughes, Daniel A. (2007). *Attachment Focused Family Therapy.* W. W. Norton & Company. New York. pp 20–28.
55. Silberg, Joyanna. (2013). *The Child Survivor: Healing Developmental Trauma and Dissociation.* Routledge. New York.
56. Wieland, Sandra. (Ed.). (2011). *Dissociation in Traumatized Children and Adolescents.* Routledge. New York.
57. Vermetten, E., Dorahy, M.J., & Spiegel, D. (Eds.). (2007). *Traumatic Dissociation: Neurobiology and Treatment.* American Psychiatric Publishing. Arlington, VA.
58. Struik, A. (2014). *Treating Chronically Traumatized Children: Don't Let Sleeping Dogs Lie!* Routledge. New York.
59. Putnam, F. W. (1997). *Dissociation in Children and Adults: A Developmental Perspective.* Guilford. New York.
60. Porgess, Stephen W. (2011). *The Polyvagal Theory: Neurophysiological Foundations of Emotions, Attachment, Communication, Self-Regulation.* W. W. Norton & Company. New York.
61. Chu, J. (2011). *Rebuilding Shattered Lives: Treating Complex PTSD and Dissociative Disorders.* John Wiley and Sons. Hoboken, NJ.
62. Porgess, Stephen W. (2011). *The Polyvagal Theory: Neurophysiological Foundations of Emotions, Attachment, Communication, Self-Regulation.* W. W. Norton & Company. New York.

2 The Neurobiology of Attachment and Trauma

Dan Siegel refers to the brain as an "open, dynamic system," meaning that it is continually changing in response to interaction with its environment, including other brains.[1] Complex trauma treatment has focused on treating the impact of early trauma on the emotional, relational, cognitive and social functioning of individuals impacted by trauma. As the field of neurobiology advances, it provides us with fascinating insight into brain development, brain function and neuroplasticity. During my early years studying children's mental health, the debate was on "nature vs. nurture." Are we the product of biology or experience? Research on brain development has fundamentally shifted this discussion. There is a new understanding of how our experiences and relationships affect the development of our biology, not just during infancy and early childhood, but throughout our lifetimes.

Through this awareness we are coming to understand that early trauma affects child development by impacting on the way children's brains grow. It isn't enough to say that trauma affects brain development. This would suggest that brain development is static, unless the child experiences trauma. All experience affects brain development, which then affects how we process and understand our experiences. In his chapter in *Treating Complex Traumatic Stress Disorders in Children and Adolescents* Alan Schore talks about the "accepted view" that our very early experience, through interpersonal neurobiology, affects how we develop and who we become.[2] Siegel states, "Though experience shapes the activity of the brain and the strength of neuronal connections throughout life, experience early in life may be especially crucial to organizing the way the basic regulatory structures of the brain develop."[3] The development of our selves is a dynamic process that is shifted and altered by experience. We are far from having all the answers, but we are beginning to learn things that support and inform trauma treatment in ways that I couldn't have imagined when I started in this field.

This chapter explores the (so far) understood ways in which brain structure and function responds and adapts to traumatic experience and in turn affects children's functioning and relationships. It is written by a nonneuroscientist for nonneuroscientists. The intent is to provide not comprehensive scientific information, but an overview of findings that inform clinical understanding and therapeutic process. This, like much of what we work with, is theoretical. Research supports findings about development, environmental impact and neurological structure.

This information is interpreted to form neurobiological theory. The theory fits with what has been observed and understood about children affected by trauma, the difficulties they experience and the types of therapy they may benefit from.

As we come to understand trauma's effects on brain development, and the purposes of the parts of the brain that are affected by overwhelming experience, coherence develops around why certain types of interventions are helpful, and what other types of interventions may prove to be. Later chapters will build on this to explore the therapeutic experiences that can contribute to the treatment of traumatised children and adolescents. Although much of the structural development of the mind occurs in response to early experience, new findings related to neuroplasticity support the idea that the brain continues to develop throughout the lifespan, and continues to be responsive to social interactions.[4] The most intense period of brain growth and development is early childhood, which suggests that the most impactful period for treatment is as early in childhood as possible. This does not mean that later interventions aren't indicated. There is good reason to believe that our brains stay open to change through experience for most or all of our lives.

The Brain

The human brain is incredibly complex, and there is no universal agreement or understanding about how the brain functions or what parts are responsible for what.[5] Figure 2.1, for example, shows a well-labelled cross section of the parts of the brain. This particular diagram is labelled in relation to many of the sections of the brain that are relevant to this chapter. It's possible to find dozens of different labelled diagrams, detailing different parts of the brain that don't enter into this discussion. Figure 2.2 shows what has been a somewhat accepted view of the functions of the left and right hemispheres. Currently there is debate as to whether these are clearly defined divisions. Emotional functioning, for example, is likely more complex; different aspects of emotional processing and expression may be spread across different parts of the brain.[6]

According to Siegel[7] the right hemisphere of the brain is usually dominant for nonverbal processing in a "holistic, parallel, visual spatial manner," self-soothing, nonverbal processing of language, the registration and regulation of body states, and the retrieval of autobiographical memory. The left hemisphere is responsible for linear processing and linguistics. Therefore, like emotional functioning, the development and understanding of autobiographical experience is dependent on both hemispheres working together.

Development

The brain is made up of millions of cells called neurons, supported by other cells called glia. Neurons are connected by synapses, which pass electrical signals between them. "Neurons and glia are organized in various levels of complexity from small clusters called 'nuclei' to larger assemblies called 'circuits,' 'regions' and 'hemispheres.'"[8]

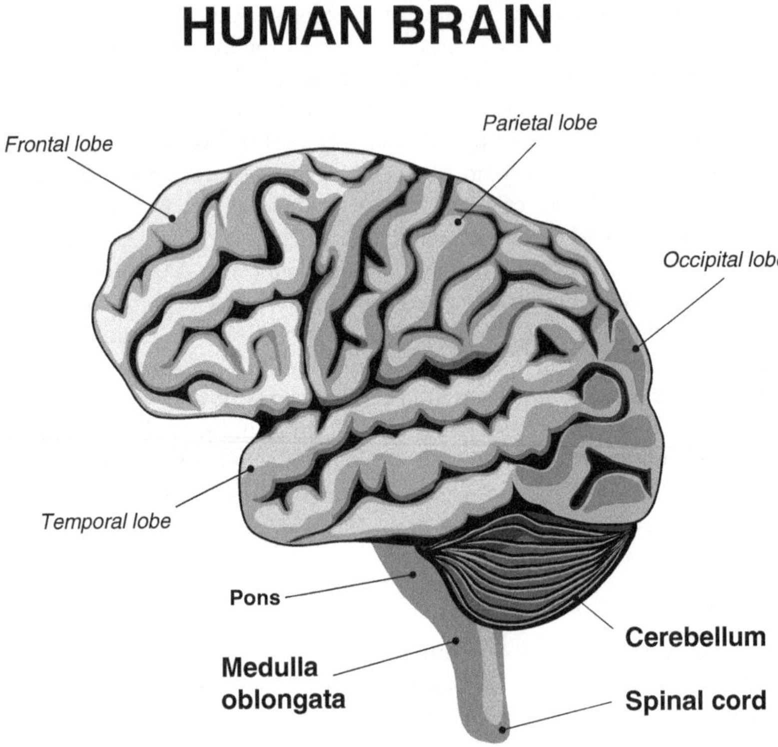

Figure 2.1 The Brain
Credit: iStockphoto

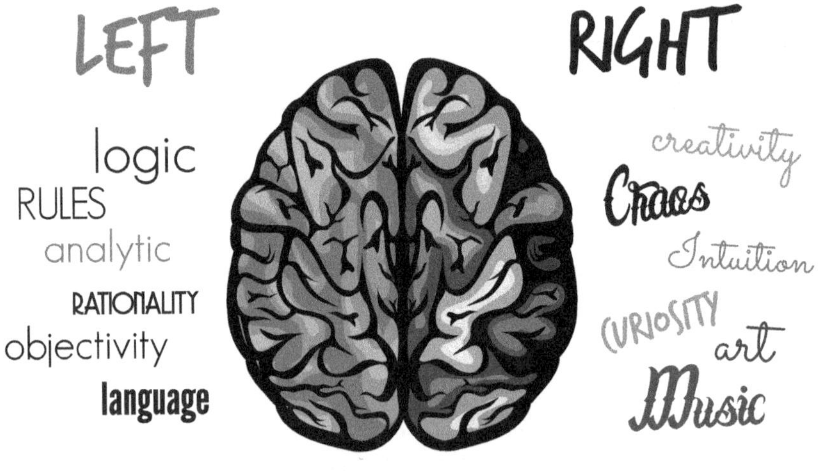

Figure 2.2 The Brain
Credit: iStockphoto

The development of our brains begins before birth and continues throughout life. The brain goes through its fastest growth spurt early in life. During the first year, total brain volume increases by 101%, and the volume of the subcortical areas by 130%.[9] The right hemisphere goes through an intense growth spurt between the third trimester of pregnancy and the second year of development.[10] The limbic system, which is connected to the right hemisphere, myelinates in the first year and a half.[11] Myelination increases the firing speed of neurons and decreases the time needed for neurons to rest before firing again.[12] The right hemisphere develops before the left hemisphere.[13,14] The cortex, or the upper part of the brain, which is responsible for higher-level functioning, develops back to front. The frontal areas are not fully developed until well into adulthood.[15]

Siegel, in his exploration of interpersonal neurobiology, describes brain development as being both "experience dependent" and "experience expectant." Our genetic makeup leads our brains to be ready to respond to our physical, social and emotional environments, which is experience expectant. Early on in our development, these experiences lead to the development and creation both of new neurons and of new connections between neurons. This development is dependent on experience. Once these neurons and connections are made, they require similar experiences to be repeated. If this does not occur, these neurons die off in a process called pruning. This, again, is experience dependent. Our brains experience the greatest growth during early childhood and the greatest pruning during adolescence.[16] During these times our brains are most susceptible to the influence of experience.

Human beings have evolved to be socially interdependent animals. In order to survive, we need to be able to build complex relationships based on nurturing and caring. We also need to be able to protect ourselves and our family from threatening or dangerous situations. During the earliest period of brain development humans are exposed mostly to the environment provided by their primary caregivers. Under optimal circumstances, these early attachment relationships create an emotional environment that leads to brain growth and development supporting connected relationships with safe others, the ability to learn to self-regulate and communicate, and the ability over time to differentiate between safe and unsafe others and environments.[17,18,19]

Memory

Long before children can encode their experiences into narrative memory, their experiences influence the programming of their brain's responses to environmental stimuli.

> Repeated patterns of children's interactions with their caregivers become "remembered" in the various modalities of memory and directly shape not just what children recall, but how the representational processes develop. Behaviour, emotion, perceptions, sensations, and models of others are

engrained by the experiences that occur before children have autobiographical memory processes available to them.[20]

In this quote, Dr. Siegel uses the term "remembered" in reference not just to autobiographical memory—the memory coded in narrative—but also to memory stored as affect and sensory experience. Early trauma and disrupted early attachment relationships impact not just the development of parts of the brain, but also the mechanisms which connect the parts of the brain into an integrated whole. Experiences are stored not just as autobiographical memory, but also as affective and sensory memories, which are stored in separate parts of our brain, and later integrated into a full memory. Think of the experience of encountering a smell or taste, or of hearing a song which brings back a memory—a memory that you might not have connected to the sensory experience which brought it back. There's a street corner in the city I live in which, when I walk past it, brings back the memory of a village in Spain where I spent the summer I was sixteen. There is something about a smell on that corner that reminds me, but I don't know what the smell is. I walk by, and suddenly I am in Denia. Only then do I notice the still-unidentified smell.

The corner of the city that triggers that memory for me is not a nice corner by any means, and yet the memory it creates is such a warm and positive one that it is now associated with good feelings for me. This isn't a unique experience; I imagine that everyone has some strange association that has grown between a sensation and an emotion.

To understand this, and to understand how it translates to our work, it's important to understand the ways in which early traumatic experience impacts on the development of a child's brain.

Trauma and Its Impacts

This chapter reviews what research and theory suggest are the likely impacts of experience, relationships and trauma on the development and functioning of the brain. Table 2.1 outlines research findings regarding impact of early trauma, neglect and emotional disruption on the development of children's brains. Different researchers examine different types of trauma and its outcomes, so the trauma that is identified in the research is named on the chart. This doesn't suggest that only these types of trauma impact on only these particular parts of the brain. In fact, clinical experience would suggest that the findings on some types of trauma could likely be generalised to others. For example, experiences which create overwhelming fear likely have similar impacts, no matter their details.

The frontal lobe, made up of the frontal and prefrontal cortex, is not fully developed until early adulthood but begins its development in infancy. It is responsive to and dependent on early attachment experience. Research supports that this part of the brain is important in emotional regulation, stress modulation, executive functioning, activating attachment behaviours, and

Table 2.1 Impact of Trauma on Neurobiology

Part of Brain	*Function*	*Type of Trauma Researched*	*Identified Impact*
Frontal Lobe	Social filters; affect regulation; impulse control; social interaction; self-awareness; neural integration; stress modulation	Neglect; attachment disruption; youth with PTSD	Thinner; less developed; shows less activity
Corpus Callosum	Connection between left and righthemisphere	Neglect; physical and sexual abuse	Less developed
Right Hemisphere	Attachment; affect regulation; stress modulation; emotion; creativity; music; colour	Relational trauma	Structural changes, lower volume, less efficient coping mechanisms
Hippocampus	Declarative memory; visual spatial skills; memory formation; connecting emotions and senses to memory	Sexual abuse	Deficits can lead to excessive cortisol, affecting ability to turn off an excessively stimulated amygdala
Amygdala	Centre for conditioned fear responses	Sexual abuse	Appears to be on hyperalert mode; larger right, smaller left
Neurochemistry	Controls on the body's response to stress including impacts on vigilance-alerting behaviours and memory processing	Abused and neglected children	Impacts on release, control, and levels of cortisol and norepinephrine

interpreting and expressing social interactions.[21,22,23,24,25] Siegel states that the medial prefrontal regions may also be involved in the integration of self-awareness, memory, emotion, regulation and attachment.[26] The development of these upper frontal parts of the brain is triggered by contact with an actively attuned primary caregiver within a secure attachment relationship.[27] Children who have experienced early neglect and chronic trauma have been found to have thinner, less developed frontal lobes and less electrical activity within their right prefrontal cortex.[28]

Difficulties in emotional regulation, integration of experience, stress modulation, executive functioning, social interaction and attachment behaviours are frequent in childhood trauma victims. Sophie, adopted at age three, is a good example. Sophie's parents were told that prior to adoption she was in one stable foster placement and had no history of trauma. Sophie had difficulties adjusting to her adoptive family. She often appeared terrified. On waking up in the morning, or when startled, she would go into a terror state, bolt and hide under a table. She found it difficult to tolerate change or new people. Her behaviour was unpredictably explosive. She had low tolerance for sensory stimulation. She often did not turn to her parents for nurturing or soothing. She sometimes engaged in trancelike behaviour during which she was unresponsive and behaved oddly. Although appearing intelligent, she struggled academically. She had social-skills deficits and was unable to make friends. During the eight years following her adoption, Sophie received many clinical interventions and received multiple diagnoses. She was assessed for autism spectrum disorders, but the results were inconclusive. She was diagnosed with attention deficit hyperactivity disorder, sensory processing disorder, dyslexia and a mild intellectual delay. She was small for her age, at twelve appearing more like a petite six- or seven-year-old. Among the treatment interventions, those which were most effective were geared towards supporting sensory integration and environmental stability. When Sophie was twelve, her behavioural therapist supported her parents' belief that her presentation matched the symptoms of a child who had experienced very early trauma and neglect. Her parents approached the adoption agency for more detailed early life information and found that during her first three years her biological parents contested her removal and proposed adoption. Over that three-year period there had been continuous failed attempts to reintegrate her into her family of origin. She experienced a tremendous amount of early instability and was transported by frequently changing volunteer drivers, back and forth almost daily between her safe and secure foster home and the home of her biological family. She had many unsupervised, partially or inadequately supervised, and often overnight visits in an environment that was identified as neglectful and possibly abusive. At twelve Sophie was referred to me for assessment and treatment of her now suspected complex trauma disorder. She was diagnosed with a dissociative identity disorder. Her parents engaged with her in attachment-focused work. She quickly displayed improved self-regulation and relationship skills in response to therapy focused on improving attachment and managing dissociative symptoms. The earlier treatment which Sophie had received which focused on sensory processing difficulties had been geared towards neurological integration. This fit with the attachment work and seemed to support the ongoing goals.[29]

Allan Schore has focused much of his research and writing on the impact of trauma and disrupted attachment on right hemisphere development.[30,31,32] Early attachment theory linked the quality of parent-infant attachment to the development of the infant's ability to cope with stress. This early hypothesis has been widely borne out by several decades of research.[33,34,35,36,37] In a series of early review articles, Allan Schore examines the impact of attachment relationships and early relational trauma on the development of the infant's right hemisphere, which he describes as "dominant for attachment, affect regulation, and stress modulation."[38,39,40] Schore writes, "An essential tenet of the interpersonal neurobiological perspective of regulation theory is that effective attachment transactions shape the cortical–subcortical emotion and stress-regulating circuits of the developing right brain during early critical periods."[41]

The attachment relationship directly influences the child's ability to develop self-regulation and identity. An attuned parent responds to their infant's affective cues. When the infant is upset, the parent responds and soothes the infant; when the infant is engaged, the parent engages as well; when the infant disengages, the parent disengages to allow the child to reorganise. All parents sometimes miss attunement cues, and either fail to respond or overengage, causing distress for the infant. This distress leads the parent to shift their response, repairing the break. It is this process of attunement, break and repair/reattunement that stimulates the development of the right frontal cerebral cortex.[42] Children who experience severe neglect or relational trauma don't receive the type of dyadically attuned connection necessary to stimulate this growth. This affects development of their attachment system, their ability to rely on or be soothed by others, and to regulate their own emotional states. Sophie again provides a good example. Even many years after her adoption, Sophie would not turn to her parents for soothing when upset; she would disconnect from them completely, reacting sometimes with fear, sometimes with rejection. If woken up suddenly she still appeared terrified, would run and hide, and would need to be coaxed out and reminded she was safe before she could be soothed. When questioned about behaviour, Sophie would lie, even about things she should have known would not anger her parents, out of fear of getting into trouble. When angry, Sophie insisted that she had no family and that no one cared about her. She enjoyed being with her mother, but when she was upset she would shut her out. She did not see her as an ally if she felt she was in trouble, and needed a lot of support to begin to explore what was happening emotionally. She often responded to her father with anger or rejection, and resisted his efforts to parent her or connect to her. Sophie has responded well to therapy. She is calmer, and gets upset if sessions are cancelled. She has begun to enjoy her relationship with her father, although at times, when upset, she reverts to earlier patterns. In therapy, at first she was chatty, but resistant to exploring emotional content, and could only tolerate brief sessions. She couldn't wait to arrive, and then couldn't wait to leave. Sophie has responded from the beginning with both interest and avoidance to the suggestion that her difficulties are related to her preadoption history. She immediately responded with spontaneous tears (unusual for her) and acknowledgment that she remembered her biological family and that the memories are frightening. She brings up emotional experiences, memories and internal experiences, but can only stay with them for a few minutes at a time. The sense in therapy, as is the sense in her relationship with her parents, is of a dependent need for connection and a resistant need to avoid connection. The experience is very much one of a disorganised attachment pattern.

The limbic system, made up of the hippocampus, amygdala and HPA (hypothalamic-pituitary-adrenal) axis, is a part of the lower brain involved in emotion, motivation, emotional memory and conditioned fear responses.[43]

The limbic system stimulates the HPA axis, which releases the chemicals and hormones responsible for our stress and fear responses, and regulates many of our body processes including digestion, immunity, sexuality, and energy storage and usage. Early trauma negatively impacts on the HPA axis and affects both the structure and the responsiveness of the limbic system, leading to excessive cortisol production and a hyperalert fear response.[44]

Using Sophie again as an example, we can see how this applies. Sophie presents as a petite, cheerful, outgoing girl. On first contact she is all smiles and chatter. Once she's engaged it's difficult for her to contain her emotional reactivity. She becomes easily withdrawn, angry or frightened, frequently dissociating in sessions. At home she can fly into a rage for no reason. If startled or suddenly woken up she becomes terrified, hides and is unresponsive even to familiar adults. If she has experienced stress at school she may verbally or physically lash out, apparently unprovoked, when she returns home.

The lower brain is responsible for maintaining physiological states, physical responses to stress including the fight, flight or freeze response, neuroimmune responses and others. Porgess has explored this process in his work on the polyvagal theory.[45] As mammals, including humans, developed to be socially dependent, it became necessary to be able to determine the difference between safety and risk, because defence against our own social group would be fatal. Through a process Porgess calls neuroception we use subtle, preconscious emotional responses to determine whether a person is familiar and safe. If we recognise the person as familiar and safe, our automatic defenses get turned off and our metabolism slows, allowing us to engage socially. As our defensive modes require a high metabolic output, this engagement state also allows our body to enter into a state of restoration and growth. Porgess also refers to a third option. When, through neuroception, we determine there is no safety, but also that fight or flight is not an option, the body shuts down; the metabolism slows, heart rate and breathing slow, and pain sensations decrease. According to Porgess's theory, it is our early attachment relationships that prime our neuroception to determine safety. Our first experience of safety is through an attuned attachment figure who responds to our emotional states. When this does not happen, our vagal system is not programmed to recognise safety. The impact of very early experience on this part of the brain determines whether we respond to the world with openness or suspicion.

Early childhood trauma does not just impact the structure of the brain. It also impacts the chemical responses of the brain. The limbic system stimulates the HPA axis, which is responsible for releasing chemicals involved in our stress and fear responses, as well as numerous other bodily responses.[46] De Kloet and Rinne[47] report that chronic childhood adversity leads to hyperresponsiveness in the HPA axis, resulting in strongly increased ACTH (adrenocorticotropic hormone) and cortisol output, creating greater vulnerability to stressors and traumatic experiences later in life. Mason et al.[48] report that emotionally engaged and reactive adult subjects with PTSD display elevated cortisol levels, while those with detached and numb presentations display lowered cortisol levels. Perry et al.[49] have noted a similar response in children. Some children, as their brains become sensitized to repeated activations, experience chronic hyperarousal. They display increased release of stress hormones marked by hyperactivity, anxiety, impulsivity, sleep difficulties and tachycardia. Other children experience an increase in epinephrine and the release of endogenous opioids, resulting in a freezing response marked by increased vagal tone, decreased blood pressure and heart rate, and desensitisation to pain. These states match both the defensive state and the freeze state described by Porgess. They also match states of activation and dissociation experienced by many of the young people we see, including Sophie.

An important area of exploration is neural integration. As Siegel points out, different parts of our brain process different parts of our experiences. This is not just a division between our left and right brain, but also our lower and upper brain, and our front and back brain. Our narrative, visual, tactile, auditory, olfactory and emotional parts of our experiences are all processed differently, in different ways, by different parts of our brain.[50] Our experiences enter our awareness, and are processed in fragments—these fragments are then integrated into a unified whole in order to be fully experienced, understood and remembered as a single experience.

The corpus callosum connects the left and right brain, integrating the functions of the two hemispheres. This part of the brain, which is required in order to connect our visual and emotional experience with our narrative processes, has been found by researchers[51,52,53] to be underdeveloped by children experiencing certain types of trauma and neglect. Dan Siegel notes that the right prefrontal cortex is involved in encoding information, and the left prefrontal cortex is involved in retrieving information. He describes the REM sleep process as one where looking first left and then right activates both hemispheres of the brain repeatedly. Siegel describes this process as necessary for the consolidation and reorganisation of memory. He hypothesizes that both the impairment of the corpus callosum and the impaired REM sleep in trauma survivors is what leads to "unresolved memories."[54] Joyanna Silberg suggests that the impairment of the corpus callosum may lead to a lack of integration between verbal coding and visual memories, which may underlie flashbacks, disconnection and dissociation.[55] Allan Schore[56] reports that trauma survivors show excessive right hemisphere activation, which suggests that emotional and body sensation memories are activated more readily than episodic memories.

Integration involves more than the flow of information between hemispheres. There are integrative fibres throughout the brain, and many parts of the brain are involved in integration and consolidation of experiences into memory. Studies have shown impairment in these integrative fibres in survivors of childhood trauma.[57,58] Seigel connects the limbic system, the right prefrontal cortex and the hippocampus to the process of memory integration. Each of these has been identified earlier in this chapter as being negatively impacted by traumatic experience, and as requiring positive, safe attachment relationships to develop adequately.

Difficulties in the integration of both current experience and of memory are evident in our young clients. Their memories are often fragmented and incoherent. Even their recent, nontraumatic memories are difficult for them to piece together. There is a striking disconnection between their verbal and visually encoded memory and their emotional experiences. At times they become flooded by emotions that seem to be triggered by memory fragments, but are unconnected to conscious experience. At other times they report deeply frightening or sad experiences with an apparent lack of emotional content. They are rarely able to connect their emotional experience to their bodily sensations either in the here and now, or when exploring difficult memories. The question itself is often met with puzzlement. These disconnections occur in varying degrees, and in their most severe forms are recognised as dissociation.

The full picture of the impact of disrupted or traumatic attachment relationships and early childhood trauma on the development of children's neurobiology provides significant insight into the complex and challenging symptoms experienced by our young clients. It also provides potential insight into the nature of therapeutic relationships and experiences that may help them heal and move forward into a more hopeful, connected future.

Notes

1. Siegel, Daniel J. (2013). *The Developing Mind: How Relationships and the Brain Interact to Shape Who We Are.* Guilford. New York. p 27.
2. Schore, A. (2013). Relational trauma, brain development, and dissociation. In J. D. Ford and C. Courtois (Eds.), *Treating Complex Traumatic Stress Disorders in Children and Adolescents: Scientific Foundations and Therapeutic.* Guilford. New York. p 4.
3. Siegel, Daniel J. (2013). *The Developing Mind: How Relationships and the Brain Interact to Shape Who We Are.* Guilford. New York. p 22.
4. Siegel, Daniel J. (2013). *The Developing Mind: How Relationships and the Brain Interact to Shape Who We Are.* Guilford. New York. p 24.
5. Siegel, Daniel J. (2013). *The Developing Mind: How Relationships and the Brain Interact to Shape Who We Are.* Guilford. New York.
6. Siegel, Daniel J. (2013). *The Developing Mind: How Relationships and the Brain Interact to Shape Who We Are.* Guilford. New York. p 177.
7. Siegel, Daniel J. (2003). An interpersonal neurobiology of psychotherapy: The developing mind and the resolution of trauma. In M. F. Solomon and J. Siegel (Eds.), *Healing Trauma: Attachment, Mind, Body and Brain.* W. W. Norton & Company. New York.
8. Siegel, Daniel J. (2013). *The Developing Mind: How Relationships and the Brain Interact to Shape Who We Are.* Guilford. New York. pp 15–16.
9. Knickmeyer, R. C., Gouttard, S., Kang, C., Evans, D., Wilber, K., Smith, J. K., Hamer, R. M., Lin, W., Gerig, G., & Gilmore, J. H. (2008, November). A structural MRI study of human brain development from birth to 2 years. *Journal of Neuroscience 28*(47), 12176–12182; and Chiron, C., Jambaque, I., Nabbout, R., Lounes, R., Syrota, A., & Dulac, O. (1997). The right brain is dominant in human infants. *Brain, 120*, 1057–1065. Referenced by Schore, A. (2013). Relational trauma, brain development, and dissociation. In J. D. Ford and C. Courtois (Eds.), *Treating Complex Traumatic Stress Disorders in Children and Adolescents: Scientific Foundations and Therapeutic Models.* Guilford. New York.

10. Mento, G., Suppiej, A., Altoè, G., & Bisiacchi, P. S. (2010). Functional hemispheric asymmetries in humans: Electrophysiological evidence from preterm infants. *European Journal of Neuroscience, 31*(3), 565–574. Referenced by Schore, A. (2013). Relational trauma, brain development, and dissociation. In J. D. Ford and C. Courtois (Eds.), *Treating Complex Traumatic Stress Disorders in Children and Adolescents: Scientific Foundations and Therapeutic Models.* Guilford. New York.
11. Schore, Allan. (1994). *Affect Regulation and the Origin of the Self.* Erlbaum. Hillsdale, NJ.
12. Siegel, Daniel J. (2013). *The Developing Mind: How Relationships and the Brain Interact to Shape Who We Are.* Guilford. New York. p 23.
13. Schore, A. N. (2002). Dysregulation of the right brain: A fundamental mechanism of traumatic attachment and the psychopathogenesis of posttraumatic stress disorder. *Australian and New Zealand Journal of Psychiatry, 36*, 9–30.
14. Schore, A. (2013). Relational trauma, brain development, and dissociation. In J. D. Ford and C. Courtois (Eds.), *Treating Complex Traumatic Stress Disorders in Children and Adolescents: Scientific Foundations and Therapeutic Models.* Guilford. New York.
15. Siegel, Daniel J. (2013). *The Developing Mind: How Relationships and the Brain Interact to Shape Who We Are.* Guilford. New York. p 18.
16. Siegel, Daniel J. (2013). *The Developing Mind: How Relationships and the Brain Interact to Shape Who We Are.* Guilford. New York. pp 22–24.
17. Siegel, Daniel J. (2013). *The Developing Mind: How Relationships and the Brain Interact to Shape Who We Are.* Guilford. New York.
18. Schore, Allan. (1994). *Affect Regulation and the Origin of the Self.* Erlbaum. Hillsdale, NJ.
19. Porgess, Stephen W. (2011). *The Polyvagal Theory: Neurophysiological Foundations of Emotions, Attachment, Communication, Self-Regulation.* W. W. Norton & Company. New York.
20. Siegel, Daniel J. (2013). *The Developing Mind: How Relationships and the Brain Interact to Shape Who We Are.* Guilford. New York. p 12.
21. Carrion, Victor G., & Wong, Shane S. (2012, August). Can traumatic stress alter the brain? Understanding the implications of early trauma on brain development and learning. *Journal of Adolescent Health, 51*(2), S23–28.
22. Czeh, B., Perez-Cruz, C., Fuchs, E., & Flügge, G. (2008, June). Chronic stress-induced cellular changes in the medial prefrontal cortex and their potential clinical implications: Does hemisphere location matter? *Research, 26*, 1–13.
23. Schore, Allan. (1994). *Affect Regulation and the Origin of the Self.* Erlbaum. Hillsdale, NJ.
24. Sullivan R., & Gratton, A. (2002, January–February). Prefrontal cortical regulation of hypothalamic-pituitary-adrenal function in the rat and implications for psychopathology: Side matters. *Psychoneuroendocrinology, 27*(1–2), 99–114.
25. Painter, Kirstin, & Scannapieco, Maria. (2013, July). Child maltreatment: The neurobiological aspects of posttraumatic stress disorder. *Journal of Evidence-Based Social Work, 10*(4), 276–84.
26. Siegel, Daniel J. (2013). *The Developing Mind: How Relationships and the Brain Interact to Shape Who We Are.* Guilford. New York. p 19.
27. Bock, J., Murmu, R. P., Ferdman, N., Leshem, M., & Braun, K. (2008, April). Refinement of dendritic and synaptic networks in the rodent anterior cingulate and orbitofrontal cortex: Critical impact of early and late social experience. *Developmental Neurobiology, 68*(5), 685–695.
28. Schore, Allan. (1994). *Affect Regulation and the Origin of the Self.* Erlbaum. Hillsdale, NJ. p 15.
29. Warner, E., Koomar, J., Lary, B., & Cook, A. (2013, October). Can the body change the score? Application of sensory modulation principles in the treatment of traumatized adolescents in residential settings. *Journal of Family Violence, 28*(7), 729–773.
30. Schore, A. N. (2001). The effects of a secure attachment relationship on right brain development, affect regulation and infant mental health. *Infant Mental Health Journal, 22*, 7–66.

31. Schore, A.N. (2002). Dysregulation of the right brain: A fundamental mechanism of traumatic attachment and the psychopathogenesis of posttraumatic stress disorder. *Australian and New Zealand Journal of Psychiatry, 36*, 9–30.
32. Schore, A. (2013). Relational trauma, brain development, and dissociation. In J. D. Ford and C. Courtois (Eds.), *Treating Complex Traumatic Stress Disorders in Children and Adolescents: Scientific Foundations and Therapeutic Models.* Guilford. New York.
33. Bowlby, J.A. (1969). *Attachment.* Basic Books. New York.
34. Korte, S. M. (2001). Corticosteroids in relation to fear, anxiety and psychopathology. *Neuroscience and Biobehavioral Reviews, 25*, 117–142.
35. Francis, D. D., & Meaney, M.J. (1999). Maternal care and the development of stress responses. *Current Opinion in Neurobiology, 9*, 128–134.
36. Levine, S. (1994). The ontogeny of the hypothalamic-pituitary-adrenal axis. The influence of maternal factors. *Annals of the New York Academy of Sciences, 746*, 275–288.
37. Schore, A. (2013). Relational trauma, brain development, and dissociation. In J. D. Ford and C. Courtois (Eds.), *Treating Complex Traumatic Stress Disorders in Children and Adolescents:Scientific Foundations and Therapeutic Models*. Guilford. New York.
38. Schore, A.N. (2001). The effects of a secure attachment relationship on right brain development, affect regulation and infant mental health. *Infant Mental Health Journal, 22*, 7–66.
39. Schore, A.N. (2001). The effects of a secure attachment relationship on right brain development, affect regulation and infant mental health. *Infant Mental Health Journal, 22*, 201–269.
40. Schore, A.N. (2002). Dysregulation of the right brain: A fundamental mechanism of traumatic attachment and the psychopathogenesis of posttraumatic stress disorder. *Australian and New Zealand Journal of Psychiatry, 36*, 9–30.
41. Schore, A. N. (2013). Relational trauma, brain development, and dissociation. In J. D. Ford and C. Courtois (Eds.), *Treating Complex Traumatic Stress Disorders in Children and Adolescents: Scientific Foundations and Therapeutic Models*. Guilford. New York. p 41.
42. Hughes, Daniel A. (2007). *Attachment Focused Family Therapy*. W.W. Norton & Company. New York. pp 20–28.
43. Siegel, Daniel J. (2013). *The Developing Mind: How Relationships and the Brain Interact to Shape Who We Are*. Guilford. New York. p 18.
44. Teicher, M. H., Andersen, S. L., Polcari A., Anderson, C. M., Navalta, C. P., & Kim, D. M. (2003, January–March). The neurobiological consequences of early stress and childhood maltreatment. *Neuroscience Biobehavioural Review, 27*(1–2), 33–44.
45. Porgess, Stephen W. (2011). *The Polyvagal Theory: Neurophysiological Foundations of Emotions, Attachment, Communication, Self-Regulation*. W.W. Norton & Company. New York.
46. Teicher, M. H., Andersen, S. L., Polcari A., Anderson, C. M., Navalta, C. P., & Kim, D. M. (2003, January–March). The neurobiological consequences of early stress and childhood maltreatment. *Neuroscience Biobehavioural Review, 27*(1–2), 33–44.
47. de Kloet, E. R., & Rinne, T. (2007). Neuroendocrine markers of early trauma: Implications for post traumatic stress disorder. In E. Vermettem, M. Dorahy, & D. Siegel (Eds.), *Traumatic Dissociation: Neurobiology and Treatment*. American Psychiatric Publishing. Arlington, VA.
48. Mason, J. W., Wang, S., Yehuda, R., Riney, S., Charney, D. S., & Southwick, S. M. (2001, May/June). Psychogenic lowering of urinary cortisol levels linked to increased emotional numbing and a shame-depressive syndrome in combat-related posttraumatic stress disorder. *Psychosomatic Medicine, 63*, 387–401.
49. Perry, B. D., Pollard, R. A., Blakely, T. L., Baker, W. L., & Vigilante, D, (1995). Childhood trauma, the neurobiology of adaptation, and "use-dependent" development of the brain: How "states" become "traits." *Infant Mental Health Journal, 16*(4), 271–291.
50. Siegel, Daniel J. (2013). *The Developing Mind: How Relationships and the Brain Interact to Shape Who We Are*. Guilford. New York.

51. De Bellis, M. D., Keshavan, M. S., Clark, D. B., Casey, B. J., Gied, J. N., Boring, A. M., & Ryan, N. D. (1999). Developmental traumatology. Part II: Brain development. *Biological Psychiatry, 45*, 1271–1284.
52. Teicher, M. H., Anderson, S. L., Dumont, M. L., Ito, Y., Glod, C. A., Vaitiuzis, C., & Geid, J. N. (2000, November). Childhood neglect attenuates development of the corpus callosum. *Society for Neuroscience Abstracts, 26*, 549.
53. Teicher, M. H., Anderson, S. L., Polcari, A., Anderson, C. M., Navalta, C. P., and Kim, D. M. (2003). The neurobiological consequences of early stress and childhood maltreatment. *Neuroscience and Biobehavioural Reviews, 27*, 33–44.
54. Siegel, Daniel J. (2013). *The Developing Mind: How Relationships and the Brain Interact to Shape Who We Are*. Guilford. New York. p 78.
55. Silberg, Joyanna. (2013). *The Child Survivor: Healing Developmental Trauma and Dissociation*. Routledge. New York. p 9.
56. Schore, A. N. (2009). Attachment trauma and the development of the right brain. In P. Dell & J. O'Neil (Eds.), *Dissociation and the Dissociative Disorders. DSM V and Beyond*. Routledge. New York.
57. Jackowski, A. P., de Araujo, C. M., de Lacerda, A.L.T., Mari, J.D.J., & Kaufman, J. (2009). Neurostructural imaging findings in children with post-traumatic stress disorder: Brief review. *Psychiatry and Clinical Neurosciences, 63*(1), 1–8.
58. Teicher, M. H., Tomoda, A., & Anderson, S. L. (2006). Neurobiological consequences of early stress and childhood maltreatment: Are results from human and animal studies comparable? *Annals of the New York Academy of Sciences, 1071*, 313–323.

3 Complex Trauma in a Clinical Setting

The presentations of children with complex trauma histories are many and varied, as are their histories. Here I will describe several different children and adolescents. Although they have all experienced disrupted attachment and trauma, their histories, symptoms and responses to therapy differ. Their life situations also differ, presenting different challenges and opportunities in addressing their treatment and attachment needs.

Beth

Beth referred herself for counselling at sixteen. She came to her first appointment, and several after that, with her boyfriend. Petite, quiet and anxious, she was afraid to leave the house alone. Her actions were restricted, based on rigid self-imposed rules. There were few foods she could tolerate eating, and they could not touch each other on the plate. When she went out, she had to have her boyfriend with her. She could not take the bus. When walking anywhere she followed specific routes, taking a predetermined number of steps on each specific part of the sidewalk. She was an excellent student and liked by her teachers, but could barely attend classes out of fear of being outside, fear of her peers and teachers, and fear of being found by her father. Although fiercely defending her mother in therapy sessions, Beth wanted no contact with her family. She saw her mother as a helpless victim likely to betray Beth's whereabouts to her abusive father. Beth engaged in therapy easily. She disclosed severe physical and emotional abuse in her first session. She and her boyfriend, Chris, were both aware of dissociative symptoms, including two alter personalities. Several months into therapy, one of her personalities shared memories of sexual abuse by her father, which Beth then disclosed in therapy. She was passive and easily controlled by others. She had had several physically and sexually abusive boyfriends prior to Chris. At sixteen she left her parents' home and moved in with Chris and his family. Initially she was dependent on Chris and followed his lead in everything. Beth did not believe that the system would or could help her. She had been let down many times. The police and child welfare had been called, but she and her siblings had been terrified to talk about the abuse. The police believed her parents that she was an out-of-control teen. When she ran away from home, the police picked her up and brought her back.

Beth exhibited many complex trauma symptoms. She has been diagnosed with a dissociative identity disorder, presenting initially with two alters. A third came to light almost two years into therapy. This part remained hidden until a sudden serious suicide attempt. Beth experienced frequent flashbacks, panic attacks and nightmares. Her sleep was disrupted and she was always tired. When asleep she lashed out physically, leaving Chris with bruises. She experienced anxiety with obsessive compulsive and agoraphobic features which restricted her daily functioning. Beth feared conflict. She was unable to identify anger and was triggered by anger or disagreement in others. She had no sense of entitlement, and apologised for every imagined infraction. Beth experienced a dependent, anxious attachment to Chris. She had very few other supports in her life.

Beth and Chris's relationship posed a dilemma for therapy. He was her only significant support, and he encouraged her to enter into therapy and recover from her trauma. It was Chris who helped her to make the referral, and who brought her for her appointments. He encouraged her to meet alone with me, although initially she was unwilling to. Chris and Beth cared about each other, and she felt safer with him than she had with anyone else. He treated her with respect and didn't talk down to her. Still, Beth's dependence on Chris, and her fear of being away from him, was a trauma symptom. It was clear that if she were to heal, the dynamic of their relationship would change. Chris insisted that he was open to this, and both Beth and Chris said they were committed to making the relationship work. They were, however, sixteen and eighteen years old. Chris had his own trauma history and his own mental health difficulties. Simply telling them about the likely impact of Beth's healing on their relationship would not help them know what to expect. This issue was discussed in detail many times during the course of Beth's treatment, and at many times became a focus of treatment. It will be discussed in more detail in upcoming chapters.

Tony

Tony, thirteen, came for counselling to address a severe single incident trauma; his involvement in a fire in which a friend had been killed. Tony had tried to save his friend, but had to leave him to save his own life. He was referred by his mother, who attended with him. The history included exposure to early domestic abuse prior to his parent's separation. Tony denied any memory of this, and his mother felt he had moved beyond these experiences. Tony's mother stated that Tony had no symptoms prior to the accident. Tony presented in session as sad and teary. He disclosed bullying at school in which he had been blamed by peers for his friend's death. Tony appeared to be a good candidate for attachment-supported eye movement desensitisation and reprocessing (EMDR; see Chapter 10). Dissociation screening was negative. After EMDR with Tony and his mother, and doing some resource installation, we did a trauma-focused EMDR session. Tony sat through the session unresponsive, repeatedly answering "nothing" to the question "What's come up for you?" He said he did not understand what he was supposed to do, or what the questions meant. He denied any experience or reaction to the process, but refused to undergo further EMDR. Over the next several weeks, Tony became increasingly anxious and obsessive. Conflict between him and his mother over his time-consuming, intrusive and repetitive behaviours escalated. His mother had reported that before the accident he had been a good student and a well-behaved teen. As the situation deteriorated, his mother began to disclose that Tony had always had difficulties with anger and disrespectful behaviour, but that it had escalated following his friend's death. He began to refuse to come to sessions. When he did attend, he would spend the time arguing with his mother about rules. When we met alone he would retreat into teary silence. For several weeks, I worked with Tony's mother, hoping to create a stronger alliance. I hypothesized that the EMDR, while targeting the helplessness experienced during the accident, had triggered preverbal experiences of domestic violence. I worked to reframe his stubbornness as anxiety. Although apparently open in sessions, and acknowledging the idea of anxiety, Tony's mother continued to respond to her son with increasing anger and rigid punishment. Eventually, Tony was hospitalised following an explosive meltdown. Hospitalisation led to a decrease in outbursts, and a new attempt at therapy. Both in individual and in parent-child sessions, Tony engaged superficially. The conflict between him and his mother again became the focus. On his own, Tony contacted the Children's Aid Society (CAS) and disclosed physical and emotional abuse by his mother, ongoing throughout his childhood. He was removed from home and placed in foster care. Tony continued to come for individual sessions, but his mother refused any contact. Although attending sessions and talking with me about a number of personal relationship and peer issues, Tony avoided talking about the accident or abuse. His foster mother, like his mother, was a matter-of-fact person who was more focused on behaviour than on his affective experience. She often sent Tony alone to appointments which had been scheduled for the two of them, calling to tell me that Tony did not appreciate her efforts, and she would not waste her time. This placement broke down. Tony's next placement, although warm and supportive, was in his old neighborhood. He was more open in therapy, but was distressed by being exposed to triggers and to peers from the past who continued to bully him. A few months into this placement, Tony made three serious suicide attempts and was hospitalised three more times in succession. During the first of these hospitalisations his mother made contact and visited. Both have since expressed a wish to work on their relationship. The situation continues to be difficult. Tony was placed in a group home. He was unhappy with the placement, but no foster home would take him because of the safety risk. His group home staff expressed interest in understanding his behaviours as symptoms, and supporting him as a child in pain. Tony struggled with trust. He avoided talking about emotional subjects. Tony's mother was cautiously willing to engage in treatment, but unwilling to "dig up the past." It was difficult for her to acknowledge the past without blame or shame.

Tony exhibits attachment difficulties including affective avoidance and a dismissive style. His mother's acknowledgment that he has always struggled with anger and defiance suggests impaired affect regulation stemming from early experiences interfering with a secure attachment relationship with his mother. This is further supported by his difficulties with trust, and shifting between wanting caring adults in his life and keeping them at a distance.[1,2,3] When placed with a foster mother he liked, Tony refused to allow her to attend therapy sessions. He didn't want her to know about his problem; in the past, everyone who he let in "used it against" him. He struggles with a damaged sense of self; he doesn't like the way he looks or who he is. Although the tragic death of his friend was a catalyst for helplessness, it is likely that these feelings are rooted in earlier experiences of abuse by his mother and witnessing violence between his parents. These experiences held in affective and sensory memory.[4,5] When triggered, they lead to overwhelming helplessness and shame. His shame about his sense of self is directed towards himself, in repeated self-harm and suicide attempts, as well as defended against by being directed outwards in dismissive rage towards his mother, foster parents and group home staff. Tony's mother's reinvolvement creates both an opportunity and a dilemma. If Tony and his mother are able to at least partly heal their relationship, it could be very helpful. However, Tony's mother is struggling with anger and shame, which makes it difficult for her to engage in attachment work. This dilemma is discussed in in later chapters.

John

John, thirteen, was brought by his social worker. He was a Crown Ward (the Canadian term for a permanent ward of the state), living in a group home. John had entered care two years previously because his behaviour at home had been explosive and unpredictable, posing a risk to his younger siblings. John had been abused and neglected by his father and witnessed domestic violence towards his mother, Shelley, from birth to age two and a half. The family had lived in a small community where his mother had no family or friends. She worked outside the home, and her husband stayed at home with John and his sister. Feeling trapped and powerless to protect herself from her husband, she convinced herself that her children were safe and it was only she who was being abused. When she found hand-shaped bruises on John's back and buttocks, she left.

John and his mother moved to the city, and she later remarried. When she gave birth to a son from her second husband, John became episodically explosive, violent and jealous towards his new half brother and his mother. John was brought into care with the hope of stabilising him and returning him home. He rapidly broke down every placement, and finally was moved to a group home. With each move, his anger and desperation increased. After more than two years in care, and ten moves, the CAS had to return him home or make him a permanent ward. John came to our first session desperately wanting help. He was brought by his worker and his mother. John and his mother told me he was being bullied and beaten up in his group home. His worker confirmed this. As in previous placements, John had quickly alienated peers, and refused to cooperate with adults. He wasn't safe, but no other placement could be found. Although John found it difficult to trust, he was willing to work with me; he was desperate for help, both with his problems and in escaping the situation he was in.

John was a puzzle to those trying to help him. He was small for his age. When I met him he was pale, drawn and underweight, with enormous dark circles under his eyes. He looked like a child in a war zone. Individually, he was a soft spoken, polite and sensitive young man. He was kind, caring and sincere. He showed insight into his difficulties, and shared detailed memories of incidents of violence and abuse he would have seemingly been too young to remember. According to his mother, the details were accurate. He often accompanied his conversations with drawings of the events. John seemed to genuinely care about many of the adults trying to help him. He remembered if someone had been ill, and took the time to ask about it, no matter how distressed he was in the moment. He offered to share his snacks. He expressed an intense protective concern over his younger siblings, and great pain over having been frightening or threatening to them. In contrast, John's narrative of current situations, although detailed and clear, differed from what others remembered. He explained his attacks on his siblings as efforts to protect them, although he couldn't explain how or from whom. He told detailed stories of events that had not occurred. In spite of his desire to improve his situation, his behaviours did not change, and in fact escalated in violence. He continued to lie, steal and instigate conflict between his peers, at his own expense.

An important element of John's story is the varying reactions that he evoked in others. He created antipathy in those who experienced him as part of a group. The staff in his group home appeared to John, his mother, and to me to be minimising physical attacks on him by his peers, in a way that was contrary to rules and out of character for the staff. They seemed to genuinely see him as exaggerating, even when the injuries were evident and he was hospitalised. My intention is not to portray the staff as negligent. My intention is to show the countertransference reactions he elicited from others. The opposite was also true. Many adults, myself included, felt compelled to support him and advocate for him even beyond what would be expected. The outcome was a system in conflict, in response to a boy who was himself in conflict. A split was created in John's external world that matched the split in his internal world. This issue is explored in Chapter 12.

Within a few sessions, John was describing his experience of himself as divided between dark and light, good and bad. His drawings showed a young man divided down the middle, being influenced by forces outside of his control. John quickly came to understand his internal world, and within a few weeks explained that his losses of control were triggered by multiple seemingly innocuous responses in others, which led to vivid flashbacks and disconnection with the here and now. A word, movement or facial expression could send him back in time, fearing for his life. He interpreted every small negative reaction from others as dismissive, belittling or threatening. One on one, or in small supportive groups, he could tolerate more challenge. In larger groups or with anyone who experienced him negatively, he had no control and no memory of the events as they occurred. This happened anywhere from five to twenty-five times a day. John spent more of his time in flashback and dissociative states than in current time.

John's mother wanted to be involved in his treatment and he wanted her to be. In sessions, when upset, he would pull far away from her, hiding his head under his jacket, and then slowly, without looking at her, he would reach out his hand towards her. On visits, when they had a good time together, he would suddenly become reactive, or steal something, and then refuse to speak to her for days after. His behaviour with his mother was typical of disorganised attachment.[6] Consistent with this assessment, John had poor affective awareness, and little ability to regulate either his affect or his behaviour. When triggered or overwhelmed he could not integrate experience; he could not connect sensory experiences with emotions or thoughts; he got memories of recent events mixed in with memories of the past; John's limbic system was in a constant state of hyperalert, and he appeared not to have learned how to experience safety.[7,8,9]

Sophie

Sophie has been described in detail in Chapter 2. Initially identified as having no trauma history prior to adoption, Sophie received multiple services, interventions and diagnoses focusing on behaviour and sensory integration. Mostly, these were unsuccessful or mildly helpful. When Sophie was twelve, her behavioural therapist supported her parents' belief that her presentation suggested early trauma and neglect. Her parents approached the adoption agency for detailed early life information and found that she had spent most of her first three years in a high-risk, dangerous environment.

Sophie was referred at twelve for assessment and treatment of her suspected complex trauma disorder. Sophie has been impacted in all the domains of functioning listed in Chapter 1. She has been diagnosed with a dissociative identity disorder, and experiences difficulties with attachment, affective and behavioural control, cognitive processing, biological development, self-concept, worldview and social development. Her parents engaged with her in attachment-focused work. She showed immediately improved self-regulation and relationship skills in response to phase one therapy focusing on attachment and dissociative symptoms.

Terra

Terra has been described in Chapter 1. Paternal grandparents gained custody when she was three. She experienced physical and emotional abuse and neglect by her mother, complicated by the sudden deaths of her father and paternal grandfather when she was six. Following their deaths, she remained in the care of her grandmother, who raised her. Initially she managed well, until being retraumatised at age eight , at which time she stopped attending school.

Terra was referred for counselling with me at nine. She was oppositional, angry and anxious, with difficulty sleeping and frequent nightmares. She was alternately dependent on and rejecting and mean towards her grandmother and the family pets.

Terra and her grandmother engaged well in phase one work, and Terra experienced both emotional relief and improved coping skills. Phase one work became extended when her grandmother suffered a serious heart attack. Initially Terra experienced a return of many of her old difficulties, but these resolved fairly quickly.

We attempted to begin trauma work just after Terra turned twelve. Each time we attempted EMDR, Terra immediately fell asleep and could not be woken up. Her grandmother described the sleep as very different from the way she slept at home. She was generally a light sleeper, easily roused and physically restless. In my office, she lay completely immobile and unresponsive. When her grandmother was able to rouse her, she would hold her arms up, like a toddler, to be picked up. Once, during a session, when she appeared distracted, she referred to having been in "gummy-bear land." I asked, and she told me she had always been able to go to gummy-bear land—that it was full of rainbows and everything was made of candy. We started to talk about other possible dissociative experiences—she became quiet and said this was "awkward" to talk about. I reassured her that many kids I worked with had these kinds of experiences, and that they weren't uncommon for kids who had had a lot of stress when they were little. Within an hour this twelve-year-old, whom I had known since she was nine, told me all about the voices in her head. She described Tarra—who had her name but spelled it differently and said bad things about her; there was also her when she was four, another twelve-year-old who was like her, but also kind of negative, and Mr. Nobody. Mr. Nobody used to be her imaginary friend—Terra's grandmother even remembered him and Tarra, from years ago. Terra said that she stopped talking about him because he isn't her friend anymore and he scares her. She can see them all in her head. She then added that she knew the little girl and the other twelve-year-old were parts of her, but that Mr. Nobody and Tarra were not. They were different because they were dead. She said that Tarra had died in a fire in one of her dreams. She was reassured, although sceptical, to know that her grandmother and I didn't think she was crazy. She was less able to consider the idea that Tarra and Mr. Nobody could be parts of herself, even if they were dead. She became quite eager to explore these experiences. A talented artist, she agreed to spend the next few weeks, during which I would be away, drawing these parts, and other internal experiences, in a sketch book that I gave her.

During the initial assessment Terra was identified as struggling with attachment issues and post-traumatic difficulties resulting in problems with affect regulation and anxiety. Terra and her grandmother engaged in successful attachment-focused work, and her ability to manage her feelings and attend school improved. Her reactions to attempts to process her trauma experiences using EMDR are suggestive of a polyvagal shutdown response[10] that was unexpected after successful phase one work. Another puzzling problem was that previously resolved issues seemed to reappear occasionally without clear triggers, and Terra seemed unable to understand or even really talk about them. The surfacing of dissociative symptoms provided answers to these questions. Children with dissociative disorders can seem to respond well to treatment which does not directly address their dissociation. However, the parts of the self that remain compartmentalised, including those parts' memories, symptoms and attachment difficulties, may not be engaged in therapy, and so remain stuck. The parts that engage in therapy learn skills to manage, and can appear to be coping better, but the compartmentalised impact of the trauma remains untouched.

Amie

When Amie first attended therapy she received traditional family therapy with her father and older sister. Amie did not engage well in family therapy. When the male family therapist discussed whether or not she wanted to continue, Amie said she would like to meet with a female therapist individually. Her family therapist referred her to me. Our first session was a month before her sixteenth birthday. As usual, I explained the limits of confidentiality and informed consent. In Ontario, Canada, any incident defined as abuse, historical or otherwise, must be reported to child welfare if the child is under the age of sixteen. After the age of sixteen, if no other child is at risk, the information is confidential. Amie asked many questions about this. She then said, "Well—I guess I have nothing to talk about right now—I'll call you in a month!" and walked out. Just over a month later, sixteen-year-old Amie was back in my office disclosing a history of neglect, physical abuse, sexual abuse and sexual exploitation dating back to infancy. Although she did have siblings, she maintained that she was the only one who had these experiences. Her mother, who suffered postpartum depression with her, had "hated her" from birth, leaving her unattended in the laundry room as an infant when her father was at work. As she grew older, she sought out her mother's attention. Maybe because she was so willing to please or maybe because her mother didn't have a strong attachment to her, she began including Amie in daytime parties. These parties happened when Amie's siblings were at school. Amie's mother found reasons for her to stay home. Amie tried to please her mother and get the attention of other guests. By age eight she was drinking, dancing sexual dances, and had a thirty-two-year-old "boyfriend." She describes her earliest "dance partners" as being her uncles, one of whom is a registered sex offender. In spite of her description of herself as having been sexually abused, Amie found it difficult to describe incidents other than the dancing.

During the first year of therapy, Amie battled suicidal ideation, and was seen at emergency psychiatry several times. In spite of being factually open, her descriptions lacked emotion. During sessions Amie's other parts began to make appearances. She was diagnosed with dissociative identity disorder about six weeks after beginning individual therapy. She disclosed the existence of six parts. Two parts spontaneously began to participate in therapy sessions. Although Amie engaged quickly in therapy and built a strong alliance, she continued to struggle with hopelessness and helplessness. She viewed herself as damaged, contaminated and good only for being used. She found it difficult to consider other possibilities. Amie's negative view of herself and the world are her greatest challenges.

Amie presented with dissociative identity disorder, disorganised attachment patterns, affect regulation difficulties, problems with cognitive functioning and cognitive integration, and a negative sense of herself and the world. Disclosure of her dissociative experiences and her history of abuse was not easy. She distrusted others, particularly those who are part of the "system," and she experienced deep shame about her experiences, for which she felt responsible. She was unable to engage in a helpful therapeutic relationship until she was able to feel in control of her own information and what would be done with it. For Amie, that meant she needed to be over the age of sixteen, so that she could be sure that her disclosures would not be reported to the CAS.

Michael

Michael, seen following a suicide attempt at seventeen, had experienced a close and connected early relationship with his mother, Linda. When Michael was eight, Linda suffered a depressive episode which left her emotionally incapacitated and unavailable for several years. By the time Michael was fifteen, Linda had received treatment for her depression, and was doing well. At that time, Michael's best friend of many years committed suicide. This impacted not just on Michael, but on his family, his school and his community. Having experienced his mother's depression for so many years, Michael became afraid of her sadness, and of the impact of the death on those around him. He contained his own feelings, while taking care of those around him. Michael began to use drugs to cope with his feelings of loss, sadness and aloneness. He began to experience severe anxiety over events he could not control. He and his mother began to argue over his missing school and his drug use. Michael disclosed suicidal feelings to a teacher at school, and was briefly hospitalised. He was diagnosed with major depression and prescribed medication. Michael's anxiety continued to escalate, and he continued to use street drugs to cope. A year after his first hospitalisation Michael overdosed on his antidepressant medication and was hospitalised again. On discharge he was brought by his mother for treatment. Michael was open and motivated. He quickly was able to consider that his anxiety and depression were related to trauma over his friend's suicide, and his difficulties in relying on others for support. Linda was willing to talk about the impact of her previous depression on their relationship. Both wanted to be closer. Michael and his mother engaged in some dyadic work followed by a process of EMDR during which Linda remained present as witness and support for her son. A while later, a school crisis led to Michael experiencing suicidal thoughts. By the time I was able to see them the next day, the thoughts had passed. I asked Michael what was different, and he replied "I've realised that I'm not alone." The day of the crisis, rather than doing drugs, or becoming overwhelmed by his panic, he had taken the day off and spent it with his mother. They had spent the day "cuddling and watching TV together." Since then Michael has experienced a few ups and downs. He has been able to rely on his mother for support, and when necessary comes in to talk. Considering the severity of his loss, Michael is displaying remarkable resilience.

Michael is an example of a young person who had a good early attachment that was disrupted when he was older. He experienced anxiety around his relationship with his mother and had become protective of her. This anxiety may not have led to major difficulties if Michael hadn't experienced a major trauma which overwhelmed his ability to cope on his own, and that also affected his mother and caused her sadness. Because Michael's relationship with his mother was generally solid, and because she was no longer depressed, they were able to work together to do repair work. Improving his ability to turn to his mother for support and to rely on her to help him coregulate his feelings when they became too much assisted him in being able to deal with the impact of his friend's suicide.

James

James referred himself at the recommendation of his school. James was a young man known for being quiet. During an argument, he had allegedly threatened a teacher. James had attended the same high school for several years, and had never been violent; the school wanted to be supportive. He was well liked by his teachers. The school also did not want to ignore a possible risk of violence.

James was a muscular, bearded young man appearing older than his seventeen years. Clearly intelligent, with a sophisticated sense of humour, James enjoyed talking about ideas. His physical appearance was somewhat different than his spoken presentation. He looked dangerous. He enjoyed intimidating people both with his appearance and his intelligence. He joked about needing to be in control. In spite of his sophisticated presentation James appeared detached and emotionally flat, almost robotic and wooden. During our first interview, he denied having threatened his teacher. "I wasn't threatening her, I was warning her. She was pushing and pushing, and wouldn't let me get a word in. She was getting right into my face, and I was going to lose control. I don't ever want that to happen. When I lose control, bad things happen. I told her if she didn't back off, something really bad was going to happen." He agreed that someone who didn't understand could see that as a threat. I asked him what would happen if he lost control. He suddenly fell back in his chair, unresponsive. After a few minutes, he regained consciousness, seemingly unaware of what happened. I asked him about it, and he answered that he had been told that this happened sometimes. James then told me that when he was much younger, in early elementary school, he had been badly bullied, both at home and at school. He had two older brothers who beat him up often, and a father who beat the three of them. At school one day, a bully pushed him too far, and he lost control. He doesn't remember what happened, but the police came to his house and after that, everyone at school was scared of him. He believes he hurt the boy very badly.

Over the next few weeks, James openly but unemotionally shared his world with me. He told me he had few memories of his childhood, but that he did remember that his mentally ill father treated all three boys violently, but the older two the worst. His older brothers took their anger out on him and regularly beat and humiliated him. He had few memories of his mother in the home, and did not know if she had witnessed the abuse and did nothing, or if she had been at work. James had never done well at school. He knew he was intelligent, but he had difficulty with the work. His report cards described him as not applying himself and as not putting in effort. This resulted in his being beaten by his father. Elementary school was alienating for James. He couldn't understand his lack of success, and his anger and frustration quickly resulted in his being labelled. James also described summers spent with his maternal grandparents on their farm. He talked about his grandfather with reverence, stating that he was his grandfather's favourite, and that he had taught him how to be a man. He described how his grandfather would beat him to get him to defend himself. He forced him to drown kittens in order to learn to manage his emotions. He told him he was the only one in the family who was worth anything, and that he would help him become strong. When James became a young teen, he decided he would become able to defend himself from his brothers, and started working out. He worked out so intensely, and developed so quickly, that his muscles inhibited the growth of his limbs. James coped with his world by taking steps to gain control, and refused to ever be out of control. He had a group of close friends at school who knew him well and supported him. He had known them since they were young, and they stood by him. Their families liked him, and when he left home, he moved in with one of them. These friendships seemed to go beyond what most teens share. His friends ran interference for him. They knew that he was worried about losing control, and that he found being around people stressful. At school, at least one, if not more, of his friends was always with him. If anything went wrong, they would physically stand around him until he felt safe again.

James told me that when upset he lost chunks of his memory. He was dependent on his friends to tell him what had happened, and to prevent him from hurting people. This system worked, and he had not hurt anyone since the fight in elementary school. James agreed to complete an Adolescent Dissociative Experiences Scale (A-DES). When James reached question nine, "I hear voices in my head that are not mine," he stopped and asked, "Do angry, feral noises count?" James's score on the A-DES was very elevated. We agreed to proceed with a diagnostic interview. James was open about his symptoms but was not able to discuss any experiences during which he felt out of control, including experiences when he had felt not present. He was given a provisional diagnosis of major dissociative disorder with dissociative identity disorder suspected but unable to be confirmed.

James has done very well in therapy. He has undergone a psychological assessment and was identified as very intelligent with a nonverbal learning disability. Once this was identified and accommodated he excelled academically. Over time he fully integrated, finished high school and has continued on to college. He has maintained strong relationships with his friends, and has been in several long-term dating relationships. He is capable of closeness and connection with others, and is able to experience a full range of emotions, including vulnerability. The theme of control and loss of control became the central theme in his healing.

Katy and Lilly

Katy and Lilly were biological sisters adopted together at age four and five. They had been removed from their family of origin due to neglect, family violence and a suspicion of abuse. Lilly, one year older, had been parentified, and was used to caring for her younger sister and keeping her safe. At the time of adoption they had been diagnosed with a reactive attachment disorder. The recommendation had been made that should they be adopted, they and their adoptive parents attend attachment-focused therapy in order to support a successful transition. A further concern identified was that the girls were being unevenly treated in foster care, with Katy being the favourite, and Lilly being severely scapegoated. This situation was having a negative emotional impact on both girls.

The girls were placed for adoption with a couple whose biological children were adults. They had expressed an interest in adopting one child, but agreed to adopt two when advised that the child available could only be adopted with her sister. They chose not to pursue therapy at the time of adoption.

Three years later, the adoptive mother requested treatment for Katy. Katy was having learning difficulties at school, as well as stealing and having trouble making friends. At home she was having explosive outbursts, and was both intensely dependent on and highly jealous of her older sister. The adoptive mother felt that Katy suffered from food allergies and from foetal alcohol syndrome. She had found the school uncooperative, and had taken Katy out for a year to homeschool her. She returned her to school because she felt that Katy needed the social interaction, but continued to struggle with the school around Katy's needs. The school felt that the mother's expectations around academics and behaviour were unrealistic, and that she was looking for a medical diagnosis to explain difficulties which they believed had to do with the mother's high expectations and strict behavioural approach. For her part, the mother felt blamed by the school, who she felt was ignoring her concerns and undermining her as a parent.

We began in sessions to address the previously diagnosed reactive attachment disorder. As we began to explore attachment dynamics, the adoptive mother became distant. She maintained that Katy had neurological issues which were not being addressed, and that we, like the school, were trying to blame her for the problems. The parents then chose to take a break from treatment to facilitate some sports and academic programs the girls were in, and did not return.

About a year later, the parents contacted me again. The girls had been placed in temporary foster care due to conflict between Katy and her adoptive mother, with Lilly caught in the middle. The placement was voluntary, but the parents very much wanted to have their children return to their care. I met with the parents together, and we agreed to treatment.

This case displays a number of challenges which can arise when working with adopted children. Engaging adoptive parents in therapy can be difficult. Adopted children with complex trauma histories are not easy to parent. Many parents, initially feeling that they have a lot to offer their children, end up feeling like failures. They become caught in needing to believe that either there was something "wrong" with the child when they adopted them, or the child's problems must be their fault. This leads to defensiveness when parents feel blamed. There is a very wide range of "good enough parenting." A behavioural approach, or high expectations, can be part of good parenting, and likely goes uncommented on when a child is doing well. The same factors can immediately be identified as "the problem" when a child begins to struggle. The parent can be left feeling alienated and defensive, making it harder for them to engage in attachment-focused work.

The Stock Family

Rose and her brother Mark were adopted from Liberia at the age of four. They were not biological siblings, and were close in age. From the beginning, they were different from each other. Rose had been a favourite in her orphanage—she was good at engaging adults, and was cheerful and social. As a result she was well fed and healthy. Just prior to her adoption, she suffered a head injury. The source of the injury was never disclosed, and she had not received medical care. She has a large scar at the crown of her head where hair doesn't grow. Mark, on the other hand, was isolated and withdrawn. He had been ignored in his crowded orphanage, and didn't turn to adults for comfort. He was thin and malnourished. Just prior to the adoption he suffered a broken femur. Again, the source of the injury was not disclosed. When his adoptive parents arrived to pick him up, he was in traction in the hospital and they had to leave him in Africa for a month, returning after his release. He had a rod installed in his leg which had to be removed later in Canada.

At home, the two children reacted differently to their new circumstances. Rose clung to her adoptive mother, following her everywhere and becoming anxious and panicky when separated. She was afraid of strangers, particularly of men. Mark was quiet, independent, and more or less ignored his parents. As the children grew older, these patterns continued. Rose struggled socially and academically. She was diagnosed with ADHD and learning difficulties. Bright, cheerful and outgoing on the surface, she couldn't tolerate negative emotions. She never acknowledged feeling bad, but had meltdowns and tantrums when frustrated or anxious. During meltdowns she would call her mother terrible names, throw things and threaten. Rose did not discriminate in what she would damage—she would break things that were important to her, or throw things that were heavy or valuable. Immediately after the tantrum was over, she would act as if nothing happened. If asked, she would say "it's in the past, it doesn't matter; everything is great now." Others learned to walk on eggshells around her. Rose didn't experience connection to others, or even to herself. She was superficial. She was afraid of being alone, and was highly dependent on others. She didn't experience empathy, so her relationships were one-sided. Rose was impulsive and a risk taker. She had little awareness of cause and effect, and thrived on excitement. She was silly, socially inappropriate and outrageous in her public behaviour.

Mark was a serious and quiet boy. He was reasonably successful in school and excelled in sports. He did well socially and had many friends. On the surface, Mark had adapted better than Rose. On a day-to-day basis he coped well. Mark did not look to adults for support or guidance. He was able to keep within the rules for the most part, if it served his interests. He was not, however, connected to the rules and expectations of his world, and would find ways to circumvent them if it met his needs. Mark had poor frustration tolerance. He would give up on things if he was not immediately successful. He was motivated by sports only when they were rewarding. As soon as he was challenged, or if he was not the best, he lost interest and his effort suffered. He became known as inconsistent and unreliable in school and on teams. He would do what suited him and his interests, and had little concern for the impact on his team. Mark's pattern was that he made an immediate good first impression, and was well liked. Over time, teachers, coaches and others felt let down by him. Mark was prone to angry outbursts, but he was much more likely to brood and hold a grudge after the outburst had passed. Mark was able to identify his feelings, but did not ever want to talk about them.

I first met Rose and Mark when they were twelve. Their parents, Marco and Angela, referred Rose for counselling due to her explosive outbursts and impulsive and sexualised behaviour. During the intake, the parents also expressed worries about Mark's position of needing to be responsible for his sister at school and the impact this responsibility and her behaviour had on his ability to have a normal childhood. Neither child expressed an interest in counselling. Rose was insistent that everything was fine and her life was perfect. Mark stated that his sister was embarrassing and got away with murder, but that wasn't going to change and he had nothing to talk about. Marco and Angela were exhausted and demoralised. They had different views of how issues should be dealt with, and different expectations of what Rose could achieve. They were experiencing conflict in their marriage and around parenting. Traditionally Catholic, they were struggling with Rose's sexual preoccupations and sexualised behaviours. Marco came from a traditional Eastern European family and was expressively emotional. Angela came from a Canadian family of British descent and was restrained and quiet. Their styles clashed and as the family situation had deteriorated, Marco had become explosive himself, damaging property and putting holes in the walls at home.

This family engaged in ongoing and long-term therapy that went through many stages and will be explored in several chapters within this book. Both children experienced many crises which gradually facilitated engagement in therapy and increased healing. Several years later, when all the children were older teens, Jessica joined the family. Prior to adopting Rose and Mark, Marco and Angela had considered adopting Jessica and her two older sisters, also from Liberia, but had felt that three children at once might be overwhelming.

Jessica and her sisters had been adopted when she was almost five, by a different family in the neighborhood. The family Jessica was adopted into was emotionally and physically abusive to her and her sisters. At fourteen, Jessica disclosed the abuse to a teacher, who contacted the CAS. She was removed from the home, became a permanent ward and entered into foster care until she was eighteen. Jessica was academically successful and at school exhibited no behaviour problems. She was eager to please adults and wanted to be seen as good and successful.

When Jessica turned eighteen, she graduated from high school and was accepted into university in a nearby city. Marco and Angelo had known Jessica for many years and had been part of a group of adults who had rallied to support her. When she moved out of her foster home, they invited her to live in their home during holidays, school vacations and weekends when she wished to return to her home city. Rose and Mark also knew Jessica, and were willing to accept having her in their home. As time progressed, Jessica's status as a young adult and the "good" child began to trigger the other children's attachment difficulties. Shortly into her stay with the family, a family member let Jessica in on the "secret" of her history—that the Stock family had considered adopting her and then had chosen to adopt Mark and Rose instead. As soon as Jessica knew this, Marco and Angela realised that it could not remain a secret. The news triggered significant attachment crises in all three children, and led to a new phase in family therapy. This was when I met Jessica.

The crisis in the family led to a deterioration in Jessica's functioning, including self-harm, suicidal ideation and academic deterioration. She started going out with Rose and the two of them began to get into trouble together. She was caught shoplifting. Jessica attended some individual sessions with me, and soon revealed dissociative symptoms, including the existence of dissociated self-states.

The therapy done with this family has involved a combination of individual work, family work, dyadic work, parenting work and sibling work. All three children have been impacted by their early trauma. Marco and Rose, although very traumatised in early childhood, have experienced several years within a family willing to work hard to provide stability. This has created an odd combination of young adults who appear stable on the surface, but who react with primitive, affective responses when their early trauma is triggered. Jessica, adopted into a critical and abusive family, learned to dissociate her trauma reactions in order to overfunction as the best possible child she could create. The dynamic of entering into a family, and then experiencing the resulting attachment crisis, triggered a breakdown of her dissociative defenses and an inability to continue to exist only as the "good" child, disconnected from her anger and shame.

The trauma in this family has been systemic, with each person's experiences affecting the others. The parents' struggles with fertility, their choice to adopt, their trips to Africa, the children's medical issues and the struggle to parent Rose and Mark impacted each of them, which in turn impacted the other and their relationship. Although their experiences don't fall into what would usually be called trauma, the parents have been overwhelmed, and both parents experience symptoms consistent with PTSD. Their involvement in Jessica's life, their understanding of the impact of their adoption choices on her life, and the impact on the family of taking her in has created a process through which the family as a whole, and each individual, is again exploring their own attachment and trauma histories through a new lens.

The Varied Presentations of Trauma

Tables 3.1 and 3.2 below compare and contrast the impacts of complex trauma issues on each of the young people in this chapter. They are subjective, based on my experiences and assessments of these clients throughout their therapeutic process. As an example, direct medical evidence of neurological impact has not been assessed, but is identified when the young person's functioning matches those described in the literature on trauma impact and neurodevelopmental theory. Physical impact ranges from none known, through scars from abuse or later self-harm, to the complex and lasting physical challenges faced by Beth. Overall, I am rating symptoms based on their presentation during assessment. The exceptions are those who had masked symptoms which appeared later. Those who are in later stages of treatment have successfully resolved some or all of their listed symptoms. Table 3.2, referring to comorbid conditions, is not based only on diagnosed disorders, but features suggestive of conditions. ADHD is endorsed if a child has been diagnosed with ADHD or provided medication to treat suspected ADHD. The table designates a diagnosed condition with a "D" and features suggestive of a diagnosis with an "F." Table 3.2 is not intended to show a cause-and-effect relationship between complex trauma disorders and other conditions. It is, however, striking to notice the prevalence of many of these issues within the complex trauma population.

Table 3.1 Impacted Domains of Functioning

	Attachment	*Physical (long-term)*	*Neurological*	*Affect Regulation*	*Dissociation*	*Behavioural Control*	*Academic and Learning*	*Self-Concept*	*Worldview*	*Social Development*
Beth	1	3	0	2	2	1	1	2	2	2
Tony	3	0	2	3	1	3	1	3	3	2
John	3	1	2	3	3	3	2	3	3	3
Sophie	2	2	3	3	3	3	3	2	2	3
Terra	2	1	1	2	2	2	2	2	1	1
Amie	3	2	3	3	2	3	3	3	3	2
Michael	1	0	0	2	0	1	1	1	1	0
James	3	1	3	1	3	1	2	3	3	1
Katy	2	3	3	3	0	3	2	2	1	3
Lilly	2	2	2	1	1	1	3	2	1	1
Mark	2	2	1	2	0	2	1	1	1	0
Rose	2	1	3	3	1	3	3	1	0	3
Jessica	3	1	1	3	2	2	0	2	2	1

0—No Impact; 1—Mild Impact; 2—Moderate Impact; 3—Severe Impact

Table 3.2 Symptoms and Comorbid Conditions

	Attachment Difficulties	*ADHD*	*Learning Difficulties*	*Nonverbal Learning Difficulties*	*Sensory Processing Difficulties*	*Anxiety*	*Panic Attacks*	*Flash Backs*	*Obsessive Compulsive Symptoms*	*Dissociated Self-States (Alters)*	*Placement Breakdowns*
Beth	Anxious					D	D	√	F	D	
Sandra	Resistant					F		√	F		√
John	Disorganised	D	F	F	F	F				F	√
Sophie	Disorganised	D	D	D	D	D		√	F	D	
Terra	Anxious		F			F		√	F	F	
Amie	Disorganised		D	F	F	F	F	√	F	D	
Michael	Anxious	D	F			F	F				
James	Disorganised	D	D	D	F	F		√		D	
Katy	Anxious	D	D	F	F	F					√
Lilly	Disorganised	D	D		F	F					√
Mark	Avoidant					F					
Rose	Anxious	D	D	D	F	D					Required respite
Jessica	Disorganised					F	F	√	F	D	√

"D" designates a diagnosed condition. "F" designates features suggestive of a diagnosable condition.

(*Continued*)

Table 3.2 (Continued)

	Physical Shutdown States	*Growth and Development Issues*	*Food Issues*	*Depression*	*Nonsuicidal Self-Harm*	*Suicidality*	*Anger*	*Sleep Difficulties*	*ODD*	*Substance Abuse Issues*	*Sexualised Behaviour*	*FASD*
Beth			√	D	√	√		√		√	√	
Sandra			√	D	√	√	√	√	F		√	
John		√	√	F	√	√	√	√	D	√	√	
Sophie	√	√	√				√	√	F		√	
Terra	√		√	F	√		√	√	F			
Amie			√	D	√	√		√		√	√	
Michael				D		√	√			√		
James	√	√		F			√	√	F			
Katy			√	F			√	√	D		√	D
Lilly			√	F			√	√			√	D
Mark							√	√		√		
Rose	√						√	√	F	√	√	D
Jessica				D	√	√		√		√	√	

"D" designates a diagnosed condition. "F" designates features suggestive of a diagnosable condition.

As can be seen from the previous tables, children with complex trauma disorders present with a variety of difficulties. These children have often accumulated multiple diagnoses prior to treatment for attachment and trauma-related difficulties. This is not to suggest that all of these difficulties in all children are related to trauma or attachment. There are many children, adolescents and adults with these difficulties who do not identify as having trauma histories. Certainly the prevalence of these symptoms and disorders in this population raises questions that are worth exploring further.

Another theme is the number of these young people seen in treatment prior to being identified as having trauma disorders. Of the thirteen young people discussed in this chapter, five of them, Tony, Sophie, Amie, Michael and James, were seen previously without their difficulties being connected to trauma. Three of them, Tony, Amie and James, were being seen in assessment and or treatment while they were being abused, and did not make a disclosure. Six of them, John, Sophie, Terra, Amie, James and Jessica, have been diagnosed with major dissociative disorders that were not identified during their initial assessment and treatment. Five of them, Tony, Sophie, John, Katy and Lilly, experienced at least some of their trauma while in care. Six of them, Beth, John, Sophie, Amie, Katy and Lilly, all had some involvement with or were investigated by the CAS and/or the police, while living in abusive situations, which were either not disclosed or were not recognised and responded too.

This is not said to identify blame or responsibility. It shows how difficult these issues can be to identify. Many abused children have been taught to keep secrets and mistrust authority. It isn't unusual for these children to have parents who were abused in care, who truly believe that the child welfare system is more dangerous than their families. Dissociation is a disorder of secrecy, and helps children to hide trauma and its symptoms. Many therapists, child welfare workers and police don't have adequate training in recognising complex trauma or dissociative disorders. This is not just about training or skill in complex trauma or dissociation, or about pointing fingers at others. Four of the children listed, and many others not listed, were seen by me for a significant period of time before the issues were recognised. Other therapists with experience and expertise in these areas have had similar experiences. It's uncomfortable to miss an important dynamic on one or more of our cases. It can be even more uncomfortable to learn that a young person we've been working with was being abused or suffered from an intrusive major disorder while under our care, without our being aware of it. It may be easier for many therapists to consider dissociative disorders as rare or nonexistent than to believe that they consistently slide under our radar, but it happens to all of us. Secrets hide. The long-term results of finger pointing, the ways in which these cases split systems (see Chapter 12), and the resulting atmosphere of mistrust and blame, is increased defensiveness and a felt need to deny the issues of invisibility.

The same approach was widespread in relation to child maltreatment within the recent past. Two prominent historic children's mental health textbooks from the fifties and sixties[11,12] do not address child maltreatment, and refer to neglect and physical abuse only in passing. A more recent textbook from the early eighties[13] contains a three-page discussion of child abuse. The possibility of sexual abuse is mentioned once in passing. Maltreatment is not mentioned as an etiological factor of childhood disorders. When our understanding of child maltreatment as an issue moved from believing it to be rare to understanding how pervasive and impactful it is, our child welfare and children's mental health system exploded in size and cost. To understand and respond to the prevalence of complex trauma, dissociation and attachment disorders will have a similar impact on the system.

Notes

1. Hughes, Daniel A. (2007). Attachment Focused Family Therapy. W.W. Norton & Company. New York. pp 20–28.
2. Porgess, Stephen W. (2011). *The Polyvagal Theory: Neurophysiological Foundations of Emotions, Attachment, Communication, Self-Regulation*. W.W. Norton & Company. New York.
3. Siegel, Daniel J. (2013). *The Developing Mind: How Relationships and the Brain Interact to Shape Who We Are*. Guilford. New York.
4. Siegel, Daniel J. (2013). *The Developing Mind: How Relationships and the Brain Interact to Shape Who We Are*. Guilford. New York.
5. Porgess, Stephen W. (2011). *The Polyvagal Theory: Neurophysiological Foundations of Emotions, Attachment, Communication, Self-Regulation*. W.W. Norton & Company. New York.
6. Main, M., & Solomon, J. (1986). Discovery of an insecure-disorganized/disoriented attachment pattern. In T.B. Brazelton & M.W. Yogman (Eds.), *Affective Development in Infancy*. Ablex Publishing. Westport, CT.
7. Teicher, M. H., Andersen, S. L., Polcari A., Anderson, C. M., Navalta, C. P., & Kim, D. M. (2003, January–March). The neurobiological consequences of early stress and childhood maltreatment. *Neuroscience Biobehavioural Review, 27*(1–2), 33–44.
8. Siegel, Daniel J. (2013). *The Developing Mind: How Relationships and the Brain Interact to Shape Who We Are*. Guilford. New York.
9. Porgess, Stephen W. (2011). *The Polyvagal Theory: Neurophysiological Foundations of Emotions, Attachment, Communication, Self-Regulation*. W.W. Norton & Company. New York.
10. Porgess, Stephen W. (2011). *The Polyvagal Theory: Neurophysiological Foundations of Emotions, Attachment, Communication, Self-Regulation*. W.W. Norton & Company. New York.
11. Gordon, H.L. (1956). *Casework Services for Children*. Houghton Mifflin Company. Boston.
12. Finch, S.M. (1960). *Fundamentals of Child Psychiatry*. W.W. Norton & Company. New York.
13. Liebert, R.M., & Wicks-Nelson, R. (1981). *Developmental Psychology* (3rd ed.). Prentice Hall. Englewood Cliffs, NJ.

4 Attachment and Attachment-Focused Therapy

Early child development is strongly influenced by the child's primary attachment relationship. Human development is both experience expectant and experience dependent; the early experiences of the infant occur within the relationships with their main caregivers.[1]

Attachment-focused therapy is based on the early work of John Bowlby,[2,3,4,5,6] who explored the impact of maternal separation on infants and toddlers. In 1969, Mary Ainsworth, through her research on infant attachment using the "strange experience" scenario, began to outline patterns of attachment that develop in childhood.[7] This work has been further developed by Mary Main working with Judith Solomon, Eric Hesse and N. Kaplan, in their exploration of disorganised attachment, adult attachment styles and the development of the Adult Attachment Interview.[8,9,10]

Infants are wholly dependent on their caregivers for meeting their physical and emotional needs. The lack of a safe, secure attachment relationship in itself creates an overwhelmingly frightening experience in an infant. A healthy early attachment is one in which the parent responds to the child's emotional cues, providing both care and soothing. An attuned caregiver who recognises an infant's cues and responds to them by caring for the infant and connecting emotionally to the infant's internal state allows for the infant to begin to recognise relationship, safety, being soothed, and eventually the ability to soothe the self.[11] This is the process through which infants begin to develop an identity of themselves as worthwhile and of adults as safe and reliable. They begin to see themselves as a part of a world in which they can rely on others and achieve some control over their environment. These changes occur on a neurobiological level.[12,13] The attuned, nurturing and soothing relationship with an attentive and engaged parent facilitates growth and development of the infant brain.

When an infant's first environment is one in which the caregiver is unavailable, detached, unengaged or overwhelmed, there is a negative impact on the development of the infant's brain, and as a result, on the child's ability to cope and function in the world. As these children get older, they don't have the ability to regulate their emotions, rely on adults for guidance or be confident in their abilities to negotiate their world.[14,15,16,17,18]

A poor or disrupted attachment relationship may lead to impairment in all of the domains of functioning referred to in Chapter 1. A child who hasn't had an engaged attachment relationship may struggle with forming other relationships. They have difficulty with trust, connection and the ability to take someone else's point of view. Neurological development is negatively impacted, since early emotional connection is required for optimal development. There is evidence that the many impacts of poor attachment can lead to long-term physical health effects resulting from a compromised immune system and poor lifestyle choices.[19] Affect regulation is the ability to experience, tolerate and cope with strong emotions. The beginning of affect regulation is learned in the attuned soothing behaviours of an attachment relationship.[20,21,22] Children who don't have solid attachment develop a low tolerance for emotions and an inability to cope with emotional experiences, leading to difficulties with anger, sadness, despair and anxiety, and eventually to dysfunctional ways of coping such as violence, aggression, substance use, suicide and self-harm.[23,24,25,26] Dissociation is the inability to integrate the experiences of memory, self and the world into a coherent whole. The attachment relationship is an important element in the development of the integrative fibres of the brain which allow this to happen.[27] When consistent and safe, the attachment relationship allows for the development of stable internalisations of the self, other and external world. Children without good attachment relationships have an increased likelihood of suffering dissociative symptoms and disorders even in the absence of further trauma.[28,29] Behavioural control, the ability to stop, review choices, and then to make choices based on possible outcomes, is affected. Children with poor attachment histories display poor impulse control and a limited ability to determine choices based on outcomes. Cognitive development has also been tied to early attachment. Brain development is affected by the lack of a secure attachment figure. Cognitive development is further impacted by poor emotional and behavioural regulation and difficulties with concentration, focus and impulse control, which affect a child's ability to learn from experience or teaching. Effective cognitive abilities rely on the ability to take in different types of information, integrate it into a coherent whole, store it in memory, and retrieve it. When the integrative fibres of the brain are not well developed, it seems likely that this is compromised. Self-concept is one's view of themselves in relation to others and the world. A child's self-concept begins within their first attachment relationship.[30,31] A child who is not responded to in a consistent and positive way won't learn to see themselves as worthy of care and nurturing; they develop a sense of themselves as ineffective or bad, and the world as hostile and unresponsive. These eight domains of development are mutually interactive, and stem from the earliest experiences of an infant and attachment relationships. Difficulties with trust, emotional and behavioural control, cognition, self-concept, dissociation and worldview lead to difficulties with socialisation and peer relationships. The outcome is children who struggle with achieving a sense of safety, self, success, belonging and interdependence.

Attachment Styles

Mary Ainsworth identified three main styles of attachment—secure; anxious/ambivalent and anxious/avoidant.[32] Main and Hesse have since identified a fourth pattern—disorganised.[33] Through early relational experiences, each of us develops an attachment style. A child can have differing attachment relationships with different adults, but their attachment style will most resemble that of the adult with whom they were most involved or that relationship which was the most impactful on their development.[34,35] As a child grows, their attachment style affects relationships. When the child becomes a parent, their attachment style impacts on their engagement with their children, forming the beginning of their child's attachment style.[36] These patterns are not created solely based on the parents' behaviours and choices. The dynamics that create attachment relationships are complicated. When we assess attachment relationships and attachment patterns, parents sometimes feel judged. Attachment is not a measure of whether or not parents love their children enough, or are good or bad parents. Although secure attachment is viewed as the healthier pattern and tends to support greater resilience and adaptability, attachment patterns are adaptations to the caregiving environment and provide strategies for coping and surviving. Many healthy, flexible people are somewhat anxious, ambivalent, preoccupied or avoidant in their relationship styles. Even disorganised attachment patterns can range in their severity and impact on functioning. Circumstances create environments which impact on a child's experience of caregivers. Events occur which may impact on the parent's ability to be attuned to their child. It's true that abuse, neglect and abandonment are factors that affect attachment, but even these dynamics are complex and rarely as black and white in a family's life as we sometimes assume. This is not to suggest that parents aren't responsible for their actions. It suggests that in working with families, we approach parents with a similar lens to that which we use with children and adolescents—with openness to their stories, empathy for their experiences and an assumption that they want to do the best with their children that they can.

Secure Attachment

A child who grows in an environment with a sensitive and attuned caregiver learns to value themselves and to see others as potentially helpful and responsive. They learn to expect others to be aware of their needs and to consider them. These early experiences allow for a sense of relative safety, encouraging exploration and learning. As the world still presents with dangers, they see their caregivers as a safe haven to turn to when they need reassurance or help. These children are well equipped to learn and explore. They are more resilient and can turn to others when they need support. They grow to become individuals who can regulate their emotions and behaviours, recognise others' needs and respond as they have learned to be responded to. They are capable of interdependence. When they become parents, they are able to see and respond to the needs of their children. Their ability to regulate their own reactions allows them to respond to their children's needs.

Anxious/Ambivalent Attachment

A child that experiences their caregivers as fairly safe and generally available, but inconsistently so may, become anxious about their caregivers availability and responsiveness. This anxiety becomes preoccupation with their caregiver and difficulty with separation from them. It is described as anxious/ambivalent because the child seeks out attachment, but rather than increasing their feelings of security, closeness triggers the anxiety of potential loss. The child can become focused on engaging the caregiver and ensuring their presence and availability. The need to focus on the caregiver makes it difficult for the child to explore and learn about the world. Being apart from the caregiver feels dangerous. Anxious/ambivalent attachment can arise from having a parent who is preoccupied or not able to consistently be attuned. It can also arise from having a parent who is unavailable due to illness or from a child having medical needs requiring intrusive treatments or hospitalisations. A parent who is generally able to be attuned to their child may become disconnected due to periods of high stress, loss or their own trauma. Some children are difficult to soothe, or have feeding or sleeping difficulties, leading to stress in parenting and fewer of the emotional cues that make attuned parenting a rewarding, engaged process. When this happens, it can undermine a parent's confidence and make it more difficult for them to enjoy and respond to the child. A parent who is being abused can become numb, focused on survival and coping, and feel the need to deny the impact on their child in order to protect their daily functioning. This denial of impact requires disattunement. A child who experiences trauma outside of the family may develop an anxious attachment due to their felt experience of the parent as unable to protect them. Events such as surgeries, illnesses, disasters and abuse are experienced and interpreted through the child's view of the world, not through the parents' intentions or experiences. Children see adults as powerful, so when bad things happen, they feel that their parent should have been able to protect them and didn't. Children who are adopted or fostered often have difficulty attaching; they see their new parents or caregivers through the working models they have already developed for the world.

Anxious/Avoidant Attachment

A child who experiences a caregiver as fairly safe but not emotionally attuned or accepting of their emotional states can develop an anxious/avoidant attachment. It is described as anxious/avoidant because the experience of closeness and connection, along with the experience of strong emotions, creates anxiety. The child begins to experience emotion as an unvalued part of themselves, a part that is likely to increase their chances of being rejected. Children and adults with anxious/avoidant attachment patterns may value logic, stoicism and the ability to cope and function in challenging situations, but avoid emotional experiences and struggle with feeling close or connected to others. Strong emotional experiences trigger anxiety. There are a number of ways in which children can receive the message that emotions are undesirable. These can range from caregivers who genuinely meet their children's physical and safety needs, but do not respond to or express emotional communication, through parents who discourage emotional expression and praise and value strength, to parents or caregivers who punish, reject and belittle a child's emotional expression. Again, these are generally not intentionally neglectful or harmful stances. Parents who are overwhelmed by their own life stresses or trauma histories may be unable to tolerate the feelings created in them by their child's emotional states, and so fail to respond or respond negatively. Parents living in stressful, challenging or dangerous situations may need to focus on survival and encourage their children to do so as well. Parents who were raised in dangerous situations may have been taught that emotions are dangerous distractions or vulnerabilities, and believe that discouraging emotion is good parenting. Sometimes when a child has been abused or otherwise traumatised, the helplessness or distress this triggers in parents or caregivers can be frightening to children, who then begin to view their emotional reactions as harmful to the people they care about. The opposite can also happen, when a parent responds by being very calm and accepting, denying their own emotions and inadvertently giving the child the message that strong emotions aren't appropriate or called for. Many people in our society view independence as a goal, and begin early to teach their children to be independent rather than interdependent. This can involve discouraging or not responding to distress. Others experience the expression of anger as being potentially violent, and children can grow up believing that anger is bad.

Disorganised Attachment

The fourth attachment pattern recognised by Main et al. in their research is disorganised attachment. This pattern is most highly correlated with mental health disorders, dissociation and severe complex trauma disorders.[37] A child who has experienced their caregivers as being chronically unsafe and unpredictable, while still being wholly dependent on them for survival needs, will need safety, security and closeness with their parent, while also being afraid of them and needing to distance themselves. In their work with toddlers Main and Solomon described children who, when separated briefly from their parent in the presence of a stranger and then reunited, would respond to their parents in a confused and disorganised manner, caught between approach and rejection.[38] These children might stop, frozen and unresponsive, or turn in confused circles. Some children might approach and move away repeatedly, or act in a trance-like, disconnected manner. When I think of disorganised attachment, I remember John (Chapter 3) on the couch in my office, physically turned and pulled as far away from his mother as possible, not looking at her or me, his hood pulled completely over his head and face, stretching out one hand and arm towards her for comfort.

Children and adolescents with disorganised attachment patterns are difficult to care for. They are threatened by closeness, and can react negatively, or even violently and explosively, to feeling connected or cared about. They are equally threatened by feeling abandoned, and can become either desolate or increasingly angered when they are successful at pushing caregivers away. John was in care because of his explosive and dangerous behaviour at home. Being placed in care had triggered increased anger and abandonment. In each placement he became more desperate, angry and defiant. No placement lasted more than a few months. Each placement increased his self-hatred and his anger at the world.

Disorganised attachment patterns are most associated with complex trauma disorders and dissociation. Many children with disorganised attachment have experienced physical or sexual abuse, domestic violence or neglect, parents with addictions problems, mental illness, or chronic, painful medical conditions. Many of the children with disorganised attachment patterns have developed dissociative symptoms or disorders. Although physical and sexual abuse is common in the histories of these children, not all of them have been abused. There is research that supports that a child who experiences their parent or caregiver as being both frightened and frightening in their manner, who is inconsistent and changeable, or who actively dissociates while parenting, may develop a disorganised attachment pattern.[39,40] We can't assume, based on attachment patterns or dissociation, what a child has experienced.

Attachment-Focused Therapy

Attachment theory has been incorporated into models of treatment for children and adults. It has become an important component of trauma work. At its best, the therapist-client relationship contains elements of an attachment relationship, providing both safety and security required for exploration, change and development.[41] Early psychodynamic work recognised the ways in which our early attachment relationships are recreated in our current relationships, and explored the way this enters into therapy in the form of transference and countertransference.[42] Family therapy developed from an understanding that family relationships are the central environment in which we grow, explore and change.

Dyadic developmental psychotherapy was developed by Dan Hughes[43,44,45] to support foster and adopted children experiencing behavioural, emotional and adjustment difficulties. His model has been expanded to use with children living with biological parents and family of origin caregivers.[46] Dr. Hughes's model supports children and caregivers in developing safe, attuned attachment relationships, and using the intersubjectivity within these relationships to support the child in coregulation of affect and cocreation of meaning. These are the early experiences that help young children learn self-regulation and develop a coherent narrative and identity. Creating these experiences in therapy supports neurological development that has been missed by children with complex trauma histories.

Dyadic developmental psychotherapy has shown itself to be helpful in supporting children in new placements. This model has been used by many trauma therapists in my community and has supported many children and families in developing safer, more attuned relationships within which the children can learn to regulate their affect and behaviour and develop a more stable sense of self. I've used many of these principles to work with children placed with grandparents and extended family members, and in modified ways, to work with children living with biological parents with whom their relationships had been disrupted or damaged.

In *Trauma and the Avoidant Client*, Robert Muller[47] explores how avoidant defenses are used by traumatised clients to protect against attachment-related distress. Avoidance, used in the context of avoidant defenses, is not to be confused with avoidant attachment patterns. Avoidant defenses can be used by those with anxious/avoidant, anxious/ambivalent and disorganised attachment patterns. Dr. Muller explores Bowlby's idea of "defensive exclusion,"[48,49] by which children learn to defensively ignore, and not internalise, information or experiences which interfere with their ability to connect with and rely on their attachment figures, leading to avoidant defenses. Avoidant defenses cause older children and adults to avoid or ignore experiences and memories which would highlight what has been ignored. Dr. Muller's book goes on to explore the impact of these defenses on relationships and on the clients' engagement in the therapy process.

Dr. Joyanna Silberg[50] has developed the "affect avoidance model" to explore the ways in which children develop dissociative processes to cope with painful attachment-related experiences. This model fits well with the ideas discussed by Dr. Muller. The child may develop multiple working models of themselves and of their attachment figures in order to manage experiences that are too painful or frightening to allow for the child to feel safe enough to rely on their parents or caregivers.

These insights into the ways many children's, adolescent's and adult's difficulties result from adaptations to their earliest attachment experiences are critical to the development of an attachment-focused phase-oriented approach to trauma treatment. The idea that the struggles and actions of both the children and the adults make sense, and have adapted as ways of coping with difficult and challenging situations, creates the safety to explore the past and present, and the freedom to move forward without self-recrimination. Exploring the ways in which mistakes, choices and behaviours make sense allows the parents to feel compassion for themselves and empathy and attunement with their children.

Attachment-focused therapy has some differences from traditional family therapy. The work is done dyadically, rather than with the whole family. In order to better help the parents or caregivers create a new and different experience with the child, it's often necessary to work with the parents for a number of sessions, either before sessions with the child or sometimes in between them. At times it may also be necessary to have individual sessions with the child. Ideally, this is a preamble to dyadic work. Occasionally, this process will suggest that one or both parties are not ready for dyadic work. When this happens, these early sessions can help to create a framework for individual work with an attachment focus. The development of the treatment frame will be discussed in more detail in Chapter 6.

Anna was brought for therapy at the age of sixteen, by her father, Tom. Tom was concerned about his daughter's low self-esteem, self-harm and history of being bullied. Anna had been at emergency psychiatry six times in the previous four months. During her most recent hospitalisation Anna talked about voices telling her life was hopeless and she should kill herself. The voices came from inside of her head, and she knew them. Although Anna lived with both parents, Tom and Anna reported that her mother, Christine, was more of a roommate, and was not really involved with either of them. Tom wanted Anna to have a closer relationship with her mother, but Anna wasn't interested because she didn't like her mother.

Both parents had experienced abuse, neglect and emotional deprivation. Tom had been removed from his mother's care around the age of two or three, and after some time in foster care, was adopted at four. He recalls frightening and abusive incidents while in his mother's care. His adoptive father died when he was seven. Christine had been raised by her biological parents, and experienced physical, sexual and emotional abuse and chronic neglect within the home. Anna does not have an identified abuse history, but she has very difficult attachment relationships. Both of her parents have severe trauma and attachment issues, and neither was able to provide stable, safe, attuned availability for her. It is this overwhelming sense of being bereft, caught between her frozen, unavailable mother and her angry and controlled father, that forms the source of her internal conflicts.

Both parents have been profoundly impacted by their own early histories, and are beginning to come to terms with the impact this has had on their child. Tom took early control of parenting Anna and allowed her mother only limited involvement. He did not feel Christine would be able to parent their daughter, although he has been unable to explain why. When Anna was a few months old, he took Anna from the home and moved with her to his adoptive mother's home. It is likely that Tom's own preverbal abuse history created a protective terror in him that led to his isolating his daughter from her mother. Christine's response was passivity. She felt unable to influence Tom's control, and so did not challenge it. This lack of response would also contribute to Anna's experience of herself and her mother. It never occurred to Christine to question her husband's right to remove her daughter. Throughout her own history, she had never been allowed to question anyone's authority. It never occurred to Anna that her mother cared that they did not live together.

When Anna was nine, Tom's adoptive mother died. Tom was devastated, and began drinking heavily. Christine took Anna to a shelter. Tom struggled for a few months, stopped drinking, and the family moved into an apartment together. Although they lived together, Christine had little involvement with Anna, and Tom remained the primary caregiver.

The death impacted all members of the family. Tom's adoptive mother had been a positive mother figure for both Christine and Anna. Anna states that when her grandmother died, both of her parents shut down in different ways. She describes herself as the only one who didn't cry. She needed to stay strong in order to take care of her parents.

Tom is devoted to his daughter. He has engaged in treatment with her, and actively engaged with a therapist in a way which he admits is uncomfortable to him. He also attends individual therapy. He has expressed being torn between wanting his daughter to engage in therapy, connect with her emotions and be able to experience healthy relationships, while at the same time wanting to avoid the same experiences. When I first met Tom, he stated that the only emotions he could identify were anger and humour. He could rage, and he could laugh. After a period of individual work he was able to connect to deep sadness, loss and loneliness. Throughout Anna's life, Tom's presence had been one of intensity and anger. Once, when Anna was attacked by a large and vicious dog at the park, Tom killed the dog with his bare hands. For Anna, this memory is both terrifying and confusing. She doesn't know whether she was more afraid of the dog or of her father's sudden, violent response. She continues to be afraid that her father will kill a person in the same way.

Christine has been barely present in Anna's life, even when they lived together. She almost never spoke to either her daughter or her husband. She had no physical contact with either of them. She worked at a job that started at five a.m. She returned from work at about three p.m., and napped for a few hours. She then watched TV or read books until going to sleep. When I first met with Anna and we talked about her mother, she said, "I don't like Chris. Chris doesn't talk and she's boring." During our first sessions, Christine presented as flat. She talked emotionlessly about her terrible childhood and her violent and abusive first marriage, about the loss of Anna, and her sense of helplessness. When I inquired about feelings, she responded, "I don't have any. I haven't had feelings in years." During our first mother-child session, Anna disclosed a frightening and traumatic adolescent experience. When I asked Christine what her reaction was, she said, "I don't feel anything. I never do." When I asked what response she thinks she might have if she were to have one she began to cry and said, "I guess I would be very, very sad for her." This show of emotion sent Anna into a panic, with the response, to me, not to her mother, "Chris can't feel—she never feels! Stop it now!"

This situation involved clinical challenges. Anna was a distressed teen experiencing great difficulties. She presented as unkempt and at times as much younger than sixteen. Her parents had to fight to get her to shower, wash her hair or brush her teeth. She had experienced bullying at school and had begun to refuse to attend. She was dependent on her father, often clinging to him. Tom was becoming uncomfortable with her physical intrusiveness. Anna appeared desperate—self-harming and at times suicidal; intense, isolated and reaching out for connection of any kind. She had been bullied and sexually exploited or assaulted by peers on more than one occasion. As I got to know Anna, she began to talk about dissociative experiences. Age regression was often observed in session. Not surprisingly she felt a lot of conflict between her alliances to her parents. Part of her was strongly allied with her father and disliked her mother, whom she found boring and detached. Yet when we met together with her mother, she was at times not just anxious to connect, but caring, sensitive and open to her mother's experience. She often engaged her mother in a playful but childlike way, poking her, caressing her or jumping on her in physically intrusive ways like a toddler. Anna was frightened by many of her parents' emotional states. She experienced them as potentially dangerous and likely to lead to frightening experiences

Shortly into an early individual session, "Martha" made an appearance—smooth, sophisticated and with a slight accent, Martha was a sardonic observer of Anna's "childish" relationships with her parents. There was also a child alter who was "little Anna," and another teenager who was confused as to whether they were male or female. In exploration with all of the parts, the difficulty that contributed to their development was Anna's conflicted desire for her mother, her alliance with her angry father and her overwhelming loneliness. This is a case in progress; those familiar with dissociative identity disorders know that many things can't be known for sure, and that new memories and details can arise at any time. I am not in a position to say that this dissociative disorder has developed in the absence of abuse. If I were to say that now, I would surely be faced with a disclosure tomorrow. Certainly Tom's anger has exposed Anna to situations of terror, whether or not she has been directly targeted. What I can say with some confidence is that I am working with dissociative parts that have split in response to desperation arising from chronically unmet attachment needs. Anna is a child raised by two parents with disorganised attachment patterns, which created an environment frightening enough and unresponsive enough to create an experience of aloneness and unpredictability.

The other side of this complicated picture is of a now seventeen-year-old girl, with parents who both present and act, to the best of their abilities, as being committed to her therapy and working towards her healing. This is an act of courage on their part. They have never chosen therapy for themselves. Their own childhoods have created immense difficulty for themselves and then for their daughter. They are both in pain. These are not parents who would usually be considered good candidates for attachment-focused therapy. Attachment work can be painful for even the most secure parent or caregiver. Yet, here is a young woman who needs parents, and parents who want to try to be what she needs. If it is possible to improve these relationships, and to help build an environment where emotional expression is safer and security of attachment is somewhat more available, than that has to be better than any alternative.

The challenges of this type of work were discussed with both parents. Each expressed a willingness to attempt doing work that could be painful to support their daughter's healing. Anna, for her part, agreed that she would be willing to work on having a better relationship with her mother.

One year later, Tom and Christine have separated. This was initially difficult and led to several crises for all of them. They have worked at removing Anna from the middle, and on building separate homes. Anna moved in with her father, but continued to attend sessions with her mother. In these sessions we focused on activities designed to facilitate attunement and coregulation. I supported Anna in communicating her needs to her mother safely, and I supported Christine in being able to hear and respond to Anna's needs. At times, Anna would spontaneously reject her mother, say she didn't like her and wanted nothing to do with her. At other times, Anna would become childlike, engaging with her mother in a playfully aggressive toddler-like way. This was difficult therapy. I needed to meet often with Christine to support her through Anna's reactions and help her understand Anna's confused and confusing behaviours. Christine has persevered, tolerating Anna's occasional rejections and beginning to enjoy her. Anna also attends sessions with her father, where she works at being able to communicate her experiences safely and he works on being able to hear her without her being afraid of his reactions. Tom has protected himself with anger for many years and it is difficult for him to tolerate being challenged. For the sake of his daughter he is willing to not only tolerate, but even hear and respond to gentle and respectful challenging. Anna attends individual sessions during which time we explore her inner world, build connections between her parts and work on inner communication.

There have been rapid improvements in both the physical and mental health of all three family members. Most striking was the dramatic decrease of severe tremors, spasms and pain that Tom had been experiencing for several years, which left him disabled and unable to work. He attributed this to a decrease in his repressed anger and sadness. Although initially unsure, and making a few false starts, Tom entered into therapy with a colleague who specialises in working with adults with complex trauma histories. Anna began to experience fewer headaches, stomachaches, and suicidal thoughts and feelings, and was able to return to school. Christine initially had the most difficult time. She had viewed their earlier family life as so much better than her earlier experiences, and had really believed that numbly going through the motions of life was a good outcome for her. When Tom chose to leave she was confused and hurt. Over time, however, she has presented as more relaxed and affectively connected. She is able to feel, identify and talk about her feelings. Christine also began to attend individual therapy.

Anna currently has a relationship with both parents. She feels caught between them at times, but is able to manage. Dissociation has been less of a problem for her, as she feels she is aware of and connected to her parts. Anna has not been hospitalised for almost a year. When there are problems, Tom's first reaction is often anger, and Anna feels hurt and rejected. She is beginning to be able to separate her father's reactions from her behaviours. She fears making new friends as she fears rejection. She continues to experience anxiety and aches and pains. She still has more than one part, with different names and ages, although she is coconscious and has good internal cooperation. Treatment is ongoing.

Notes

1. Siegel, Daniel J. (2013). *The Developing Mind: How Relationships and the Brain Interact to Shape Who We Are.* Guilford. New York.
2. Bowlby, J. (1969/1982). *Attachment and Loss: Volume 1. Attachment* (1st and 2nd eds.) Basic Books. New York.
3. Bowlby, J. (1973). *Attachment and Loss: Volume 2. Separation: Anxiety and Anger.* Basic Books. New York.
4. Bowlby, J. (1979). *The Making and Breaking of Affectional Bonds.* Basic Books. New York.
5. Bowlby, J. (1980). *Attachment and Loss: Volume 3. Loss: Sadness and Depression.* Basic Books. New York.
6. Bowlby, J. (1988). *A Secure Base.* Basic Books. New York.
7. Ainsworth, M.D.S., & Wittig, B. A. (1969). Attachment and exploratory behaviour of one-year-olds in a strange situation. In B. M. Foss (Ed.), *Determinants of Infant Behaviour* (Vol. 4). Methuen. London.
8. Main, M., & Solomon, J. (1986). Discovery of an insecure-disorganized/disoriented attachment pattern. In T. B. Brazelton & M. W. Yogman (Eds.), *Affective Development in Infancy.* Ablex. Norwood, NJ.
9. Main, M., Hesse, E., & Kaplan, N. (2005). Predictability of attachment behaviour and representational processes at 1, 6, and 18 years of age: The Berkeley Longitudinal Study. In K. E. Grossmann, K. Grossmann, & E. Waters (Eds.), *Attachment from Infancy to Adulthood.* Guilford. New York.
10. Hesse, E., & Maine, M. (2000). Disorganized infant, child and adult attachment: Collapse in behavioural and attentional strategies. *Journal of the American Psychoanalytic Association, 48,* 1097–1127.
11. Hughes, Daniel A. (2007). *Attachment Focused Family Therapy.* W. W. Norton & Company. New York. pp 14–20.
12. Siegel, Daniel J. (2013). *The Developing Mind: How Relationships and the Brain Interact to Shape Who We Are.* Guilford. New York.
13. Porgess, Stephen W. (2011). *The Polyvagal Theory: Neurophysiological Foundations of Emotions, Attachment, Communication, Self-Regulation.* W. W. Norton & Company. New York.
14. Teicher, M. H., Andersen, S. L., Polcari A., Anderson, C. M., Navalta, C. P., & Kim, D. M. (2003, January–March). The neurobiological consequences of early stress and childhood maltreatment. *Neuroscience Biobehavioural Review, 27*(1–2), 33–44.
15. Porgess, Stephen W. (2011). *The Polyvagal Theory: Neurophysiological Foundations of Emotions, Attachment, Communication, Self-Regulation.* W. W. Norton & Company. New York.
16. Schore, A. N. (2009). Attachment trauma and the development of the right brain. In P. Dell and J. O'Neil (Eds.), *Dissociation and the Dissociative Disorders. DSM V and Beyond.* Routledge. New York.
17. Schore, A. (2013). Relational trauma, brain development, and dissociation. In J. D. Ford and C. Courtois (Eds.), *Treating Complex Traumatic Stress Disorders in Children and Adolescents: Scientific Foundations and Therapeutic Models.* Guilford. New York. p 4.
18. Schore, A. N. (2001). The effects of a secure attachment relationship on right brain development, affect regulation and infant mental health. *Infant Mental Health Journal, 22,* 201–269.
19. Felitti, V. J., Anda, R. F., Nordenberg, D., Williamson, D. F., Spitz, A. M., Edwards, V., Koss, M. P., & Marks, J. S. (1988, May). Relationship of childhood abuse and household dysfunction to many of the leading causes of death in adults: The Adverse Childhood Experiences (ACE) Study. *American Journal of Preventive Medicine, 14*(4), 245–258.

20. Bowlby, J. (1969/1982). *Attachment and Loss: Volume 1. Attachment* (1st and 2nd eds.) Basic Books. New York.
21. Hughes, Daniel A. (2007). *Attachment Focused Family Therapy*. W. W. Norton & Company. New York.
22. Siegel, Daniel J. (2013). *The Developing Mind: How Relationships and the Brain Interact to Shape Who We Are*. Guilford. New York.
23. Schore, A. (2003). Early relational trauma, disorganised attachment, and the development of a predisposition to violence. In M. F. Solomon & J. Siegel (Eds.), *Healing Trauma: Attachment, Mind, Body and Brain*. W. W. Norton & Company. New York.
24. Felitti, V. J., Anda, R. F., Nordenberg, D., Williamson, D. F., Spitz, A. M., Edwards, V., Koss, M. P., & Marks, J. S. (1988, May). Relationship of childhood abuse and household dysfunction to many of the leading causes of death in adults: The Adverse Childhood Experiences (ACE) Study. *American Journal of Preventive Medicine 14*(4), 245–258.
25. Struik, A. (2014). *Treating Chronically Traumatized Children: Don't Let Sleeping Dogs Lie!* Routledge. Sussex.
26. Silberg, Joyanna. (2013). *The Child Survivor: Healing Developmental Trauma and Dissociation*. Routledge. New York. pp 1–16.
27. Siegel, Daniel J. (2013). *The Developing Mind: How Relationships and the Brain Interact to Shape Who We Are*. Guilford. New York. pp 8–10, 336–377.
28. Hesse, E., Maine, M., Abrams, K. Y., & Rifkin, A. (2003). Unresolved states regarding loss or abuse can have "second generation" effects: Disorganization, role inversion, and frightening ideation in the offspring of traumatized, non-maltreating parents. In M. F. Solomon & J. Siegel (Eds.), *Healing Trauma: Attachment, Mind, Body and Brain*. W. W. Norton & Company. New York.
29. Jarari, D., Bakermans-Kranenburg, M. J., & van-Ijzendoorn, M. J. (2007). Attachment, disorganization and dissociation. In E. Vermettem, M. Dorahy, & D. Siegel (Eds.), *Traumatic Dissociation: Neurobiology and Treatment*. American Psychiatric Publishing Inc. Arlington, VA.
30. Hughes, Daniel A. (2007). *Attachment Focused Family Therapy*. W. W. Norton & Company. New York.
31. Siegel, Daniel J. (2013). *The Developing Mind: How Relationships and the Brain Interact to Shape Who We Are*. Guilford. New York.
32. Ainsworth, M.D.S., & Wittig, B. A. (1969). Attachment and exploratory behaviour of one-year-olds in a strange situation. In B. M. Foss (Ed.), *Determinants of Infant Behaviour*. (Vol. 4). Methuen. London.
33. Main, M., & Solomon, J. (1986). Discovery of an insecure disoriented attachment pattern: Procedures, findings and implications for the classification of behavior. In T. Brazelton T. & M. Youngman (Eds.), *Affective Development in Infancy*. Ablex. Norwood, NJ.
34. Hughes, Daniel A. (2007). *Attachment Focused Family Therapy*. W. W. Norton & Company. New York.
35. Muller, R. T. (2010). *Trauma and the Avoidant Client: Attachment-Based Strategies for Healing*. W. W. Norton & Company. New York.
36. Muller, R. T. (2010). *Trauma and the Avoidant Client: Attachment-Based Strategies for Healing*. W. W. Norton & Company. New York. p 9.
37. Hesse, E., Maine, M., Abrams, K. Y., & Rifkin, A. (2003). Unresolved states regarding loss or abuse can have "second generation" effects: Disorganization, role inversion, and frightening ideation in the offspring of traumatized, non-maltreating parents. In M. F. Solomon & J. Siegel (Eds.), *Healing Trauma: Attachment, Mind, Body and Brain*. W. W. Norton & Company. New York.
38. Main, M., & Solomon, J. (1986). Discovery of an insecure-disorganized/disoriented attachment pattern. In T. B. Brazelton & M. W. Yogman (Eds.), *Affective Development in Infancy*. Norwood, NJ: Ablex.

39. Liotti, G. (2006). A model of dissociation based on attachment theory and research. *Journal of Trauma & Dissociation, 7*(4), 55–73.
40. Liotti, G. (1999). Understanding the dissociative processes: The contribution of attachment theory. *Psychoanalytic Inquiry, 19*(5), 757–783.
41. Hughes, Daniel A. (2007). *Attachment Focused Family Therapy*. W. W. Norton & Company. New York. p 1.
42. McWilliams, N. (2004). *Psychoanalytic Psychotherapy: A Practitioner's Guide*. Guilford. New York. pp 70–71.
43. Hughes, Daniel A. (2004). An attachment-based treatment of maltreated children and young people. *Attachment and Human Development, 6*, 263–278.
44. Hughes, Daniel A. (2006). *Building the Bonds of Attachment* (2nd ed.). Jason Aronson. New York.
45. Hughes, Daniel A. (2007). *Attachment Focused Family Therapy*. W. W. Norton & Company. New York.
46. Hughes, Daniel A. (2007). *Attachment Focused Family Therapy*. W. W. Norton & Company. New York.
47. Muller, R. T. (2010). *Trauma and the Avoidant Client: Attachment-Based Strategies for Healing*. W. W. Norton & Company. New York.
48. Bowlby, J. (1980). *Attachment and Loss: Volume 3. Loss: Sadness and Depression*. Basic Books. New York.
49. Muller, R. T. (2010). *Trauma and the Avoidant Client: Attachment-Based Strategies for Healing*. W. W. Norton & Company. New York. pp 10–14.
50. Silberg, Joyanna. (2013). *The Child Survivor: Healing Developmental Trauma and Dissociation*. Routledge. New York.

5 Phase-Oriented Psychotherapy

Abreaction, the expression of repressed, disconnected or dissociated strong emotions connected to trauma, has often been seen as the goal of trauma work.[1] Over the years, I have met many parents bringing their children to therapy hoping that they will "open up" about their feelings and "talk about what happened" to them. A lot of older children and adolescents come with the idea that talking about trauma is what will help them "get over" their experiences. There is truth in the idea that talking about their experiences is part of healing from trauma. Getting children to talk about trauma, however, is not the same as getting them to eat their vegetables. It's not an end in itself that simply leads to better health if we can just find a way to get them to do it. Trauma work can be a painful, frightening process that can lead to regression, destabilisation, increased dissociation, rejection of therapy and placement breakdowns.[2] For children and adolescents, and also for adults, trauma work needs to be approached carefully and sensitively, in the context of a safe and protective environment and a well-developed therapeutic relationship.[3]

Tom, age nine, and his sister, twelve, were referred to me by a child psychiatrist who had assessed them at emergency psychiatry after they had been removed from their mother's care. The CAS made the unusual decision to take them to the hospital for assessment, because they spoke between themselves in a made-up language and said they lived together in a secret world. When apprehended they disclosed a history of physical abuse and isolation. They had been homeschooled with little contact with other children. The child psychiatrist who had seen them recommended that they be assessed for dissociative disorders.

When I first met Tom, the situation was complicated. His mother denied maltreatment of the children. They had been removed after Tom's sister had run away and called the police, stating their mother was planning to murder them. Both children disclosed abuse, but their disclosures were inconsistent, vague and confusing. Both presented as unstable and as much younger than their reported years. Some of the allegations were extreme and unusual. It was difficult to know what had happened to them. In the early weeks, there was considerable worry that they would be returned home due to lack of evidence. Tom was in a foster home that he loved. There were several other children, so the home was very busy, but his foster mother was skilled, kind, nurturing and committed to him. Tom engaged well with me. He loved coming to sessions and having me and his foster mother to himself for an hour. After years of isolation he had a voice and people who were willing to listen to what had happened to him. He wanted to talk.

I generally do not assess or treat children until investigations are completed and legal issues are resolved. The children I work with have often had their trust betrayed many times, and therapy needs to be a safe place where a child can experience safety. There is a difference between therapy and an assessment for child welfare and legal purposes. These differences need to be respected in order to ensure the safety of the therapeutic relationship. A child's right to confidentiality is important, and undermining that is another betrayal. Canadian therapists are subject to subpoena, and so are unable to provide confidentiality when a situation is under investigation or before the courts. I met Tom many years ago, however, before these issues were clear to me. Also, Tom's situation appeared to be an exception. He was anxious to talk about the abuse. He was also anxious to have his information heard by the police and the courts, and my responsibility to report any new abuse allegations did not appear to undermine his trust in me. He wanted me to pass this information on; he viewed me as part of this new group of people that would protect him from his mother. The opportunity to have a voice and be heard was important to him. Initially, our plan had been to do a brief assessment to determine the degree of dissociative symptoms and to develop an understanding of his placement needs. Tom wanted to continue, and seemed to find it helpful. After his first few sessions he seemed happier, more relaxed, and began to engage appropriately with peers in his foster home and school.

During the first few weeks of therapy, Tom disclosed physical abuse, emotional abuse, deprivation and confinement. A few weeks into therapy Tom began to talk about and draw pictures of the other children inside his head. It soon became evident that not all parts of Tom were happy that he was talking about his mother, and not all parts wanted to stay in care. Some parts were aligned with Tom's mother and denied the abuse. Other parts believed that Tom's mother would find and kill him for talking. Tom began to destabilise. He arrived in sessions with an internal pressure to talk about his abuse. He found change threatening, and the new relationships had been rewarding. He was resistant to taking a break or changing the pattern of our time together. During sessions he had multiple switches, becoming increasingly agitated. I made many attempts to slow down the process, but Tom rigidly held to the pattern. There was a battle between the parts that wanted to talk, and those that didn't. Tom began to struggle outside of therapy. He became explosive and verbally abusive to others. He began to self-harm and some parts expressed suicidal ideation. Tom needed increased supervision in order to keep him safe. After two months of being unable to slow down the pressured disclosures and emotional and behavioural instability, Tom's foster mother realised that she needed to make a choice between the five other children in her care, and Tom. Tom had to move. This was traumatic for Tom and heartbreaking for his foster mother. His placement had been a positive one. His relationship with his foster mother had been stable, loving and unconditional. Many parts of Tom had begun to experience the world outside his mother's home as potentially safe and caring. Having to move was experienced as abandonment, betrayal, and above all, a reinforcement of his earlier experiences. He felt he was being sent away because he was too "bad" to be loved.

This was not a failure of his foster mother, or the foster system. When Tom first entered into care neither the CAS nor I had any idea of what we were dealing with. This was early in my involvement with dissociative disorders, and Tom was, at the time, the youngest such child I had worked with. Tom initially presented as a frightened boy who was relieved to be safe and anxious to talk. He was not ready to process the traumatic material he felt so pressured to disclose. Once he began, he became increasingly unstable. He could not be safely contained in a placement with many other children. He needed more support and supervision. It would be easy to see the problem as being that Tom was too difficult to maintain in a foster placement. If, however, we want to meet the needs of traumatised children, we need to learn to understand and respond to them. It may have worked better for Tom if we had moved much slower, getting to know what was inside him. With children and adolescents who dissociate, we need to assume that what we see is not all that is there. This is not always obvious or easy and the outcome could well have been worse. It was only Tom's disclosures that kept him safe. The court chose to make him and his sister permanent wards based solely on the strength of his disclosures and the degree of his emotional fragility. Unfortunately "talking about" the trauma also contributed to his decompensation and the breakdown of his placement.

Phase- or stage-oriented psychotherapy was developed to support adults with complex trauma issues in engaging in treatment without becoming overwhelmed.[4,5,6,7,8,9,10] A stage- or phase-oriented approach to adult treatment is included in both the International Society for the Study of Trauma and Dissociation (ISST-D) and the International Society for the Study of Traumatic Stress (ISSTS) treatment guidelines.[11,12] The ISST-D Child and Adolescent Treatment Guidelines do not refer directly to stage- or phase-oriented psychotherapy but stress maintaining stability in functioning and an appropriate developmental trajectory. Should stability be compromised they recommend examining and reorienting treatment to help the client return to a more normalised age-appropriate life experience. As well, the section of the guidelines focusing on treatment cautions against overwhelming children when processing traumatic memory and recommends the use of ego-strengthening techniques and calming techniques to avoid this.[13]

Dan Siegel[14] refers to a "window of tolerance" (Figure 5.1) for emotional stimuli. This window of tolerance describes each person's optimal range of emotion before becoming hyper- or hypoaroused.

In Chapter 1, I referred to my working definition of trauma as being "extreme stressors which have overwhelmed the child or adolescent's ability to

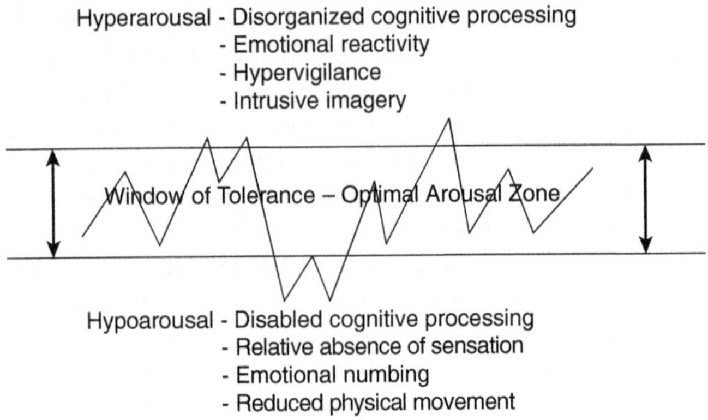

Figure 5.1 Window of Tolerance

Adapted from Siegel, D. (2011). *Mindsight: The New Science of Personal Transformation.* Bantam Books. New York.

cope." It is this experience of being overwhelmed which takes a person outside of their window of tolerance and interferes with normal integration of experience. Overwhelming experiences lead to affective overwhelm, which leads to hyper- and or hypoarousal, which leads to the inability to integrate and process information. This is the basis of the neurological impact of trauma. Children's brains, when exposed to chronic trauma, adapt to living in a high-risk environment.[15,16] Some children become primed to identify dangerous experiences quickly and efficiently; they become hyperalert. Other children protect themselves from becoming overwhelmed by becoming detached and numb; they are hypoalert. Some children do both depending on the situation. In all of these examples, their windows of tolerance have become smaller. Events that take children out of their window of tolerance support this adaptation to a high-risk environment by reinforcing the neural pathways that create hyper or hypoalert responses.[17,18] When therapy takes children out of their window of tolerance, triggering either hyper- or hypoarousal, it is, in effect, retraumatising. Not only do these experiences reinforce the neurological impact of earlier trauma, but once working on a memory leads the child to a state of hyper- or hypoarousal the attempt to process the memory fails; the child is unable to process and integrate information in this state. Phase-oriented psychotherapy for children supports our young clients in processing and integrating their traumatic experiences without retraumatising them, by helping them and their caregivers create a stable base for remaining within their window of tolerance.

There are variations of phase-oriented trauma therapy developed for adults, and the names or number of phases differs. Many therapists break therapy down into three phases.[19,20,21,22] Frank Putnam described eight stages of treatment.[23] Each of these models describes a similar process, with the main ideas being well established and generally agreed on. All the components of Putnam's eight phases are covered in the three phase models. These models describe a progression of steps, but they are not a systematic program of treatment. Each person has different needs and different experiences. Therapy involves movement back and forth within and between phases depending on the needs of the client. Some children or adults have good stabilisation skills, affective and behavioural control, and stable relationships. Others may enter into therapy with few supports, struggling to cope with daily life. The length of each phase is variable, and so is the length of treatment. Children and adolescents are often able to move through treatment fairly quickly, compared to adults, but some children and adolescents still need a lengthier course of treatment. Depending on the supports in the young person's life, as well as how well they are able to engage in positive relationships, their ability to self-regulate and their willingness to take on challenges, treatment can range from a few months to a number of years. Some children benefit from entering into and out of treatment as needed, rather than staying for a lengthy period. Flexibility in responding to the needs of the child or adolescent and their family provides the best outcome.

I approach this work thinking of three phases of treatment. The phases I use are adapted for young people from the models developed for work with adults. I think of phase one as "stabilisation and relationships," which focuses on building and strengthening attachment relationships, affective and behavioural regulation, and general daily coping skills; phase two as "trauma processing and integration"; and phase three as "moving forward," which focuses on helping the child return to their appropriate developmental trajectory and to "get a life," so to speak. These phases will be described in detail in upcoming chapters.

Notes

1. Kluft, R.P. (2013). *Shelter from the Storm: Processing the Traumatic Memories of DID/DDNOS Patients with the Fractionated Abreaction Technique*. R.P. Kluft. North Charleston, SC. pp 19–22.
2. Chu, J.A. (2011). *Rebuilding Shattered Lives: Treating Complex PTSD and Dissociative Disorders*. John Wiley and Sons. New York. pp 109–128.
3. Chu, J.A. (2011). *Rebuilding Shattered Lives: Treating Complex PTSD and Dissociative Disorders*. John Wiley and Sons. New York. pp 109–128.
4. Janet, P. (1973). *L'automatisme psychologigue*. Paris: Société Pierre Janet. (Original work published in 1889).
5. Scurfield, R.M. (1985). Post trauma stress assessment and treatment: Overview and formulations. In C.R. Figley (Ed.), *Trauma and Its Wake: The Study and Treatment of Post Traumatic Stress Disorder*. Brunner Mazel. New York.
6. Brown, D., & Fromm, E. (1986). *Hypnotherapy and Hypnoanalysis*. Lawrence Earlbaum. Hillsdale, NJ.
7. Putnam, F. W. (1989). *Diagnosis and Treatment of Multiple Personality Disorder*. Guilford. New York.
8. Herman, J. (1997). *Trauma and Recovery: The Aftermath of Violence—From Domestic Violence to Political Terror*. Basic Books. New York.
9. Chu, J.A. (2011). *Rebuilding Shattered Lives: Treating Complex PTSD and Dissociative Disorders*. John Wiley and Sons. New York. pp 109–128.
10. Van der Hart, O., Nijenhuis, E., & Steele, K. (2006). *The Haunted Self: Structural Dissociation and the Treatment of Chronic Traumatization*. W.W. Norton & Company. New York.

11. International Society for the Study of Trauma and Dissociation. (2011). [Chu, J.A., Dell, P.F., Van der Hart, O., Cardeña, E., Barach, P.M., Somer, E., Loewenstein, R.J., Brand, B., Golston, J.C., Courtois, C.A., Bowman, E.S., Classen, C., Dorahy, M., Sar, V., Gelinas, D.J., Fine, C.G., Paulsen, S., Kluft, R.P., Dalenberg, C.J., Jacobson-Levy, M., Nijenhuis, E.R.S., Boon, S., Chefetz, R. A., Middleton, W., Ross, C.A., Howell, E., Goodwin, G., Coons, P.M., Frankel, A.S., Steele, K., Gold, S.N., Gast, U., Young, L.M., & Twombly, J.]. Guidelines for treating dissociative identity disorder in adults, third revision. *Journal of Trauma and Dissociation, 12*, 115–187.
12. Cloitre, M., Courtois, C.A., Ford, J.D., Green, B. L., Alexander, P., Briere, J., Herman, J.L., Lannius, R., Stolbach, B.C., Spinnazola, J., van der Kolk, B.A., & Van Der Hart, O. (2012). *The ISTSS Expert Consensus Treatment Guidelines for Complex PTSD in Adults.* Retrieved from: http://www.istss.org/ISTSS_Complex_PTSD_Treatment_Guidelines/5205.htm
13. International Society for the Study of Trauma and Dissociation. (2004). [Joyanna Silberg, PhD. Members: Frances Waters, Elaine Nemzer, Jeanie McIntee, Sandra Wieland, Els Grimminck, Linda Nordquist, Elizabeth Emsond. The committee thanks Peter Barach, James Chu, John Curtis, Beverly James, John O'Neil, Gary Peterson and Margo Rivera]. Guidelines for the evaluation and treatment of dissociative symptoms in children and adolescents. *Journal of Trauma and Dissociation, 5*(3).
14. Siegel, Daniel J. (2013). *The Developing Mind: How Relationships and the Brain Interact to Shape Who We Are*. Guilford. New York.
15. Siegel, Daniel J. (2013). *The Developing Mind: How Relationships and the Brain Interact to Shape Who We Are*. Guilford. New York.
16. Porgess, Stephen W. (2011). *The Polyvagal Theory: Neurophysiological Foundations of Emotions, Attachment, Communication, Self-Regulation*. W.W. Norton & Company. New York.
17. Siegel, Daniel J. (2013). *The Developing Mind: How Relationships and the Brain Interact to Shape Who We Are*. Guilford. New York.
18. Porgess, Stephen W. (2011). *The Polyvagal Theory: Neurophysiological Foundations of Emotions, Attachment, Communication, Self-Regulation*. W.W. Norton & Company. New York.
19. Janet, P. (1973). *L'automatisme psychologigue*. Paris: Société Pierre Janet. (Original work published in 1889).
20. Brown, D., & Fromm, E. (1986). *Hypnotherapy and Hypnoanalysis*. Lawrence Earlbaum. Hillsdale, NJ.
21. Herman, J. (1997). *Trauma and Recovery: The Aftermath of Violence—From Domestic Violence to Political Terror*. Basic Books. New York
22. Chu, J.A. (2011). *Rebuilding Shattered Lives: Treating Complex PTSD and Dissociative Disorders*. John Wiley and Sons. New York. pp 109–128.
23. Putnam, F.W. (1989). *Diagnosis and Treatment of Multiple Personality Disorder*. Guilford. New York.

6 Bringing It Together

The Treatment Frame

We refer to early trauma combined with disrupted attachment as complex trauma for a reason. Children affected in this way have complex impacts and needs. The skills we use to cope with trauma develop through early attachment relationships. When adults experience trauma, even when it involves betrayal by someone close, these experiences are mediated by earlier experiences. When trauma happens to children, they not only don't have the skills and resources to cope, the impact is compounded by a disruption of their developmental process.[1,2] When adults experience trauma, we either support them in using skills they have already developed, or support them in developing skills they missed. When therapy is finished, they are still adults. Separation from the person who supported them through this process makes developmental sense. When working with kids, we are working within their developmental time frame to develop skills that would be developed outside of therapy within their attachment relationships. Most children develop trust, build attachment and, through attunement and coregulation, develop self-regulation and a sense of themselves and the world. As they grow and mature, they continue to rely on their attachment figures as a secure base from which to explore the world, gradually achieving individuation and interdependence as they are ready. When children enter into therapy, build a trusting relationship with an attuned therapist, and use this relationship to grow and develop, an artificial situation is created; the therapist takes on the role of the primary attachment figure. This creates a conflict. Children and adolescents are not ready for emotional independence. When therapy ends, they continue to be dependent on the adults in their lives. These are not the ones by whom they have been supported in facing their challenges and developing their identity. Principles of transference suggest that our clients are seeking to re-create parent-child relationships with their therapists.[3] The difference with child clients is that it is age-appropriate to want and need a parent-child relationship. The therapist taking on this role in therapy leads to new losses for the child.

Attachment-focused therapies solve this by helping the child and caregiver to either build new attachment relationships, or to repair the existing relationships which have been damaged. Phase-oriented attachment-focused therapy aims to build or repair attachment relationships between the child and their caregiver, and then to work within these relationships to guide the caregiver in supporting the child to explore, resolve and integrate their traumatic experiences.

Ideally, this approach meets many ends. We now realise that when children's developmental trajectories are altered by trauma and disrupted attachment, the impact occurs on the level of brain development, affecting both discrete parts of the brain and neurological integration.[4,5,6] The theory of neuroplasticity suggests that by helping children experience connection, attunement and coregulation with an attachment figure that they missed during early development, they can strengthen the parts of their brains that may not have adequately developed earlier.[7] By building these connections with their caregiver, the child can then use their caregiver as a source of soothing and coregulation, thereby developing their self-regulation skills. By building and using their attachment relationship, the child's ability to trust and rely on their caregiver is improved. The use of this relationship to support the child through the resolution of their trauma supports the child and family to cocreate new meanings of the experiences, and supports the child in developing a stronger, more positive sense of self and others that is shared by the caregiver. When therapy ends, rather than losing an attachment figure, the child has gained one.

The Treatment Frame

The model of phase-oriented attachment-focused trauma therapy that I've developed incorporates an attachment figure, usually the caregiver or caregivers, into each phase of treatment. Achieving this requires gently challenging assumptions held by caregivers and children about therapy and therapists. Adults and children often arrive in my office with expectations of what therapy does and how. They also arrive with ideas of what they do and don't want. It's important to respect the goals the clients bring with them when developing the treatment plan. Many times the child's and caregiver's goals conflict. It can be a fine balance to engage each party, allow them to experience hope, and still maintain the attachment and healing focus of the therapeutic process. It helps to be aware of the ideas that our clients bring into the room. Below, I explore how many of these fit or don't fit into the treatment frame, and how they can be talked about in a way that is helpful to both the adult and the child or adolescent.

Common Assumptions about Trauma Therapy

1. The goal of therapy is for children to talk about what happened in order to "get it out" and "get over" what happened to them.
    - Talking about traumatic events is part of processing and integrating them into the child's experience. Talking about trauma is a tool, not a goal. The act of talking is not enough to heal the impact of the trauma. Talking with trusted people who are able to openly witness, support

and empathise with them helps the child or adolescent cocreate a different, healthier, more balanced meaning to their experiences. Even within the context of an attachment experience, merely using words to describe events is not enough to work through traumatic experience.

2. Traumatic experiences change or "damage" a person, and the goal of therapy is to undo the damage and return the child or adolescent to who they were before their trauma.

    - All of our experiences change us, and no one goes through life without trauma in one form or another. No therapy undoes experiences or makes trauma un-happen. The goal of trauma therapy is to help guide the child or adolescent through their experiences and take control of change, so that they can grow in a positive, healthy and adaptive way. No one returns to who they were before any life-changing event, nor should they, but the changes can be positive and adaptive.

3. Traumatised children need individual therapy, because they are more likely to talk about what happened to them if their caregivers aren't in the room. Caregivers often suggest that their child or adolescent should be seen alone. They have tried to talk to their child, and their child hasn't opened up. Often the child will agree that they prefer to talk without their caregivers.

    - Most often the child or adolescent isn't comfortable talking with their caregivers. I begin the first session with the child and caregivers together to talk about the treatment plan and outline the first few sessions. During the early part of therapy I meet with the child and parents separately at least once in order to build the relationship and negotiate the treatment frame. Often the parents and children see themselves on different sides of a battle over control. They are on the same side regarding wanting the child to be happier and wanting to have a better relationship. Children and adolescents who have histories involving trauma and disrupted attachment don't talk to the adults in their lives; they expect that caregivers won't understand and can't be trusted to hear them. Almost always, they will agree that they would like that to be different and are willing to have the therapist meet with their parents a few times to see if it might be possible. For the parents and caregivers, it's often easy for them to agree to try a different approach if we are nonjudgmental. Underneath the arguing they are more concerned about their child's mental health than about winning the arguments. They are invested in the arguments because the child's behaviours are harming the child and the family, and they believe they have to change these behaviours to help their child. Parents and caregivers often believe that "being in control" of their child means they are good parents. I shift this to the idea that understanding and supporting their child and helping them move towards self-control is also good parenting.

4. The goal of therapy is to improve children's behaviour.

    - Both children and adults share this idea, but with different effect. Children see us as another adult being brought in to help make them behave. When their behaviours are discussed in session, they experience their caregiver as "telling on them," which increases shame. Living together and experiencing the struggles daily can lead parents to view symptoms as "the problem," and to believe that changing the behaviour will mean that the child is "better." They see the therapist as an adult ally in achieving this goal. Their intentions are to help the child, but the child experiences this as proof that they are bad, and that their parents want to change them. For traumatised children being controlled is threatening.
    - Part of these early meetings is to help the clients know that my interest in behaviour is as clues that help me know what the child is experiencing. It isn't my job to make them behave, to control them, or to help someone else control them. My interest is in understanding them so that I can help them feel better and be more in control of themselves. I also help caregivers understand that this is my goal while reassuring them that children who are well attached and emotionally healthy have better self-control and don't engage in the kinds of behaviours that are causing so much worry and conflict.

5. A primary attachment figure needs to be a parent or caregiver.

    - Ideally, all children or adolescents would have a parent or long-term caregiver who is open and available to participate in therapy. Ideally, of course, children and adolescents also would not need attachment-focused trauma therapy. The children we work with don't live in the ideal world. We need to adjust treatment to what is available and possible. Many teens refer themselves for treatment, having left abusive and neglectful homes, or while living with adults with whom they don't feel safe and don't want involved in their treatment. Some children and adolescents live with caregivers who are not emotionally or physically available for therapy. Others live in group homes with inconsistent staffing, or in temporary foster placements, and are not willing to build trusting relationships with people who have limited investment in their lives. We also encounter children who aren't emotionally ready to engage with and trust the adults who are available to work with them. Sometimes there are other people in the child's life that can be a supportive attachment figure. When we aren't able to find or build an appropriate attachment relationship, there are techniques that can be used to incorporate attachment-focused work into individual treatment. These possibilities will be discussed in Chapter 7.

6. In order to participate in therapy the attachment figure needs to have fully resolved their own and their child's trauma and be fully focused on their child's emotional needs. This involves preparation with the therapist and may involve the caregiver attending individual therapy before attending with the child.

    - Participating in attachment-focused treatment is difficult for the adults in a child's life. This is particularly true if the adult is a parent or kinship care provider who has a connection or involvement in the trauma. If the parent or caregiver has had their own therapy, or has been able to resolve and come to terms with their own and their child's experiences, this creates an ideal situation, but there isn't always a caregiver who has done this. As long as the caregiver is open and willing to understanding that their child's experience and perspective may be different from theirs, and that their child needs their support to work on their experiences, a way can be found to support improved attachment. If the parent was involved in the child's trauma, the parent needs to be able to work within the child's understanding and perspective of their role and to take responsibility for their part. I do a fair amount of individual work with attachment figures, but I intersperse them between dyadic sessions, on an as-needed basis. I try to avoid delaying the child's therapy to work with adults. When working with caregivers who are struggling, or whose own trauma and attachment histories continue to impact on their availability, I work more slowly and cautiously during dyadic sessions, and am more tentative in focusing on moments of attunement and connection. Sometimes I intersperse individual sessions with the child into the therapy in order to work on issues that the caregiver is not ready for. Although this can be challenging and more limited work, the small moves within these dyads can be very meaningful and lead to improved connections within families that have been very troubled. An example of this, in the case of Anna and her parents, is discussed in Chapter 4.

7. For therapy to be successful children need to trust their therapist.

    - In the earlier days of trauma therapy, James Chu said, "The most common trap for therapists, particularly those unfamiliar with the treatment of trauma survivors, is the assumption of the presence of trust."[8] In 2002, when I was attending the ISST-D Dissociative Disorders Training Program, Clare Pain clarified this further. She said, "Most of us, when we say that our clients don't trust us, believe they think we will fail them or let them down. What they really believe about us is what they believe about everyone—that we are waiting for them to let their guard down so we can rape and murder them!"[9] I found this difficult to believe. I knew it may be true about some clients when in dissociated states, but I couldn't imagine that the children and adolescents who sat in my office, engaged, safe and relaxed, were in a state of continuous fear. Over time, I have checked this out with many of the young people I work with, and without exception, they have all acknowledged some degree of active fear that I will hurt them in a real and physical sense. Understanding this has made me a better therapist.

- Joyanna Silberg says that everything our clients do makes sense.[10] Both not trusting us and behaving as if they do make sense when we understand their experiences. I approach every client from the position of assuming lack of trust and am open about it. Issues around trust and safety in therapy form an important part of phase one therapy and are discussed in Chapter 7.

8. For therapy to be successful children and adolescents need to want therapy.

    - Therapy is a voluntary process. We can't work with people against their will, and when working with children and adolescents who have been traumatised, it does more harm than good to try. This knowledge, however, gets misused in an oversimplified way. I have heard the argument made that children need to want to attend, and so should never be seen at all unless they say they want to be there at the beginning of the first session. A related argument is that trauma-focused therapy is only OK if they say they want to talk about what has happened to them. If, before or at the beginning of therapy, they say they don't want to talk about it, they should be referred for therapy focusing on present functioning. As well-meaning as this seems, there is a difference between the right to control and the right to make informed, well-thought-out choices. Not many young people would choose to attend school, go to the dentist, or get a good night's sleep, if they were given the opportunity to make the choice based on what felt most comfortable in the moment. Engagement in therapy is a process, and we have the ability and the responsibility to lead this process. No child or caregiver can make a choice without having a good understanding of what is involved in the types of treatment available and what the outcome of choosing not to attend, or choosing not to "talk about it," will mean. This does not mean imposing trauma work on children against their will. It does mean negotiating a process of treatment that is focused on what will be most helpful to the child and which is co-led by the child in a way that feels safe to them. I take the approach that we will take time to get to know each other and figure out what directions will be best for them. I may encourage them to move towards difficult conversations, but they determine the pacing of the work, and they do not have to talk about something that is overwhelming until they have the skills to do it without being overwhelmed. If after attending a number of sessions with me, we can't work out a mutually agreed-on direction, and they are unwilling to attend, I will not continue to meet with them, even if their parent or guardian wants me to. This has almost never happened. When it has happened, I've worked with the parents or caregivers to help them find ways to work with the child in the home. The child or adolescent always eventually returned.

9. Therapeutic boundaries must involve objectivity and professional detachment.
    - Boundaries are critical, and the boundaries of the therapist-child relationship need to be clear. There are many issues that pull on these boundaries, and therapists working with children and adolescents with attachment and complex trauma issues need to maintain a high level of self-awareness. At the same time, these are powerfully intense, long-term relationships that have enormous significance in the child's life. A therapist who doesn't acknowledge that these relationships also have an enormous significance in their own lives is not being honest with themselves. These boundaries need to be clear, but they also are different from those in other therapy relationships. We need to be real, genuine human beings with our clients. Our feelings and reactions are an important part of the process. This applies to our relationships with parents and caregivers as much as to children. We are joined together in a journey of major exploration, and it is a journey we are sharing.
10. The reason therapists assess family relationships and involve parents is because the parents are "part of the problem."
    - The reason for parents and caregivers to be involved in therapy is that they are the people who the child or adolescent will be relying on for connection and support on an ongoing basis. I will be involved for a few weeks, months, or a year or more. They will see me about once a week. Their parents or caregivers are the ones who are there day in, day out, year after year. It may be easier and quicker for a child to learn how to open up to a stranger in an office, but it is more useful to learn how to open up to the permanent adults in their life, and for those adults to learn how to make it safe for this to happen.
    - It's easy for parents to experience family-focused interventions as being blamed for their child's problems. The chances are that they have been blamed by schools, doctors, child welfare, the police and their child. They have almost definitely blamed themselves. If the parents or caregivers are part of the child's family of origin, there may be a lot of self-blame and blame from others. I often work with parents who had some part in the child's trauma or attachment difficulties. Even if the child was adopted or fostered, or placed with a relative who was not involved in the early parts of the child's life, caregivers feel responsible for their difficulties in reaching the child and helping them overcome their difficulties. Traumatised children

can be difficult to parent, and parents find themselves thinking and responding in ways that don't meet their own expectations. They are ashamed of their responses and angry at the child for raising these reactions in them. This is a fine line to walk for a therapist. We need to find ways of helping parents experience therapy as a safe, non-judgmental experience. It is easier for humans to take responsibility for their mistakes if they aren't being shamed or shaming themselves. Marsha Linehan describes the approach of "accepting people completely for who they are, while still expecting change."[11] This is one of the basic approaches of my treatment frame. It's our job to help parents understand that their mistakes, no matter how big, somehow made sense; only if they can accept that and have compassion for themselves can they help their child move forward.

- Usually, it's easy for us to be supportive and have compassion for the caregivers we work with, which makes it easier for them to feel safe enough to let us in. Adoptive parents, foster parents, grandparents, aunts and uncles are often caring, loving, protective adults who have taken wounded children into their home and done what they can to be helpful. Even those who are angry and rejecting by the time we see them can be understood as trying to do the best they can with children that have difficulties greater than they were prepared for.
- Some of the parents we work with can be a greater challenge for us. Parents who have had addictions, who abandoned, neglected or abused their children, or who didn't protect them from abuse, can trigger anger and mistrust from therapists and from others in the helping system. Sometimes these parents are open; sometimes they are highly defended against internal shame and external blame, and need a lot of support to engage. If these parents pose a risk to their child, it is of course important that we not encourage the child to trust them in a way that's unsafe or unrealistic. At the same time, when parents have reached a different place in their lives, or when older adolescents have no one else in their lives to rely on or build a connection with, it can be helpful to repair these relationships as much as possible.
- In all cases, I work with parents around realistic responsibility for the past rather than getting caught up in guilt or shame. I let them know that I'm including them as part of the solution. I do not and will not judge them for the past—I truly believe they are with me now because they want to make things better, that I can't possibly understand what their past experiences or situations have been, and that I believe they did the best they could in whatever situation they were struggling with. This is not just a stance. This has to be genuine. If I can't find something in a parent to like and respect, than I should not be working with them. Just like I understand that children's behaviours make sense somehow, I also understand that the parent's behaviours have made sense too. The

minimum requirement that a parent needs to be helpful in therapy is a willingness to accept that bad things happened in the past, that the child may have experienced the parent as having some responsibility, and that the parent has to be able to be open to the child's experience. If the parent did have some responsibility, they need to acknowledge that for themselves and the child. This does not have to be the starting point, but there needs to be openness to move in that direction.
- I'm open to their needing me to understand the hows and whys of their situation, if it helps them to feel less shame, but they need to agree to not place this burden of understanding and forgiveness on their child or adolescent.

11. Therapy is for the treatment of mental health difficulties. This means that children who need therapy are mentally ill, or "crazy."

    - Many of the children we work with think they are "crazy" or worry about being "crazy." Often the adults who bring them for therapy have the same worries about them. This can be particularly true for children with dissociative symptoms. Hearing voices, losing time or denying things that they were seen to do can seem like mental illness to people who don't understand the impact of trauma. When children lie or are secretive about simple things, have outbursts of rage or fear, or engage in self-abusive or self-defeating behaviours, they and others may assume they are "crazy."
    - When we begin to understand the kids we work with, we realise that their behaviours make sense.[12,13] They are sane adaptations to having lived in a crazy world. When we help them make sense of this, they realise they aren't crazy. It's a relief to them to hear, and then to understand that their symptoms make sense, even if we are not at first sure how.

12. Dissociation in children and adolescents is a symptom of trauma which will resolve naturalistically during good trauma therapy.

    - This assumption makes sense at first glance. Earlier I mentioned that I don't focus on changing behaviours because they are symptoms, and that symptoms are likely to resolve as trauma is resolved. The difficulty with this lies in the nature of dissociation. Dissociation involves compartmentalisation of part of the consciousness, and as such, prevents that part of the consciousness from being accessed during the regular therapeutic process. Whether that part involves a fully dissociated self-state, or whether it involves an affective experience or memory, this part is not integrated into the whole self. Often, when therapy should be working, but somehow isn't, this is because dissociation has not been identified or directly addressed.
    - Jake was an eight-year-old boy being seen by a skilled child therapist. She had been working with Jake and his father for over a year.

Jake resisted talking about abuse that he had previously disclosed in detail, and that had been verified by the Children's Aid Society and the police. He continued to have explosive episodes at home, and his father was reaching the end of his rope. After more than a year of therapy, Jake was hospitalised for a serious suicide attempt. There had been no indication that he was suicidal. The therapist began to explore possible dissociation. She identified dissociation, including periods of lost time and altered consciousness. As this was addressed, Jake began to stabilise and became more able to access traumatic memories in treatment. A few months later, when asked about the abuse in a session, Jake shook his head. He then said, "That happened to the second Jake. He's orange."

- Sometimes trauma appears to be resolved, but is not. This can be more dangerous, as the parts carrying the trauma learn during treatment to be better at keeping secrets. This was the case with Beth, who nearly died from a suicide attempt by an unidentified alter when treatment appeared to be going well, and with Terra, who appeared to be coping much better and then had a sudden deterioration (Chapter 3).

13. When children or adolescents have dissociated parts, the goal of therapy is to make the parts, particularly the "bad," "dangerous" or "scary," "go away." These parts were created by trauma and when they go away, the child will be "better."

    - Many kids and most caregivers at first think the parts should go away. The parts do not share in this view, and are likely to undermine therapy if it is not clarified.
    - This view is adopted by many children and caregivers once they become aware of dissociated parts. This may occur before therapy if a child or adolescent is aware of parts or voices that they experience as separate, or it may occur during therapy as awareness surfaces. Few children, adolescents or caregivers find it easy to be open to some or all of the parts. Most kids will say something like, "No way—I don't want anything to do with her. She's horrible!"
    - Parts aren't symptoms. The separation of the whole into parts is a symptom.
    - We all have parts of ourselves that we would like to disappear. Getting rid of a part that we don't like or that we are afraid of would serve about the same function as getting rid of a part of our car. Even if the car part isn't working, or we don't know what it's for, it's there for a reason and we need it.
    - Every dissociated part has a purpose, a reason, and something important to say. Accepting the child involves accepting the whole child. There may be parts that have adapted to a world that is no longer their reality, and that may mean that the part will grow or change in some way, but getting rid of it isn't helpful. A more useful

goal is to decrease the boundaries so that the parts work as a team, and ideally move close enough together to form a cohesive whole.

14. When children are removed from abusive and/or neglectful homes, this is in their best interests and therapy can help them realise that they are better off. This also applies to children who have experienced difficult, painful and frightening medical procedures. The assumption is that actions that are truly necessary are benign, and the child's resentment is based on misunderstanding or misperception that needs to be corrected.
    - Children often do need to be removed from dangerous situations for their own safety, and they do sometimes need medical care that is difficult, painful or frightening. This does not mean that these actions don't also cause harm. As adults, or as a society, we are often in the position of having to choose the less traumatic of several traumatic options. It is still trauma. Therapy allows for the experiences of anger, sadness and loss.
15. Parents who hurt or neglect their children are bad. Therapy needs to help children accept this.
    - This is a tricky area, particularly when we are working with children who are angry at their parents, and view them as "bad." It's easy as a therapist to empathise with the child and mirror their experiences. This can be a trap. The child's views of their parents are often mixed, and sometimes the opposing views are held by dissociated parts. When we side with the part of the child that is angry at the parent, we are not leaving space for the parts of the child that are aligned with the abusing parent or desperately want to be loved by that parent. When parts are alienated from therapy, therapy is likely to fail.
    - Another difficulty with this assumption is that if the parent's bad behaviours mean the parent is bad, then the child's bad behaviours may also mean that the child is bad. People are complex, and buying into the easy idea that there are good and bad people limits the child's ability to explore all aspects of themselves and to accept the parts of themselves that have acted out or are aligned with their abusers.
    - A third complication caused by dismissing abusive parents as bad is that it limits options for healing. Many children and adolescents choose to have some form of relationship with their parents. If the child has been able to come to terms with the idea of their parents as flawed human beings, they do not have to categorise them as good or evil. Acceptance of their parents as flawed allows for a realistic evaluation of what can and can't be hoped for in the relationship.
    - The view of abusive or negligent parents as complex and flawed doesn't mean that we excuse abuse or work to reunite children with

abusers. It means that we separate behaviours from people, and work with our clients to develop an age-appropriate understanding of their lives and experiences. Realistic narratives aren't comprised of black-and-white thinking and neat categories.

Lessons Learned from Brief Therapy

Over the past several years, in addition to complex trauma work, I have also trained in and practiced brief, single-session therapy on a walk-in basis. This has been a tremendously valuable experience. Historically there is mistrust between trauma therapists and those who work with a brief model. I suspect this comes from a belief that the two models are in competition for funding dollars. Those who do long-term work are worried that funders and insurers will favour briefer therapies due to lower costs. Those who work in a brief way worry about being discounted as not as effective by long-term therapists protecting their territory. My experience suggests something different. The availability of brief models of treatment opens options for clients and allows greater freedom for therapists to invest long-term resources where they are needed. My work with single-session therapy has taught me important ideas and skills needed for long-term work.

1. Every session needs to stand on its own.
   - When working longer term, it's easy to take time for granted. Treatment becomes more effective when we think of each session as potentially the only session. The concept behind the single-session walk-in model is not that the session will be the only session the person attends. Clients have the option of returning when and if they need to. Each session needs to work within the context of what is important in the moment. Each session needs to be relevant to the client in the here and now, and be responsive to what they are bringing with them. Long-term directions and plans are fine, but if we get caught up in them we risk losing sight of what our clients need right now.
2. Every session is an intervention.
   - Something helpful and significant should happen in every therapy session. Trauma therapy is a daunting process that requires determination and motivation. Many of the caregivers and young people have been struggling for a long time, and have tried many things. It's not enough to reassure them that things will be better eventually. They need to feel hope, possibility and connection now. They need to have tools to address day-to-day struggles. They need support in dealing with external systems that are adding to their challenges and increasing their feelings of helplessness. What is helpful depends on the client, the situation and the session. It may be a new way of seeing the situation that can give them hope; it may be the experience of feeling

heard, understood and not judged; it may be a realisation that their parent does want to understand why they are struggling, and may be open to hearing what is inside them. These are small shifts that have big impact. Other possibilities are techniques for coping with a meltdown before it gets too big, or a way of managing sleep problems so the child doesn't feel ashamed of being afraid. Sometimes something practical is necessary, such as a note to a teacher that helps the child's needs be understood, or prevents them from being suspended for refusing to do a Father's Day assignment. Even a plan for what direction treatment will take, and how the child will be heard and understood, is something that can help them feel hope and agency in their own healing. The more each session is meaningful and provides the child with something they did not have before, the more engagement they will have in treatment, and the more likely they are to continue.

3. Our work needs to stay focused and intentional. We should never be treading water or passing time.

    - When working long-term, it is easy to coast. Sometimes our clients will arrive tired, sometimes we will. Often there will be many things going on in everyone's life and it can be tempting to sit and chat, check in, and update, without doing intentional, focused work. Of course there will always be sessions that are not earth-shattering, or that fall flat, but we need to make the best use of our time and of our client's time.

4. Our clients are our partners. Therapy is led by them and done together, not something we do to them.

    - Children who have experienced trauma have experienced very little control over their experiences and relationships. They have often lost people who were important to them, and some of them have been moved from place to place with little experience of being heard and understood. Many of the kids we see do not want to come to therapy and do not want another adult telling them what to do. It's our job to listen, hear them, try to understand them and help them have a voice. Trauma therapy is best when it helps them regain some control in their lives. The best way for us to support this is to see them as partners. As guides, we help them go where they want to be. Because they might not know where that is, we can help them know what is possible. We can share our opinions and ideas, but we can't choose their direction.

5. The here and now is important. Our clients need actual solutions to current problems.

    - We need to balance the work we do to support our clients not only in developing stable attachment relationships and resolving traumatic experiences, but also in negotiating the challenges of daily life. Although we aren't focused on getting children to behave, we can help them cope. They may not want to be controlled, but they don't want to be out of their own control either. When meltdowns, angry outbursts, dissociative switches, sleep difficulties and other symptoms mess up their lives, our first challenge is to help them experience stability and safety. Some of this is achieved by helping them learn skills to cope with internal experiences, some of it is achieved by helping them build relationships with caregivers that can provide them with needed support, and some of it is achieved by working with systems to help them understand and meet the child's need for support, containment and stability.

6. Therapy is more interesting to therapists than it is to our clients.

   - Most children and adolescents are not that interested in spending endless hours talking about their trauma. When they are, it reflects a sad reality that they aren't often heard and listened to by adults who take interest in what they have to say. It's a sign of good health when children have better things to do than come talk to us, and we should encourage it. This means working around things that are important in a child's life, rather than expecting to take priority. If children don't want to schedule at a particular time because they don't want to miss gym, or drama, or an after-school activity, work around it. I always cancel or reschedule appointments to accommodate a school trip or activity. When a teenager suddenly misses a regular appointment and then apologetically tells me they forgot because they were at the park with their friends, I celebrate their flight into health rather than complain that they weren't there. This is different than consistently missing or cancelling appointments. The reverse is also true. If a child wants to schedule ten a.m. appointments because they want to miss math class, or want to sleep in a bit later, I work around that as long as they are not failing the subject or haven't been refusing to attend school.

The treatment frame described here is flexible, responsive and respectful. The treatment frame and relationship are interventions in themselves. We can't help children heal by engaging in disempowering, disrespectful practices. We help them heal by showing them another way.

Notes

1. van der Kolk, B. A. (2005). Developmental trauma disorder: Towards a rational diagnosis for children with complex trauma histories. *Psychiatric Annals, 35*(5), 401–408.
2. Cook, A., Blaustein, M., Spinazzola, J., & van der Kolk, B. (Eds.). (2003). *Complex trauma in children and adolescents* [White paper]. National Child Traumatic Stress

Network Complex Trauma Task Force. National Centre for Child Traumatic Stress. Los Angeles. Retrieved from: http://www.nctsnet.org/nctsn_assets/pdfs/edu_materials/ComplexTrauma_All.pdf

3. McWilliams, N. (2004). *Psychoanalytic Psychotherapy: A Practitioner's Guide*. Guilford. New York. pp 70–71.
4. Siegel, Daniel J. (2013). *The Developing Mind: How Relationships and the Brain Interact to Shape Who We Are*. Guilford. New York.
5. Schore, A. (2013). Relational trauma, brain development, and dissociation. In J. D. Ford and C. Courtois (Eds.), *Treating Complex Traumatic Stress Disorders in Children and Adolescents: Scientific Foundations and Therapeutic Models*. Guilford. New York.
6. Porgess, Stephen W. (2011). *The Polyvagal Theory: Neurophysiological Foundations of Emotions, Attachment, Communication, Self-Regulation*. W. W. Norton & Company. New York.
7. Siegel, Daniel J. (2013). *The Developing Mind: How Relationships and the Brain Interact to Shape Who We Are*. Guilford. New York. p 143.
8. Chu, James A. (1988, December). Ten traps for therapists in the treatment of trauma survivors. *Dissociation, 1*(4), 24–32.
9. Pain, Clare. (2002). International Society for the Study of Dissociation. Dissociative Disorders Training Program. Toronto, Ontario.
10. Silberg, Joyanna. (2013). *The Child Survivor: Healing Developmental Trauma and Dissociation*. Routledge. New York.
11. Linehan, M. (1993). *Cognitive Behavioural Treatment of People with Borderline Personality Disorder*. Guilford. New York.
12. Silberg, Joyanna. (2013). *The Child Survivor: Healing Developmental Trauma and Dissociation*. Routledge. New York.
13. Hughes, Daniel A. (2007). *Attachment Focused Family Therapy*. W. W. Norton & Company. New York.

7 Phase One—Stabilisation and Relationships

Process and Conceptualisation

The goals of phase one are to establish the treatment frame, build relationships, and help the child and family develop and maintain enough stability to cope with daily life and be ready for trauma work. When approaching this from an attachment focus, the goals include identifying and engaging an attachment figure to work with you in the child's therapy, and creating enough safety within the attachment relationship for the child to move forward in treatment. Sometimes this is straightforward, but most of the time it's like juggling. Early in treatment, the challenge is to prioritise. The juggling act involves maintaining safety while building relationships with children whose first view of you is as a potential enemy and with adults whose first view of you is as someone who is judging them. Safety is first priority, but we need to be careful not to sacrifice trust, or engagement in treatment won't happen. It's during early sessions that being genuine and open may be a therapist's best tool. Our young clients find it difficult to trust us regardless, but they have radar for manipulation and subterfuge. If we are dishonest or caught in our own agenda, they will know.

Traumatised kids often come to therapy reluctantly. They are likely to see treatment as an attempt to control rather than help them. Even those who self-refer are sceptical. In order to engage in treatment these kids need to experience that something new and different is possible. That "something" is being heard, felt and understood: the beginnings of the possibility of attachment. This connection, and the experience of being heard and felt, becomes their motivation to continue in therapy.

It's important, from early on, to remain aware of possible dissociation. It may not be obvious. Even when we assess for dissociation early, it can remain hidden well into treatment. When possible we need to be aware of dissociation and work to connect with whatever is disconnected. When we aren't sure, we still need to stage our interventions in ways that include possibilities that may be outside of the child's active awareness. For example, we need to assume that even emotions or reactions that seem clear may be mixed or confused under the surface; that a child who seems open or engaged may internally be suspicious or angry; and that a child who says that they trust us likely does not trust us as completely as we want to believe.

Assessment and Early Interventions

It's not unusual to meet a young client and their caregivers for the first time in crisis. It's often crisis that brings people to therapy. It's the nature of trauma work that crises can be intense experiences involving safety risks and potential relationship breakdowns. Children and their caregivers often feel desperate, hopeless and failed by the systems that are supposed to support and protect them. We are part of this system. There are dangers to being identified as part of the system, and there are dangers to being identified as separate from it. This is part of the early dance. When children and families are struggling with trauma and attachment, the systems often become split and conflicts are frequent. This is not always avoidable, but keeping this dynamic in our consciousness is critical. Black-and-white thinking around right and wrong, good and bad, support and harm, success and failure is endemic. Initially the "right" or "good" side appears to be obvious, but it rarely is.

There are many balancing acts to be accomplished during early sessions. We need to build relationships with the child, who will struggle with trusting us, and with the adult, who may struggle with being involved in the therapy. While establishing these relationships, we want to ensure that the child experiences us differently from other adults who they have felt were allied against them, while not being experienced by the parents or caregivers as being overly aligned with the child at the adults' expense. During this delicate period of building relationships we also need to keep aware of the need to create and maintain safety for the child and family. Safety concerns for both the child and other family members are created by the child's symptomatic behaviours, and are often the reason the child has been brought to therapy. Often self-destructive or aggressive behaviours have resulted in the child being labelled as "bad," "crazy" or "out of control."

Because of the need to balance priorities, and because there are several that need to be first, there is no linear approach to phase one. The major tasks that need to be accomplished are safety planning and stabilisation; engaging caregiver and child; strengthening attachment relationships; meltdown management; affect regulation skills; sleep management; and school stabilisation. Rather than linear, the initial sessions look more like Figure 7.1.

Internal Conflict, Dissociation and Alliances

Assessment is an ongoing process; no matter how thorough and careful we are, our initial assessment won't give us all the information. There will often be something hidden that jumps out to startle the therapist, the caregiver and the client. Because of difficulties with trust, I suspect that few people tell their therapists everything early on. When working with trauma, we need to hold the possibility that enormous amounts of information are withheld. Some of this is intentional, and some less so. Even when intentional, we need to be accepting of it. Control of their information is a necessary part of our clients' ability to be in control of their healing.

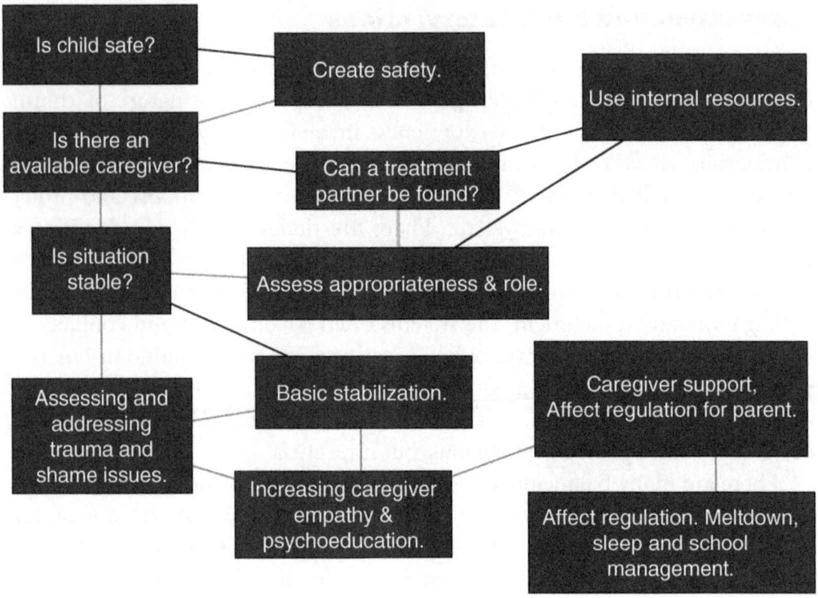

Figure 7.1 Weighing the Tasks of the Initial Session

Issues around dissociative processes are rarely clear or easy to access, but it's important to stay aware and open to the possibilities. Dissociation can add many layers to phase one work, because it masks internal conflict. Any alliance we make with a child can mean we are making an alliance against a different aspect of the child we are not aware of. This is equally true for the relationships which caregivers have with their children, and can be the source of a great deal of the child's difficulties in building relationships, adjusting to placements and benefitting from treatment. Not all internal conflict is dissociated, but when it is, it can create confusion for the child, family, therapist and system.

Internal conflict is inherent to attachment trauma. When a child is harmed by a person on whom they are dependent, it creates conflict between dependency and safety. The child needs to maintain attachment to the same person they need to be protected from. As the child develops working models for themselves, the world and others from their early relationships, this conflict creates confusion as to how a child comes to understand themselves, others and their place in the world. Many theorists suggest that this irresolvable internal conflict is one of the pathways leading to dissociation.[1,2,3,4]

Consider the situation of John (also discussed in Chapters 3 and 12). John experienced early abuse and domestic violence from which his mother could not protect him. Eventually, his mother left his father, remarried and had another child. John became so disregulated and out of control that he could not safely live at home. When John was brought to therapy, he described dissociation, including alter personalities. Table 7.1 outlines some, but probably

Table 7.1 Possible Conflicting Experiences of Self and Others for John (age 13)

Self	*Father*	*Mother*	*Stepfather*	*Younger Half Brother*	*Group Home Staff*	*Child Welfare*	*Peers*	*Therapist*
Helpless and alone Fear	Evil abuser Rage	Neglectful and unprotective Rage	Rescuing mother at his expense Abandonment	Loved replacements Anger, abandonment, jealousy	Controlling and uncaring Anger, mistrust, self-protection	Interfering and uncaring Anger, fear, mistrust	Dangerous abusers Anger, fear	Potential ally Hope, need, dependence
Self-protecting defender Bravery	Powerful abuser Fear, respect	Helpless victim Shame, anger (at father), pity	Potential abuser Anger, fear	Evil usurpers Self-righteous rage, suspiciousness	Possible source of material resources Self-interest, neediness	Abusive and evil Rage, powerlessness	Potentially dangerous but possible to manipulate Suspicious, superior, powerful	Possibly useful Superiority, hope, suspicion
Useless failure at protecting mother Shame	Misunderstood and abandoned Anger (at mother); sadness	Rejecting and angry Rage	Possible source of new life for mother Love, hope	Deserving replacements of failed self Shame, jealousy	Uncaring source of possible refuge Fear, obligation	Empty bureaucrat Helplessness, mistrust	Alien strangers—confusing and incapable of understanding Alienation, aloneness, anger	Potential source of empathy Hope, need, fear, despair
Stupid and bad; deservingly abused and rejected Shame	Sick and not responsible for his actions Pity, sadness, protectiveness	Uncaring and self-absorbed Rage, blame	Mother's rescuer; John's replacement Jealousy, fear	Mother's new life Abandonment, jealousy, aloneness	Jail guards Rage, hatred	Source of punishment Fear, anger, shame	Weapons of punishment Anger, shame	Potential rejection; dangerous source of false hope Suspicion, rage,

(*Continued*)

Table 7.1 (Continued)

Self	*Father*	*Mother*	*Stepfather*	*Younger Half Brother*	*Group Home Staff*	*Child Welfare*	*Peers*	*Therapist*
Weak and deserving abuse Shame	Loving father Love, connection, protectiveness	Cold and uncaring Rage, unimportance	Mother's rescuer—her means to leave John and the past behind Love, protective self-sacrifice, sadness, loss	Potential victims of mom's selfishness Protective; anger and suspicion at mom	Keepers of the discards Shame, anger	Controlling Anger, helplessness, obligation	Wished-for companions Loneliness, isolation, shame	Ally with the keepers and controllers Suspicion, anger, helplessness
Bad and deserving of abuse Shame		Loving mother Love, protectiveness	Uninterested in John—uncaring Rejection, anger, sadness	Potential victim of abuse by mom or stepfather Protectiveness, anger and suspicion at mom and stepdad	Potential abusers Fear, anger	Interfering busybodies Anger, indignance, suspicion	Rejecting bullies Loneliness, isolation, anger	Help against the keepers and controllers Hope, need, dependence
Bad and powerful like abuser Anger, alienation			Usurper Suspicion, jealousy	Deserving of abuse and rejection Self-righteous superiority, anger	Potential rejecter Shame, obligation	Stupid Superiority, rage	Potential victims or dupes to be manipulated Powerful, self-righteous superiority	Potential abuser Fear, suspicion, anger
Misunderstood and abandoned like father Sadness, aloneness, anger			Intruder Suspicion, anger, fear		Potential saviours Hope, fear, obligation, need, helplessness			

not all, of the conflicting experiences John had of himself and others. Some of these reactions were held by dissociated parts which prevented the internal conflict from overwhelming him with confusion. This table identifies both his internalised view of himself and others, and the affect states these views created in him.

The interpretations and combinations are many. The problems created are multilayered. John presented as a sad and frightened boy who had experienced severe bullying and abuse by peers at his group home. He loved his mother and wanted to be with her. He was remorseful about his behaviour. He was open, motivated and insightful. He worked hard in sessions. He responded to me positively and was hopeful because I seemed to understand and accept him. All of this was genuine. It also created a dangerous minefield. It was a real part of John, but only one of many.

An alliance with this sad and frightened John could lead to being dismissed as stupid and irrelevant by the angry part of him, which controlled others in order to ensure his own survival. An alliance with the John who wanted to gain control of his angry outbursts could be experienced as threatening by the parts of John that needed his anger to feel safe and in control of his environment, or as rejecting by the parts that saw him as being bad and evil. An alliance with the part of John who loved his mother and wanted to be part of her new family would anger the parts of him that saw her as manipulative, rejecting or abusive, or that saw the new family as a way to leave her past, John included, behind her. Adding to this picture and complicating it further is that the John who initially presented himself in therapy was different from the John who was fighting to survive in his group home. To see the John that I knew as the whole John would mean that I was dismissing both others' experiences of him and *his* other experiences of himself and the world. Although there is a lot to be said about focusing on strengths, all of John's experiences and feelings, and all of his ways of seeing himself and the world, were equally important. The parts of John that came to therapy felt validated and cared about, and participated openly. The parts of John that were at his group home did not like or trust me at all. If I allied with the parts that I saw, therapy would be easy and pleasant—I would get to feel liked and trusted while hanging out with someone who wanted to be there with me. It would also be ineffective. Large chunks of John would be excluded from treatment. The part of John that first came to therapy was not the part of John that was causing so much chaos and pain in his life.

Another part of this dilemma leads to damaging splits in the treatment system. John was a different boy in different situations and with different people. The very different ways that John presented, and the very different views he expressed to different people, led to an atmosphere of mistrust between different parts of the system. This is a common issue, which will be discussed in Chapter 12 on external systems.

The solution to the dilemma created by these internal conflicts is to maintain a stance of openness and acceptance towards all parts of the child and to support the other adults in the child's life in doing the same. This is challenging, as some parts of the child represent the feelings, attitudes and behaviours that brought the child to counselling in the first place. Often the child themselves is resistant to accepting these parts of themselves, and the adults fear that accepting these parts of the child will lead to increased acting out. Sixteen-year-old Steve believes he has a demon living inside of him. This demon is fascinated with graphically violent images and craves human blood. Steve himself is a gentle, kind young man. He has no desire to hurt anyone, and keeps his "demon" relatively under control by eating very rare beef. Before coming into therapy he tried to understand this presence by studying about demonology and talking to his foster mother, Sandra, about his demon. His foster mother was sceptical about the idea and frightened by Steve's desire to drink blood. Sandra's understandable reaction was to say, "I don't want talk like that in my house." Before coming to Sandra's home seven years ago, Steve had been bounced between six different foster homes in two years. His understanding of her reaction was that the demon part of him was not welcome, and should he talk more about it, he would have to leave the only stable and loving home he had known. Sandra and her husband see Steve as a son; they consider his place in their home to be permanent and unconditional. She was shocked to learn that Steve's escalating depression and isolation from the family came from his exhausting attempts to hide his demon, and to learn about his belief that losing his family was inevitable.

Accepting the angry, alienated, suspicious parts of a child can be difficult. Sophie's adopted mother loves her daughter and empathically understands the impact of the abuse and chaos that marked Sophie's early years. She understands the necessity to accept the whole of her child unconditionally, but emotionally it is difficult for her to accept the parts of Sophie that threaten her family, use horribly foul language and seems to enjoy frightening their younger daughter.

For parents, children and therapists it can be difficult to accept some parts. The stance for achieving and modeling this is rooted in dialectical behavioural therapy.[5] "The most fundamental dialectic is the necessity of accepting patients just as they are within a context of trying to teach them to change."[6] This stance is at the core of phase-oriented, attachment-focused trauma therapy. Joyanna Silberg recommends a similar stance when she describes the need to feel and communicate a "deep respect for the coping techniques" that are often seen as self-destructive symptoms of behavioural and emotional difficulties.[7] Dr. Silberg stresses that all of our clients' behaviours, disregulations, suspicions, and other challenging and confusing symptoms make sense, even if it isn't clear how they make sense.

The importance of accepting the children and adults we work with in order to move towards growth and change becomes clear when we understand the role of shame in maintaining stuckness and clinical avoidance. Donald Nathanson discusses shame as a fundamental emotional experience in his work *Shame and Pride: Affect, Sex and the Birth of the Self*. "So much discomfort does shame produce, that people will go to great lengths to avoid it."[8] Nathanson uses the model of the "compass of shame" to diagram the directions avoidance takes. For young children, shame happens when the experience of attunement and coregulation with the attachment figure is broken; when their activity is interrupted by a disapproving parent; or when there is discipline or upset expressed by the parent. The child becomes upset, and the parent, in most cases, soothes the upset child.[9] This is the experience of break and repair described in Chapter 4. In small, healthy amounts the need to avoid shame leads us to choose socially acceptable behaviours. When shame gets too big, as happens with trauma and disrupted attachment, avoidance can take less adaptive directions. As displayed by Nathanson's compass (Figure 7.2), many of the symptoms which bring people to therapy are means of avoiding shame, and so are many of the difficulties which lead people to avoid therapy, or once there, interfere with their being able to fully engage in and benefit from treatment.

The young clients we work with struggle with shame arising from trauma, abuse, rejection and abandonment. The adults we work with as treatment partners are also struggling with issues of shame. With biological parents or family

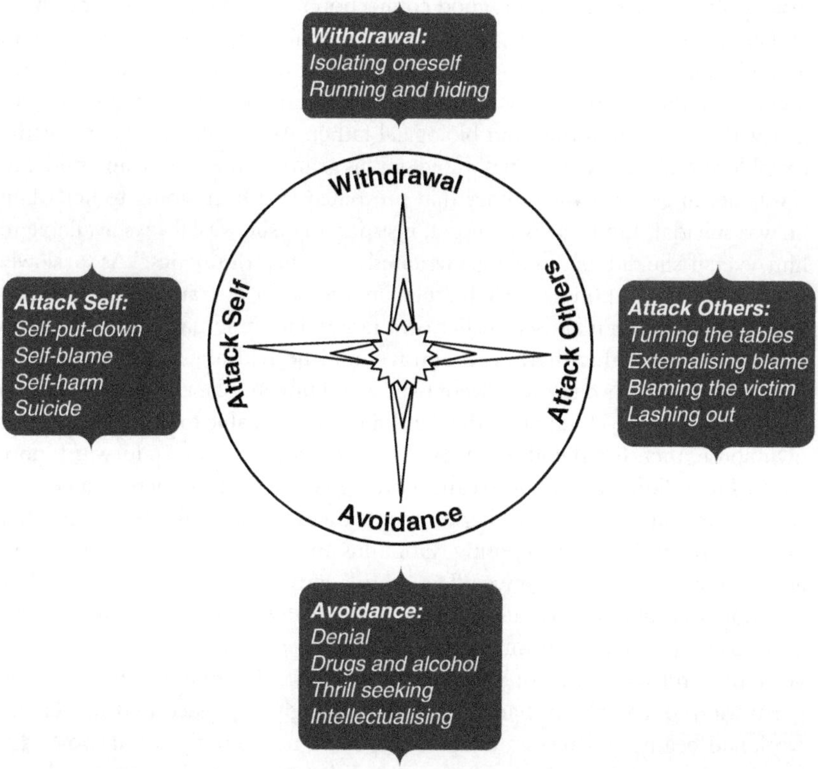

Figure 7.2 Compass of Shame

Based on the Compass of Shame by Nathanson, D. L. (1992). *Shame and Pride: Affect, Sex and the Birth of the Self.* W. W. Norton & Company. New York. p 312.

members, the shame that may interfere involves shame over failing to protect the child, shame arising from having shared the abuse or trauma with the child, or shame over having contributed to the child's trauma. Foster parents, adoptive parents and treatment staff may be struggling with shame at their inability to reach, connect, help or possibly like the child. They may also be struggling with shame arising from their own trauma histories and retriggered by their experiences with the child. When their shame is triggered, it can result in avoidant responses that can retrigger similar responses in their child, leading to a downward spiral.

Fourteen-year-old Shaun was brought to me by his grandmother, Linda, following a serious suicide attempt. Shaun lived with his grandmother and step-grandfather, who had adopted him at birth. Although he had contact with both parents, he had never lived with them. His grandparents' home was caring and loving. Shaun's grandparents attended sessions to support their grandson. They talked about the bullying Shaun had experienced in school that they felt had contributed to his depression. They had worked with the school and with Shaun to deal with the bullying, which had stopped. When taking Shaun's history, Linda talked about his good connection to her and her husband. Both of her daughters had struggled with mental health and addictions. She had limited contact with them, because of the conflict they caused at family events. Shaun's mother shared adult information with him and involved him in conflict with his grandmother and biological father. As we talked, Linda became irritable and defensive. Shaun pointed out his grandmother's tone and said that it was her anger over his feelings that prevented him from going to her when he was suicidal. Linda became upset, insisting that she was always available to him, even if she did sometimes get irritated about his "dramatics." As we slowly unpacked these responses to each other, another layer of trauma began to surface. Linda had been abused by her own father. Her first marriage, to Shaun's biological grandfather, had been abusive, and he had abused his daughters. Linda left when her daughters were twelve and fifteen. She rationalised that as her mother had never left her father, and she had been able to move beyond her own abuse, then her daughters should have been able to move forward more easily. Their difficulties triggered anger and rejection towards them as a defense against her shame for not having protected them. Linda defended against her own trauma by focusing on positive emotions and her family's ability to survive adversity. She avoided negative affect, particularly in family relationships. She had not been able to tolerate Shaun's confused feelings towards his parents, and was unwilling to hear any positive reflections on her daughters. As Shaun got older and wanted to understand more about his situation, there was no permission to ask. Shaun had become increasingly depressed and his schoolwork had begun to deteriorate. Linda appeared not to notice or acknowledge that he was struggling. He then began to self-harm, cutting his wrists and legs. When Linda learned of this she became angry and grounded him. It was not until Shaun attempted suicide by overdose, and then contacted a friend who called 911, that the family acknowledged that Shaun was in pain. Even then, the explanation for his pain involved historical bullying which had ended a year prior. Shaun, when given permission, was able to talk about his confusion about his parents and the other conflicts and secrets in his family, and about his grandmother's difficulty tolerating negativity, sadness or anger.

The challenge is not simply in learning about the history and using it to understand the family silence. The same shame that led Linda to blame her daughters and avoid talking about negative experiences was compounded by Shawn's alienation and suicidality. Making a connection between the two would feel to Linda that she was being blamed for Shaun's difficulties, putting her in the position of needing to deny the connection in order to protect herself from further shame. This could only feed into Shaun's belief that his feelings were bad and that he was disloyal for having them. The result would be either withdrawal from therapy or continued avoidance of the issues.

The closed-off areas needed to be opened gently. I needed to help Linda to reduce the shame by empathising around the terrible binds she had been in throughout her life—surviving an abusive childhood, coping with an abusive first marriage, building the courage and strength to leave in order to protect her daughters, only for them to continue patterns of addictions and abuse. She had remarried a kind and caring man and started a new life, only to have to constantly deal with painful reminders, witness her grandchildren being abused and abandoned, and finally find herself again raising children as an older retired person. My empathy for her would not be enough. I needed to help her experience empathy for herself.

When working with adults or children, another balancing act is between empathising and granting absolution. When we accept our clients' behaviours and choices we are accepting that these make sense, that they did the best they could at the time and that they were struggling with situations that they were ill-prepared for. Acceptance offers the possibility to put aside binding shame; it doesn't remove responsibility. Anyone is capable of mistakes, even terrible ones, when faced with impossible choices and multiple frightening outcomes. It's not ours to forgive our clients, nor is it up to us to get the children we work with to forgive the adults in their lives. It is up to us to not judge them, and to help them have compassion for themselves so they can take responsibility and move towards change. It is also up to us to help the adults understand the meaning of their children's behaviours and reactions enough that they can experience genuine empathy for them.

Safety Issues in Early Treatment

Early in treatment, safety issues are common. Our young clients are often referred due to one safety issue or another and early therapy sometimes involves managing and containing recurrent safety crises. Safety concerns can be related to the safety of the child or adolescent, or risk to others through the child or adolescent's symptomatic acting out. Although physical risks around self-harm, suicide attempts and aggressive behaviour can be serious problems, the question of safety is global. Safety involves emotional safety; relationship safety; safety from placement breakdowns and rejection; safety from physical, emotional and sexual exploitation of many types, risks from substance abuse, and dangerous risk-taking behaviours; the safety of having physical and emotional needs met in a way that's appropriate to a child or adolescent's age and developmental and treatment needs; and safety from emotional retraumatisation resulting in therapy.

When we engage with clients, we need to hold on to the earlier discussion of trust and honesty. There are lots of ways to assess safety, but we can't assume that our clients can always tell us what they're thinking and feeling. We need to create permission for open discussions, while making sure that there are safety plans in place. Creating safety is one of the parts of early work that needs to be checked individually. Children and adolescents may not discuss safety issues with caregivers present, and caregivers should not discuss concerns about their own safety in front of children. Even when our clients appear to be open and motivated to create safety, we can't assume that there aren't dissociated parts with different ideas. I was shocked when Beth, two years into successful, well-engaged therapy, was suddenly hospitalised. I had regularly checked in with Beth and her alters about safety, and neither suicide nor self-harm had been issues for well over a year. I was not the only one who was shocked. When Beth was discharged a week later and returned to therapy, she was frightened and confused. She had had no idea that she had another alter, Chloe, who had been planning suicide and secretly stockpiling medications. Following her suicide attempt, Chloe introduced herself to Beth and me, and brought in a secret journal she had hidden which described the plans to kill herself. Following this discovery treatment moved forward smoothly.

We also can't assume, even when our clients are telling us what they are thinking, that we can judge how they are feeling and reacting to treatment. There is often a disconnect between thoughts and feelings, and the ability to hide feelings is a survival technique for children who have grown up without trusting. Many years ago I worked with a mother and two children who had been referred by a clinic in my community. They had been seen only twice there, for the beginning of an assessment. During the first session at the other clinic, the therapist took a family history. She asked the mother if she had been abused as a child. The mother answered with apparent calm that she had been sexually abused. When the session ended the family left with no incident. The mother had not disclosed the abuse previously, and had been told by her father that if she told anyone he would find her and kill her. Her apparent calm was a numb, dissociated state. After leaving the clinic she panicked and had nowhere to turn. She became suicidal, and with no supports to manage the crisis, she looked up the therapist in the phone book and phoned her at home. The terrified therapist helped the mother to stabilise, and provided her with numbers for crisis lines and adult services. When the family returned for their second session the therapist presented the mother with a contract agreeing that she would never again call her at home, and insisted that the contract be witnessed by the program secretary. Mortified, the mother refused to return.

Many trauma survivors cope with overwhelming feelings by self-harming. Nonsuicidal self-harm can range from picking at skin and nails and superficial scratching through self-inflicted burning and deep cutting. Many young people engage in some form of self-harm at some time, and it is not always an indication of a trauma history. Overwhelming emotions are common in young people, and many of them don't have the resources to cope with them. Self-harm in itself is a common reason for young people to be referred for counselling.

Managing self-harm is an early task that balances safety and control. Although self-harm is a maladaptive coping strategy, it's still a coping strategy. It isn't easy for some of our clients to give up self-harming. Creating external controls to prevent it can leave them feeling powerless and out of control. For many of the young people we see, self-harm has been viewed as a "bad behaviour." Measures such as threats, rewards, punishment, restricted privileges, angry, hurt or upset responses, restrictive supervision, or turning the issue of self-harm into a "trust issue" either drive self-harm underground, leading to shame and secrecy, or turn it into a power struggle that no one can win. One of the reasons trauma survivors give for self-harming is that it provides a sense of control over their bodies and their pain. This arises directly out of the trauma-related experience of not having control over their bodies and their pain. To try to deal with this by taking away the control can be retraumatising and counterproductive.

This is another balancing act. Control, even control over our own bodies, has limitations. To create safety, I need to take safety seriously, and this includes safety from self-harm. Many of the young people I work with feel a strong need to self-harm. I neither want to give the message that this is a helpful way of dealing with emotions nor do I want to add to their shame and powerlessness. The message I send is that they have other choices. I understand that they feel they need to hurt themselves, and it's this need that I'm hoping they'll work with me on. I expect them to work with me to find other ways of coping. I am clear that if their actions become dangerous or life-threatening I will have to find some way of keeping them healthy and alive, even if that means a betrayal of their trust. Suicide is not an option, any more than homicide or assault. The limit to the control we have over our bodies involves the impact that our actions have on others. Suicide is not a victimless crime. The desire to kill themselves is common for childhood trauma survivors. It's OK for them to have and explore feelings about wanting to die, just like it's OK to explore fantasies about violence and revenge. The feelings are nothing to be ashamed of, but the choice is not an option and I will do everything in my power to keep them and others safe. I work to negotiate with them and their parts to find other solutions to self-harm and to suicidal feelings. This is described further in Chapter 9 on phase one intervention strategies.

Related to self-harm, and potentially more lethal, is the tendency to engage in dangerous behaviours. Sometimes these appear as compulsions, other times they involve confusion and internal pressure around sexual behaviours, thrill-seeking arising out of a need to feel emotion other than sadness, anger or despair, or an alter who is acting out one of many feelings or urges with little concern about the impact it has on the whole self. Amie would sneak out and hang around street corners at night in a neighborhood known for young prostitutes. She maintained that she wasn't planning to engage in prostitution, but she enjoyed the excitement of being approached by men for sex. She was never sure she would say no until the moment came. She also would go out drinking, sneaking into bars while underage. Because she had been given alcohol at a very young age by her mother and her mother's male friends, alcohol and the feeling of being drunk triggered the activities of a sexualised alter who liked to taunt the police and then run away through back alleys while they chased her. John liked to walk on railroad bridges and jump off when the train was coming. He felt numb and empty, and enjoyed the rush of adrenaline he would get. Kalli had an alter who craved excitement and didn't feel fear. She would cruise BDSM (bondage, discipline, sadism and masochism) chat rooms, pick up men and arrange to have them take her to parties.

These behaviours are life-threatening, frightening and often more clinically challenging than self-harm. These are complicated symptoms that have multiple motivations and secondary gains. When there is a self-harm component, it's often hidden. In the examples above, the young people denied trying to hurt or kill themselves. "Fun," excitement and challenge were more likely to be given as reasons. At the same time, risk of harm or death weren't enough to stop the behaviours, because these young people saw injury and death as more acceptable than feeling numb or empty. Many of the children and adolescents I work with refer to themselves as being "bored." This word frustrates adults, but it often means something other than the way we understand it. *Bored* is the word that best describes the emptiness of feeling no meaningful connection or emotion. Escaping this numb emptiness is motivating, and yet to connect to real feelings, our young clients would need to experience the overwhelming pain connected to their trauma and loss. In order to solve this dilemma they get caught up in an escalating search for "excitement."

Dealing with risk-taking behaviours involves exploration and negotiation. Too strong an attempt to stop them, without exploration of the behaviours and the reasons for stopping, communicates disapproval, leading to shame and secrecy. This is one of the areas in which the gradually improving attachment relationship helps to support treatment. When the internal motivations for change are less than the internal rewards for the behaviours, the young person needs a different kind of motivation. The experience of being heard, felt and still cared about becomes a powerful motivator. When this feeling comes from the therapist, it can motivate change, but creates a focus on having other dependency needs met. Very quickly we can reach a fine line between moving towards safety in order to gain connection, and maintaining risk and danger in order to maintain the need to keep the relationship. It can create a difficult bind for our young people to stay alive just because a therapist wants them to. When they are able to feel that there is someone else who actually cares about whether or not they make it, it becomes safer for them to move forward.

Many traumatised children and teens are brought to therapy when the adults around them have begun to feel frustrated and helpless. The commitment of the adults has begun to deteriorate, and rejection and placement breakdown may be a real risk. When placements don't break down, the atmosphere of conflict and blame can escalate to reinforce the child's view of themselves as bad and unlovable. In more extreme situations the parents or caregivers have begun to respond with emotionally or physically abusive behaviour. Sometimes the child has become scapegoated by their peers, and the adults around them have stopped protecting them. Children can't benefit from therapy when they aren't safe. Even adults who are caring and knowledgeable can feel helpless in the face of trying to parent a traumatised child with an attachment disorder. This can lead to good, stable placements becoming unsafe over time. This isn't the fault of the child. It is a result of the impacts of trauma.

Affect Regulation

Affect regulation, touched on in Chapters 1 and 2, is a major focus of phase one work. Young people with histories of complex trauma have difficulties with affect regulation which disrupt their lives, the lives of family members and communities, and create risks to themselves and others. In Chapter 5 I talked about the "window of tolerance." Those who haven't had the opportunity to learn affect regulation skills, and those who have grown up in a dangerous environment which taught them to be hypervigilant, are frequently outside of their window of tolerance. We begin with teaching affect awareness and connection; we help expand their window of tolerance; and we work within the attachment relationship to teach first how to accept soothing, and over time how to self-soothe. This is done gradually rather than through focusing on intense, overwhelming feelings. Moving too fast can lead to being overwhelmed.

Attributions

The word *attributions* refers the ways in which we understand events, actions and people based on the meanings we ascribe them. These attributions arise out of experiences, beliefs, values and personalities. A car accident could be viewed as an act of carelessness, the actions of a vengeful god, a test by a loving god, an expression of karma, or a random event. The meanings attributed to children's behaviours affect the ways adults respond to them, and ultimately the way the children are perceived. The meanings children attribute to adults' behaviours affect the ways in which children respond to them, the way they perceive them, and ultimately the way they perceive themselves and their own actions as well.

Consider the following example. Julie, an eight-year-old living with her aunt and uncle, attends parent-teacher night with her aunt. Partway through the interview, the teacher suggests Julie show her aunt her work, and Julie quietly shakes her head, looks down and says, "No." Her aunt tries to encourage her, and Julie turns, yells, "No," and tries to run out of the classroom. Embarrassed and worried about what the teacher thinks, the aunt tries to grab Julie's arm, and Julie turns and tries to hit her. The teacher responds by saying, "Julie, don't hurt Aunt Sue." Julie responds, "I want to hurt her; she's mean and I hate her." This scenario can lead to misattributions on everyone's side. Aunt Sue, hurt and embarrassed, sees Julie as intentionally embarrassing her. She also experiences herself as a failure for being unable to manage Julie's outburst, and she experiences the teacher as judgmental and unable to understand how hard Julie is to deal with. Julie experiences her aunt grabbing her, and her angry silence on the way home as mean and rejecting. She experiences the whole situation as proof that she is bad and her aunt can't possibly care about her. Julie's teacher sees the whole event as proof that Julie is out of control and her aunt is not taking care of her. When they get home, Julie is told how hurt and embarrassed Aunt Sue is, and sent to her room.

How is this different if Aunt Sue, Julie and the teacher have a different understanding of Julie's reactions? Julie was removed from a home where nothing met the expectations of her mother and stepfather. No matter how hard she tried, she would be belittled and punished for her efforts. Her resistance to showing her work was an attempt to protect herself. As the situation escalated, Julie became frightened, experiencing a flashback, accusing her aunt of being mean to her. If Sue and the teacher both understand this, the situation may not escalate to the point of triggering a flashback. Even if it does, the understanding would make repairing the situation and recreating safety much easier.

There are many behaviours, ideas and words that are understood in ways that lead to negative attributions which don't help us to understand the kids we work with. Broadening understanding helps our clients and the adults in their lives change their experiences of themselves and each other. Many of the words we use to describe the actions and behaviours of young clients are emotionally loaded and hold negative value judgments. This is not to say that the behaviours should be encouraged or allowed. Part of the exploration of phase one work involves understanding these actions, and working to develop a more empathetic meaning for why the child does things. Once these conversations are opened and the shame involved is diminished, it is possible to come to solutions.

Defiance—Understanding the defiance of a complex trauma victim is helpful in understanding many of the other behaviours we are asked to address. The kids we work with don't follow the rules, and they don't respond to behavioural controls. Even those who appear compliant and passive engage in secretive rule breaking. Willingness to follow rules involves acceptance of a social order. Acceptance of a social order requires some belief that the rules are there for our own good and protection. In children, this understanding grows through attachment to an adult or group of adults who respond to their emotional and developmental needs in a generally helpful and protective way. A child who is raised by adults who are primarily focused on meeting their own needs has little reason to see the social order as something they are part of. Without trust there is no loyalty, and without loyalty there is no engagement. Some compliance can be taught through harsh and punitive behavioural controls. This is why some young people with complex trauma histories are well behaved and compliant. They see the appearance of belonging and trusting as a means of creating safety and security. However, real engagement is missing, and secretive rule breaking, manipulation and dishonesty may be hidden issues.

Manipulation—The word *manipulation* is used in mental health to refer to indirect ways in which children, adolescents or adults manage information and situations in order to be in control. This is seen as being negative and dishonest. The young people we work with have learned manipulation skills instinctively as ways of staying safe in situations where exerting control openly was dangerous. Keeping some control of the way others see and respond to them without being direct about it has helped them stay safe. These children have learned that being direct and honest is dangerous.

Splitting—Splitting is a particularly disruptive form of manipulation in which a child or adolescent interacts in different ways with different adults, carefully managing what information they share and how, in a way that creates conflict, competition and mistrust among the adults involved. The classic splitting is best demonstrated by the common way in which one child plays their parents against each other in order to get their own way. When working with traumatised parents and traumatised children, splitting can be a more complex, multilayered and destructive pattern. Often young people aren't aware that they are splitting, both because they are instinctively building alliances in whatever way feels safest, and also because different dissociated self-states may have different relationships and alliances with different adults. Because these adults have different experiences of the child and see the child in different, often opposing ways, this creates mistrust and conflict within the treatment team. Splitting is discussed in Chapter 12, on larger systems.

Lying—Like manipulation, lying is experienced as a dishonest, negative behaviour. Because the young people we work with consider the truth to be dangerous, they learned to lie as a way of staying safe. Young people who dissociate are often believed to be lying because they deny actions that they have been witnessed doing. They may not remember these actions, or don't consider themselves to have been the ones doing it. When I asked Sophie to talk about money she took out of her mother's purse, Sophie said, "I never take money out of my mom's purse!" This was a surprise to both me and Sophie's mom, because the subject had been talked about before. I then asked, "Can you tell me if anyone inside took money from your mom's purse?" Sophie responded with, "Yes, that was the five-year-old; she doesn't know it's wrong to take things!"

Stealing—The issue of stealing comes up often with children with early deprivation and attachment histories, and can be intractable in treatment. Children and adolescents may steal from home, school, friends, extended family and the community, creating conflict with family members, peers and teachers, leading to anger, rejection and social difficulties. The simple answer is that children who have experienced physical and emotional deprivation steal and hoard items to fill a sense of emptiness. This can be particularly true for children who steal and hoard food, although it generalises to other types of theft. Children sometimes steal to feel a sense of connection to someone. Sophie would steal items from her mother that she carried with her, and sometimes from peers at school that she liked or wanted to be like. Dissociation lends further layers to stealing. Often the part of the child that steals is a dissociated part and other parts are either unaware of the stealing or feel helpless to control the part that steals. The child comes to therapy, is motivated to stop stealing, works hard to stop stealing, and then stealing happens anyway. This sets the child up to look insincere and dishonest to the parents and therapist. Another complication is that sometimes the part that steals is a very young child part, without the maturity to understand issues around ownership and right and wrong. We deal with a two-year-old who takes things differently from a thirteen-year-old who steals. We don't even use the word *steal* when we are dealing with a two-year-old. Sometimes we are dealing with a two-year-old part who is stealing in a thirteen-year-old body.

Aggression—Aggressive outbursts, bullying and assaultive behaviours are difficulties which bring young people to counselling. For complex trauma survivors this can have one or more of several interrelated presentations. Aggressive outbursts, either apparently spontaneous or resulting from conflict, are often triggered responses related to the child or adolescent suddenly finding themselves outside their window of tolerance, becoming overwhelmed, and responding to perceived and experienced risk of danger, injustice or rejection. For some children, these outbursts are related to dissociative switching—an experience triggers the emergence of a terrified or enraged alter whose role it is to take over in situations needing a violently aggressive, defensive response. This can add anger and confusion, when the young person seemingly sincerely denies any knowledge of the chaos and damage they have been witnessed causing. Seven-year-old Josh, placed with his mother after being removed from the home of his abusive father, was flying into uncontrolled rages at home, threatening his mother and destroying furniture. Afterwards, he would act as if nothing happened, deny any wrongdoing and get upset, often flying again into a rage if there was an attempt to hold him accountable for his outbursts. Josh's mother, Joanne, had previously had regular overnight access visits with Josh with no difficulties. He had been a sweet, caring, fun-loving boy. Between outbursts, Josh was the same lovely boy at home as he had been on visits. When we explored their earlier relationship, Josh told me that on visits, his mother had been fun—not trying to get him to do homework, maintain a regular bedtime or take showers. She had never had to parent him, having him only on weekends when they spent fun time together. It was being parented, and told what to do, that triggered reminders of Josh's father's punitive control. This reminder triggered the emergence of Angry Josh, who reacted to Joanne as if she was his father. When the outburst was over, Josh had no memory of his actions and was puzzled and frightened by his mother's anger. When she tried to talk about or consequence his behaviour, Angry Josh would return.

Attention Seeking—There's a story I tell the parents. When I was a young university student, studying developmental psychology for the first time, behavioural psychology was in style. I was talking to my mother about the tantrums a friend's toddler was throwing, after having moved with his mother from an extended-family situation into an apartment. I knowingly (in the all-knowing way of first-year university students) said something about him "just trying to get attention." My mother's response was, "If he wants attention that much, somebody probably should give him some!" This was my introduction to attachment-focused therapy. I tell this story because it has become one of my central beliefs about parenting, especially for children who, like my friend's son, have lost important people and been uprooted in their experience of their world. Children, adolescents and even adults seek attention, because they need it. They seek attention inappropriately because the usual ways in which children have to get attention haven't worked. Because of their pain, insecurity and losses, they need more attention than others do. They communicate in a loud voice, because a quieter, more respectful voice is not heard. Shaun was brought in for therapy by his grandmother after a serious suicide attempt. Shaun had been depressed and withdrawing for several years. He had begun self-harming two years before. His grandmother attempted to stop his self-harming by treating it as behaviour. Shaun's first hospitalisation resulted from an incident of serious nonsuicidal self-harm. On discharge, the hospital referred him for counselling. Although Shaun's grandparents intended to bring him, another issue in the family interfered, and it didn't happen. Finally, Shaun took a significant overdose late at night, and told some friends online. These friends' parents called the police. Shaun had immediately told a trusted person following his overdose. It would be easy to brush this off as an "attention-seeking" suicide attempt, manipulative in nature. The problem here is not with that understanding of the event—of course Shaun was seeking attention and manipulating people to get it. The problem is in the negative meanings attributed to this and the harsh and punitive ways in which emergency and mental health staff respond to such attempts. Shaun was desperate to communicate his pain and get some sort of help. Any other way he had tried over several years had not been heard. Shaun's grandmother's own shame and her belief that family problems should stay in the family had led to her minimise Shaun's need for help. It was not that she didn't love and care about her grandson. She was devastated to realise how much he was suffering. It was that she had been trying so hard to see her family as normal and coping that she couldn't bear to allow herself to see her grandson's pain until it became impossible not to.

Dependency—We have decided as a society that we should be raising children to be independent. This is so accepted as a value that even therapists rarely question this as a goal. During casual parenting conversations with other therapist parents I have had some ask me, "Don't you think parenting your son that way will make him dependent on you?" I wanted my son to be dependent as a young child. I wanted him to know even as an older child that it is always OK to need and ask for help; that you don't need to be ashamed to be afraid, lonely, sad or confused, and that nobody should ever have to negotiate these experiences alone. As he matured, I also wanted him to know that others would feel that way, and that he could be helpful to them. We are an interdependent species. It's unlikely that without resources created by someone else, anyone could survive on their own without help and companionship. Humans are mammals, and mammals give birth to infants that are dependent on their mothers for a long time. We are also pack animals. We are dependent not only on our mothers, but on our families and communities for shared resources, safety and companionship. The core of the polyvagal theory is that our brains have developed in a specific way, in order to allow the lowering of our defensive instincts when we are in the presence of safe others. This allows us to divert valuable energy and resources to higher functions, allowing for greater evolutionary success. I work with families to recognise the difference between dependence, interdependence and independence. The mythical goal of independence is a barrier to be overcome before a child or adult can engage in therapy. They are convinced that they should be able to "do it alone!"

Age-appropriate—The idea of age-appropriate development of behaviour, self-regulation, thinking, morality and relationships is based on normative developmental trajectories for children who have had normative experiences. What is considered age-appropriate in one culture can be different in another. Even from family to family, expectations around maturity, responsibility and behaviour differ. The young people we deal with have had different experiences from what is normative, and so have a different developmental trajectory. Because of poor attachment situations, young people with complex trauma histories often have poorly developed affect and behaviour regulation skills. They may not have the ability to empathise with others, or to identify morally appropriate choices. Because of issues around self-regulation, the impact of stress and anxiety on concentration, and irregular school attendance, our young clients are often behind academically. Lack of neurological integration may impact on learning abilities and lead to learning difficulties and struggles with information processing. When clients have dissociated self-states, alters van vary in age, causing a thirteen-year-old to sometimes present as if they are two, seven or even nineteen years old. Paradoxically, many of these young people are pseudomature in their presentations and life skills. Both Beth and Amie were doing laundry on their own, cleaning the house and caring for younger siblings by the age of four or five. Jessica began work, cleaning her adoptive parents' store and stocking shelves, from the age of six. Amie was taught how to be sexually seductive and how to strip and pole dance at the age of eight. Kalli was in a position of responsibility for her emotionally and physically disabled mother throughout her life. At three she was responsible for monitoring her fragile physical health and calling 911 when there was a crisis. By ten she could negotiate with an angry landlord, pack and move their entire apartment on a moment's notice, and knew the address, hours and rules at every food bank in town.

In order to work with these young people around their developmental profiles, we need to be working with where their development is and what they need in order to facilitate a more even and balanced development. We can talk to them about how they can learn skills that they will find helpful, and even that others their age may have developed. It isn't helpful to think and talk in terms of what they should be able to do. It doesn't help a fourteen-year-old to be told that they should be able to go to sleep by themselves, or that they should be able to keep their homework organised without adult help. It does help them to understand that if they can't do these things, it's because the world that they learned in prepared them for other necessities. In a home where drunken partiers are likely to find their way into your bedroom, the ability to sleep soundly alone in your room without fear is a liability, not a skill. The ability to focus on homework and organisation may not take priority when a child needs to think about how to arrange enough food for supper for their younger brother, or how to explain their bruises to their gym teacher. We want to honor the skills they have that others don't, while helping them learn what they may need in the world they now live in. At times we have to relate our interventions to the developmental stage of the child, at other times to the developmental stage that was missed. A child who has not learned grade one and two math can't simply start at grade three math. A child who has not learned affect regulation may need to be responded to affectively the way we would respond to a very small child.

Attachment Partners

Very often, the adult or adults who we engage in therapy will be an obvious choice. Our first hope is to engage with an adult with whom the child or adolescent lives, who is committed to the child's care and with whom the child is willing to build a closer relationship. Biological parents, adoptive parents, foster parents, grandparents, aunts or uncles, and even group home staff are good options. Sometimes the best choice is an adult who does not live with the child. John was a permanent ward of the Crown, but maintained a close and connected relationship with his mother. Including John's mother in therapy was critical. Anna lived with her father, but she and her mother wanted to improve their relationship and so Anna's mother attended the majority of appointments with her.

There are times when the choice of adult partner is not obvious. For some teens, an older sibling or even a close, supportive peer, or a friend's parent, may be the best choice. These situations aren't ideal, and we need to be realistic about what role older teens and young adults can play. The person chosen may not have a permanent role in the child's life, and when that is the case, it becomes important to consider this in the work. Teachers, child and youth workers, and friends' parents can be helpful and supportive, but if the commitment isn't a very long-term one, that needs to be clear and openly discussed.

Usually, these relationships aren't perfect. This can be part of a process of change and development. Most attachment relationships are not perfect, and some can be deeply flawed, while still providing needed support and guidance. For Shaun, his grandmother was committed and willing to be present, but had limitations in her abilities to be accepting when Shaun was dealing with issues around family trauma history and his parents, aunts and uncles. Shaun was able to explore this difficulty, and made decisions about which parts of his trauma work he involved his grandmother in, and which parts he chose to process in individual therapy. Beth was initially dependent on her boyfriend, Chris. He attended her early sessions and was caring and supportive. Beth and Chris worked on developing attachment, attunement, connection, emotional responsiveness and soothing. During early stages of treatment, Chris's presence was important and helpful. Without his support, continuing would have been difficult. We discussed the challenges that individual therapy sometimes creates in couple relationships, but Chris chose not to engage in his own therapy, in spite of identifying struggles of his own. As Beth grew and became more independent, she and Chris struggled. As we moved forward, Chris became controlling, and eventually, verbally abusive and threatening. Beth ended the relationship. Rose did effective attachment work over the years, as well as some trauma work. At eighteen, she chose to do more trauma work, but asked that her boyfriend attend to support her. They had been together a year, and her parents agreed. At eighteen, it's appropriate that a young woman would look to the support of a peer over her parents. I was surprised to find that she was much more relaxed, engaged and open about trauma with her boyfriend in the room than she had been on her own or with her parents. For his part he was supportive, caring, interested and respectful.

Sometimes, for various reasons, an appropriate attachment figure is not available and we need to be more creative. I have worked with dogs, fictional characters, physically absent or dead family members, and spiritual beings and images. During these situations, the therapist takes more of a role as an attachment figure, but continues to use the alternative ideas as a means of mediation and exploration.

Notes

1. Chu, J. A. (2011). *Rebuilding Shattered Lives: Treating Complex PTSD and Dissociative Disorders*. John Wiley and Sons. New York. p 67.
2. Freyd, J. (1994). *Betrayal Trauma: The Logic of Forgetting Childhood Abuse*. Harvard University Press. Cambridge, MA.
3. Silberg, Joyanna. (2013). *The Child Survivor: Healing Developmental Trauma and Dissociation*. Routledge. New York. p 21.
4. Liotti, G. (2006). A model of dissociation based on attachment theory and research. *Journal of Trauma & Dissociation, 7*(4), 55–73.
5. Linehan, M. (1993). *Cognitive Behavioural Treatment of People with Borderline Personality Disorder*. Guilford. New York.
6. Linehan, M. (1993). *Cognitive Behavioural Treatment of People with Borderline Personality Disorder*. Guilford. New York. p 19.
7. Silberg, Joyanna. (2013). *The Child Survivor: Healing Developmental Trauma and Dissociation*. Routledge. New York. p 52–53.
8. Nathanson, D. L. (1992). *Shame and Pride: Affect, Sex and the Birth of the Self*. W. W. Norton & Company. New York.
9. Hughes, Daniel A. (2007). *Attachment Focused Family Therapy*. W. W. Norton & Company. New York. pp 177–179.

Beginning Phase One

First Session and Assessment

Our early contacts set the tone. When working with motivated clients who trust in the process, there is room for error. With many of our clients, the early sessions may make or break treatment. This is a chance to engage the child or adolescent and caregiver, get their attention, provide them with hope, arouse their curiosity and help them open themselves to different ideas of what treatment can be.

Transparency and Use of Self

I've developed the habit of transparency. From the first session, I explain what I do and why. I want to avoid the suggestion that I am leading, manipulating or dishonest. I keep in mind that the early experiences in which my clients have learned about relationships and interactions are different from mine. Their rules of engagement are different, and I can't assume that they will experience my actions the way I intend. If they experienced actions as they were intended, their attachment difficulties would have resolved on contact with good, well-meaning people. If they need attachment-focused therapy, their experiences have led them to be both hard- and soft-wired for protection and suspicion rather than connection and engagement. When I ask questions, I explain why I am asking. If I'm exploring an idea, I explain my intentions. For example, when a young teen called to cancel an appointment and said, "I'm not coming in. I had a rough night and I'm tired," I asked why she'd had a rough night. As I heard her hesitate, I jumped in and said, "I'm not checking up on you—I want to make sure you're OK. Was it rough because something happened, or did you have trouble sleeping? I'm not upset about you cancelling—I want to know how you are." I use this type of transparency and labelling possible misinterpretations throughout therapy. If I'm giving a screening tool, I explain why. If I ask to speak to someone alone, or to contact someone, I explain why. If I get up to walk across the room to turn on a light, I say so first. I often preface questions by saying things like, "This might seem like a weird question . . ." or "This might be a tough question . . ." or "This might be awkward, and you don't have to tell me . . ." I remind them often that what they share is their choice. I'm open about myself, and try to own my own faults, mistakes and errors. I use examples of my own mistakes in conversation. I talk about my feelings and reactions. If I hope my clients will be open with me, I can expect no less of myself. I want to be experienced as a fallible human being who's trying to figure things out with them, not as an expert who will tell them what to do.

The flip side is that I don't assume I understand what my young client or their caregiver means. I check assumptions. If someone begins to cry, I reassure them that crying is OK and safe in my office and that many people, including me, have cried there. I then ask them, "Why are you crying? I know that sounds like a crazy question because we're talking about things worth crying about. I'm not asking because crying doesn't make sense. I want to know exactly what part of what we were talking about led to the tears." I don't want to accept any experience or emotion at face value—I want to understand their experience of it, not mine. If they don't know, or can't answer, I might list many different possibilities, and be open to more.

I'm open about who I am, my experiences, and my thoughts and feelings in a session. I work at being myself and being present as a person. I believe that trauma therapy is a uniquely intimate and mutual relationship. We can't work closely with somebody for months or years, share intimate details of their lives, watch, listen and support them while they grow and develop, and have it not be deeply personal. Mutual does not mean equal and personal does not mean unboundaried. My openness about myself may come across as relaxed and laid back, but everything I share is intentional and has a purpose. The purpose is always centred on the needs of the therapy, the client and the session—not on my need to be seen or experienced in a particular way. The intention is to be genuine, and to never create or increase shame by my approach or questions. Genuineness can't be faked, especially with our clients. They will know. If I am finding it hard to be genuine with someone, I need to examine my reactions and find out what is getting in my way. When I find out, I talk to them about it. For example, Valerie's mother was a strong, assertive woman, who had little patience for disorganisation and little trust for authority or the system. A single mother, she had become involved in the antipoverty movement and her neighborhood development committee and had accomplished great things. I am notorious for my chaotic style and my difficulty with being on time, and she called me on every slip. A few sessions into our relationship, I said to her, "I have to tell you, Janice, you're a strong woman and a great advocate. It's hard to raise a family and harder as a single parent. You've done so much for your kids and your community; you've worked hard at fighting for them and protecting them. I really admire you [which in fact I do—it wouldn't work otherwise and she would have called me on it in a second] and I get why you fight so hard. You and I are different. I'm not good at organisation and time—I'm good at some things, but not those ones. I know it bugs you. You don't trust many people; when I screw up, maybe you think it means I don't have what it takes to help Valerie, and you want to protect her from me. It's true I've screwed some things up, and I probably will again, but I think I can help you two, and I want to be able to work with you. My problem is now I've gotten worried about screwing up, and it's distracting me from being able to work at my best. I don't want to be scared of you—I want to work with you. I love that you can scare people into getting things done—it's helped you be there for your kids, but for me, I wonder if we can become partners and work together. You don't have to trust me completely or anything, just get to know me and work together." This not only helped us get past some of the earlier challenges, but also helped prepare the way for when, later in treatment, Valerie needed to talk to her mother about how scared she was of Janet's anger and criticism when she felt she couldn't meet her mother's expectations.

First Interview

The first face-to-face contact is arguably the most important. The young person is often brought in by an adult, and is unsure about being there. It does happen that adolescents self-refer or ask to be referred, but even then they are nervous and unsure that we have anything to offer. The first interview involves several critical tasks. The first is engagement. We need to engage the child and adult without engaging one at the expense of the other. A second task is to provide hope to both the child and the adult that we can do something together that will help.

When a child comes in with a parent, foster parent or group home staff, some therapists meet with the child first, to put them at ease, and some meet with the adult first, to gather information and history. Because I am being transparent I meet with both for the first part of the first session, to talk about shared information and to plan what will happen in the rest of the session. Both the child and the adult have expectations of what will happen, and so I describe my plan and goals for the appointment. I tell them that I'm going to spend a few minutes with everybody together, but that I will then break things up and meet with each of them on their own. I want them to know they'll have a chance to talk alone. I then start by explaining the need for some "boring" paperwork, and go over my consent for service forms. This is an opportunity to talk about confidentiality and its limits. I am outlining not just what can't be kept private, but also what is kept private, especially from each other. I explain that I'm required to disclose situations where a person is a risk to themselves or others, but also that this refers specifically to suicide and serious harm to themselves or another person. This means that I am not *allowed* to disclose nonlethal self-harm, substance use, or risky and delinquent behaviour. These are clinical issues, and become a focus of treatment; of course I encourage and work with a young person to talk to their caregiver about risky behaviours, but without their permission, I simply can't disclose. This apparent piece of administrative business helps clarify that I'm not aligned with the parents, and that I'm not gathering information for them. I also clarify that the same rules apply to the adults. If they tell me something that involves a life-threatening risk, or that a child is in need of protection, I can't keep their information private either. There is a difference between privacy and secrecy. My goal, which I'm open about, is to work towards the child and adult being able to talk to each other, not to me. I'm working with each of them towards making it safe for them to work together. At first, this may be hard for them to imagine, so I make sure they know I won't push it until it feels OK. I don't share privileged information, but I am also not looking for it. I ask the adults, in the child's presence, not to tell me things about their child that they don't want the child to know that I know. During this same session, I review information about mandatory reporting around child protection issues. Both adults and children know that even historical child protection information is not confidential. I met Amie a few months before her sixteenth birthday—the age at which she would no longer be a child under local child protection legislation. After discussing the limits of confidentiality, she chose to delay treatment until she turned sixteen. Even though the legislation is important and children need and are entitled to protection, I need to make sure that they know the rules. This is the nature of informed consent.

I tell them what to expect during our first few sessions. Our first job is to get to know each other, and I don't expect them to make up their mind about whether to work with me until after we've gotten to know each other. It takes time for the child and adult to work together, so during the getting-to-know-each-other process I meet with each of them alone once or twice, and then together. Then we will meet together to see if we can come up with a plan that's going to work for them. A lot of kids have announced that they would only come to the one appointment. I ask them to agree to do the getting-to-know-each-other part, and reassure them that if they decide not to come back, I won't agree to see them. This is usually a surprise, and I don't think I have ever had a child refuse to attend at least the assessment, after finding out that they will have some control over the outcome. I explain that during the getting-to-know-each-other stage, I'm going to ask them a lot of questions, because that's what I do. I tell them I expect they don't trust me much, because from what I know of them, they've had the kind of experience that has taught them not to trust a lot of people that they are supposed to be able to trust. If they have learned from their experiences, that shows wisdom. It's OK for them not to answer all of my questions, and if they need to lie to me, I won't be upset about it if the truth comes out later. I think everyone lies to their therapist at least a bit. Collecting information isn't important to me. I'm asking questions to get to know them, not because I want to know things *about them*. I tell them they can ask me any questions they want to, but that there might be some I will choose not to answer either. At first they almost never do. The idea seems strange to them.

At this point, I break things up. I ask the child if they want to meet with me first, or if they want their caregiver to meet with me. I say something like, "Sometimes kids don't want to meet first, because they think I'm going to tell their parents everything afterwards. Sometimes they don't want me to meet with their parents first, because they think their parents are going to tell me things behind their back, and get me to see them the way their parents do. This is just a chance to talk on our own. You can say or not say as much as you want, and I'm not going to think I know who you are from what someone else tells me. I'm telling you and your mom now that if she wants to tell me things about you without you here, I'm going to want you to know about it when we meet together at the end." Usually, unless the child is young or frightened of strangers, they agree to meet with me for a few minutes. Sometimes the adult stays outside the door, sometimes they go to the waiting room. I tell parents before they leave the room that I have no idea whether we will be five minutes or a half hour, because it's up to the child to decide how much to say, and I'm not interested in torturing them. Often, the child, the adult and I are surprised by how long the child stays and talks to me.

During the individual part of the first appointment I don't ask a lot. The goal of this session isn't getting information, it's giving it. The information I want to give the child or adolescent is that I want to hear them and get to know them on their own terms, that I respect their choices and control, and that rather than seeing them as bad or crazy, I see them as reacting normally and protectively to a bad or crazy experiences. I might ask them a bit about friends, school, activities, interests, video games or TV shows to break the ice and widen the focus to seeing them as a whole person. I ask if there is anything they want me to know. I ask them what they were expecting, and what they think about the plan for getting to know each other. I ask them whose idea coming to therapy was (usually their parent or caregiver) and why. I ask if they think the reason makes sense to them, and if not, can they think of things about their life and how they feel that they would like to make different. I tell them that my job isn't like the job of other adults in their lives—I'm not there to help control their behaviour or get them to go to school. I'm interested in their behaviour because my job is to get to know them and what it's like to be them. Knowing about their behaviour is like getting clues to a puzzle. For younger children or for those who dissociate, I repeat this often throughout therapy so that it gets heard and remembered by all parts. I also tell them that I know that everything they do makes sense[1] so they don't need to worry about me being shocked, upset or angry. I'm not in charge, so they aren't disappointing me or letting me down. I let them know that I have ideas that they might not be sure about, like their parents being part of therapy. I have these ideas because I know that when I can make it happen, it works the best, but that if I can't make it happen, we will figure out another way of making things work. They are in charge, and if they don't feel OK about certain things, we'll stop what we are doing and figure it out or slow it down. The purpose of therapy is them. It's their therapy—I'm their guide, because I've done it lots, but I won't make them do things until we can get it to feel safe enough. This is usually not what kids expect, and it helps them decide to continue.

When I meet with the adult alone, I have a similar conversation. I begin by asking what led them to bring their child to me. If the motivation was an outside influence, such as school, hospital or child welfare, I want to know if they agree, and what worries they themselves have. I want a good understanding of what they are struggling with, and to provide them with hope that I can help.

Parents or foster parents who bring their child because they are told to struggle with being part of treatment, more so if they feel blamed by others for their child's problems. Sometimes the goal we agree to work on is to get the school to stop harassing them or to get child welfare to close their file. Helping the child manage and cope better is usually the best way to achieve this. We need to hear and support how difficult it is for caregivers to cope with the challenges of an attachment-disordered traumatised child. I try to help caregivers see their child's difficulties as symptoms rather than behaviours. I want them to know and understand that the behaviours make sense and have meaning. If the adult is a biological parent who has had direct involvement in their child's trauma, such as a previously addicted parent, an abused ex-partner of an abuser, a parent with mental health difficulties, or a parent who has been abusive, this needs to be approached with empathy, not blame. Helping them understand the difficulties as trauma symptoms can lead to increased shame. Increased shame does not lead to good engagement. Even if the adult's choices or behaviours led to trauma for the child, too much shame over the past will derail treatment. The way around this is to approach the parents with the same stance that I approach the child. Like their child's behaviours, whatever choices they made in the past, no matter how negative, made sense somehow. The goal now is to do something different.

For parents and caregivers, it can be upsetting to hear that my focus is not on controlling the child's behaviour. Parenting a child with attachment and trauma issues is exhausting, overwhelming and sometimes dangerous. John became a permanent ward because his behaviours were dangerous to his much younger brother. Jake tried to kill himself twice, once by setting his bed on fire. The kids we see are cutting and burning themselves, threatening others, destroying property and creating chaos. These are serious difficulties demanding immediate response. The caregivers are desperate for help with these behaviours for good reason. I explain that because the behaviours are symptoms, direct attempts to take control of them won't work. If it was possible, good, caring parenting would have already made it happen. The reason they haven't been able to take control isn't because of lack of parenting skills. It is because taking control isn't the answer. I want to deal with the cause of the symptoms because healthy, connected young people who are heard, felt and have good self-regulation aren't a danger to themselves and others. They don't fly into uncontrolled rages, burn themselves with cigarettes or refuse to attend school. Focusing on the child's healing helps shift away from a power struggle with the child over control to a shared journey towards greater connection and self-control. In the meantime, we work together to develop safety plans and strategies to contain dangerous and self-destructive behaviours. This approach tends to give more relief faster, than focusing on behaviour.

By the end of the first session, I hope that I've helped the child or adolescent to see that therapy might help them achieve some of their own goals, feel better about themselves and their relationships, and that I am not there to side with their parents against them to make them change against their will. I hope that

I've helped the adults experience a possibility of change that doesn't involve winning a fight for control, and that they see a role for themselves in therapy; I make sure they know that exploring different ways to respond to their child's needs does not mean that they've failed. Finally, I hope that I have given both the child and the parent hope that things can be better.

First Session Goals

- Engagement
    - Helping the child experience the possibility that they can be safely heard and understood.
    - Helping the caregiver see a possible role for themselves in their child's therapy that does not translate to being a failure.
    - Helping the child and adult experience the possibility of a different relationship with shared goals.
    - Helping child and adult choose if this therapy is a good direction for them and if I am a good match for them.
- Supporting the caregiver in not seeing their child's difficulties as their failure. We all sometimes need to learn new skills for new situations. Traumatised attachment-disordered children are not easy to parent.
- Clarifying my role as being the child's therapist, and as working towards the child's emotional well-being, rather than the adult's improved control of the child.
- Reframing difficulties the child is experiencing as symptoms that make sense and need to be understood.
- Creating hope that life can be better.
- Interventions are discussed in the Chapter 9. Choosing one for the first session that best fits a challenge the child and parent are struggling with provides them with something concrete and helpful to use before the next session.

Assessing Attachment Figures

Providing support for a child during attachment and trauma work is challenging, emotionally draining work. If the child has a history with the attachment figure, there are dynamics that make this more challenging still. Biological parents may have the greatest struggles. John's mother, Shelley, had been abused by John's father. Trapped and alone, she had convinced herself that her son was not being harmed. In order to support John in treatment Shelley had to face her own and John's feelings not just about the abuse, but also about her inability to protect him.

Family members caring for a child may be impacted by the child's trauma and resulting symptoms. Shaun's grandmother had protected herself by minimising the impact of her own children's abuse. Her grandchildren's trauma symptoms challenged her defenses, leading her to become angry and resistant when Shaun talked about his feelings.

Terra had been abused by her mother, but was also impacted by her father's murder and her grandfather's sudden death. Her grandmother had put her own grief aside to focus on raising her granddaughter. In order to support Terra in treatment, she had to face her grief about the deaths of her son and husband.

Because traumatised and attachment-disordered children do not smoothly adapt to a new placement, difficult dynamics can develop even in the most balanced families, once a child has been moved into the home. A functional family can become less functional. Adopted children, if they've been with their parents for a period of time, develop added symptoms to cope with these dynamics. At adoption, Katie, who had been the favorite in foster care, reacted negatively to their new parents' attempts to treat her and her sister Lilly equally. This led to conflict in the family and Katie becoming seen as the "bad one." For Katie and Lilly's parents, it was easier to focus on the girls' preadoption history and prenatal alcohol exposure. It took time for their parents to be able to challenge the new dynamics and look at the current relationships in the family.

Children in foster care and residential care have different challenges. Often they have moved around and find it difficult to trust in a new caregiver, even one meant to be long-term. Engaging in therapy with a long-term but nonpermanent caregiver can be difficult. Foster parents and residential staff are sometimes unavailable for therapy, or feel that it isn't an appropriate role for them. When the focus of treatment becomes on relationships and ways of addressing behavioural and emotional challenges, foster parents and treatment staff may not feel the need to work on these areas. When I met John, he was living in a residential treatment setting. John had difficulty tolerating a behaviourally focused program and managing relationships with peers. He developed a role of instigating conflict, stealing from peers and manipulating power dynamics. John wanted to leave the group home, and many of the staff wanted him to leave. By the time I became involved the staff did not want to be involved in therapy, and he didn't see them as allies. He had become scapegoated and targeted, and the staff focused on the ways he instigated abuse from his peers rather than on trying to understand his internal experiences or protect him.

For an adult to be a good addition to therapy they need to be willing and able to engage with the child and experience attunement and empathy for the child's experiences. They need to be able to have insight into attachment needs and relationships and to the role this has in their child's life. They need to be able to tolerate exploration of trauma, and to hear their child's experience of it. The caregiver needs to be able to tolerate the child's experience of themselves, of the adult, and of their relationship. They need to acknowledge the child's right to a different experience, even if that feels unfair or hurtful to the adult. They don't need to agree with the child's experience, but they need to be able to hear it and not defend against it. They also need to be able to hear and feel that the therapist, hearing the child's experience, will not judge them by the same lens as the child. The adult needs to be able to understand that "correcting" the child's experience, even to reassure the child, is not helpful.

All this means that the adult attachment figure needs to be able to tolerate strong emotions in themselves and others; to have relatively good affect and behavioural control; and the ability to build trust, experience empathy and attune to the child. They need to have a reasonably long-term commitment to the child and they need to have relatively good ego strength. This does not mean that the adult needs to be able to do all this perfectly all the time, and it doesn't mean that they need to do it without assistance, guidance and support.

When I started learning about dyadic attachment work I had the impression that the caregiver needed to have a permanent role in a child's life, to be fully resolved in regards to their own attachment and trauma history, and to completely understand attachment and intersubjectivity, before treatment started with the child. These ideas would create certain difficulties. For many of the kids I work with, there is no such person. Even when permanent, committed, stable caregivers are available, to fully teach them delays treatment. Although this may be worth it if it ensures treatment success, many caregivers aren't willing to attend several sessions while waiting for their child to get treatment, and many children experience this as the therapist building an alliance with their caregiver before getting to know them. I tend instead to work with the child and adult together, addressing issues around coping and containment, while integrating individual psychoeducational and supportive sessions in between dyadic sessions as needed.

During sessions, as conflicts or difficulties arise, I explore what is happening between them and how it may be reflective of trauma and attachment issues. I work with them together to try to have a different experience of their relationship. I will sometimes stop a session and ask to meet with one or the other, or I set up individual appointments to process a thought or issue that has come up. I try to create a warm atmosphere so that it's possible to challenge an interaction without it being a criticism. Because I say early and often that the directions I'm guiding them in are not directions that come naturally to most people, redirection is not suggested as a criticism but as an experiment. At the age and developmental stage we are working at, the type of attunement and interaction is a grown-up-in-content version of early childhood interactions. This can seem unusual and awkward, which is helpful. Parenting attachment-disordered children can be counterintuitive. No caregiver could have been expected to figure it out.

An example of this would be a session between Anna and her mother. Anna was angry at her mother, who had lost her job and didn't have money for something Anna needed. In exploring individually with Anna, she was aware that the situation had triggered anger from earlier experiences of being let down and feeling unimportant. She knew that her mother was trying her best in the situation, but many of her parts were still very angry. Christine, for her part, also understood this, but was hurt and rejected by cruel things that Anna had said to her in the previous week. In our session, I labelled the anger, and Christine acknowledged the past of having been unavailable to her daughter. She became sad, which Anna was able to tolerate without panicking or rejecting her, as she had in the past. Anna acknowledged that in spite of her anger, she had parts who still wanted their mother. She said that she thought her mother might need to start with the younger parts, who had felt the most rejected, and also needed her mother the most. Anna sat on an exercise ball facing her mother, and they listened together to a lullaby Christine used to sing to her. They were able to make eye contact and to become more attuned to each other. At the end, Anna was able to say that she could be angry at her mother and still love her. They left together.

Assessing attachment figures isn't about meeting a caregiver and figuring out if they can fit into treatment. It's more about getting to know the caregiver and figuring out how the treatment can be designed to help them become more connected and available. If there isn't an adult who can be fully available, is there one who can be there and supportive for part of the treatment? Is there more than one person who might take different roles during different parts of the work? Is there an attachment figure who is committed to the child, and who may not be able to manage the trauma work, but who can work on improving their responsiveness and attunement, becoming more connected to the child and helping them to be more stable, grounded and regulated when needed? The ideal is an adult who can attend with the child, build an attachment relationship, support the child through the trauma work, support the child through creating a new, healthier daily life and future, and remain connected to the young person after therapy and into the future. If this isn't possible, the more we can work with one or more adults to support and care for the child, and the more we can improve the availability and attunement of the adults in the child's life, the better.

Assessing the Child and Their Treatment Needs

As I've mentioned, when I begin working with a child, I am more interested in getting to know them than getting to know about them. My first goal is to assess what will bring them into therapy. Why are they there, do they want to be there, and what might be something they can imagine getting out of being there. Some young people are determined not to engage, and others want to feel heard and understood. Many are conflicted. If they feel heard and respected by me, they agree to come back. Next I want to know how the child feels about the adults in their lives, and what that means in relation to attachment work. Many children want an improved relationship with caregivers, and are intrigued by the idea that their caregiver might be interested in understanding them and hearing what they have to say, rather than changing them. Some children and adolescents see their caregivers as potentially on their side, but don't know how to go about getting it to happen. Other young people feel that their parent is not emotionally available to them, and that that is not going to change. Sometimes they are right. This is a part of the initial sessions that is best handled individually. It's surprising how many kids who openly defy rules and refuse to comply with expectations grudgingly admit that having rules make sense if their parent is not in the room with them.

I want a good understanding of safety and violence issues that the child has. If they are in danger of seriously harming themselves or someone else, I need to assess their willingness and openness to work towards gaining control of this quickly. I draw a line between these issues and other types of behaviours. Safety and creating safety is first priority. I assess whether the child or adolescent is willing and able to develop a safety plan. Usually, they are. Sometimes, with young people who have dissociative self-states, this has to be assessed and negotiated in a more complex way. This is discussed elsewhere.

Along with safety I assess self-regulation—both affective and behavioural. I want to understand how in or out of control a young person feels, what that means to them, and what is getting in the way. Emergency interventions around grounding and affect regulation are good first-session interventions because they provide hope and mastery to both the client and caregiver, and often address the greatest worries that they agree on. Many times the adult sees the child as in control. Often this is not the experience of the child. The child might be as frightened and worried about outbursts as the parent, and more ashamed. Once this is identified, it is easy to make it a shared goal.

I want to understand the child's environment. What is school like for them? How much does the school know about the situation? What can be done to improve the child's school experience? Is there an adult support or ally at the school? Does the child have friends? Are there areas that they enjoy or do well in? Sometimes young people cope well at school and not at home. Sometimes it's the reverse. Some children struggle in both environments. Is there something the caregiver, or myself, can do to help the environment be more supportive?

I want to understand the safety, both experienced and actual, in the child's environments. Sometimes these are the same, sometimes they are not. A child can experience danger in a safe environment, and they can experience safety in a dangerous environment. They can also identify dangers that others are not aware of. For example, Anna's mother is dating a new man. Anna thinks he's "creepy." It could be that she has seen him hurt her mother, or it could be that he looks at Anna in a sexual way that she can't pinpoint, but she feels something is wrong. It could also be that he is fine, but that she is uncomfortable about any man, or about her mother being with a man. Beth at first felt completely safe with Chris. Even after she became less dependent on him, and he began to become increasingly controlling, she did not recognise the red flags because he was not violent in the way she was accustomed to with her father and previous partners.

I want to understand the child's post-traumatic symptoms. Do they experience fear, anxiety, depression or sadness? Can they identify emotions, name them and make sense of them? Are they aware of how their emotions feel in their body? Are they aware of their bodies in general? Does their mistrust mean that they are afraid of being harmed by others, or do they simply see others as self-involved and dishonest? Do they have flashbacks or panic attacks, and how do they cope with them? Are they attending school and learning? Do they have regular routines, and can they manage them? Do they have friends, interests and activities? How do they sleep? Sleep is often at the core of other difficulties, and can be difficult to shift. Do they have nightmares, night terrors, or difficulty falling asleep or staying asleep? A child or adolescent who is not sleeping well will have difficulty functioning, coping and self-regulating. Sometimes if you can address the sleep difficulties other problems decrease.

Assessing Dissociation

Identifying and assessing dissociation early is important. Unidentified dissociation can undermine treatment and lead to split and chaotic relationships within the treatment team. Dissociation can be almost invisible. It's a symptom of secrecy. It develops to help a child hide information from themselves and others. The media portrays dissociative disorders as dramatic; this is only a small part of reality. Dramatic changes in presentation happen, but often only in situations where it is either safe for this to happen or there is a trauma trigger. Some dissociative symptoms seem to have become accepted as "normal" responses to trauma that many therapists believe will resolve as trauma is addressed. Dissociation may be a "normal" response to trauma, but symptoms such as age regression, traumatic amnesia, pseudoseizures, lost time, trancelike episodes, flashbacks and hearing voices do not resolve organically with trauma treatment. Dissociation is an indication that parts of the child's consciousness are separated from the rest. In dissociative identity disorder these parts take the form of alternate personalities. In less severe dissociation these parts can be memories, parts of memories, emotional states or sensory experiences. Parts that are dissociated from consciousness are not experienced as part of the whole, and are not affected by treatment unless they are directly accessed and intentionally engaged.

Once a therapist is familiar with dissociation, they recognise the subtle signs more easily, but that doesn't mean it is easy or obvious, or that a therapist experienced with dissociation will always see it. Once a therapist has worked with one or two clients with recognised dissociative symptoms they do begin to identify it more often. That is probably true with most symptoms. Even with experience, it can be easy to miss. I had worked with Terra for four years before she revealed the existence of an imaginary world and several alter personalities. More than a year after Beth was diagnosed with a dissociative identity disorder, and after two years of what appeared to be effective treatment with Beth and her two known alters, a third suicidal alter surfaced. If a young person, or their parts, does not want to be seen, they won't be. The solution is to approach the client with openness and acceptance, creating as much safety as possible, while continuing to check in around experiences and clues as they come up. Everyone wants to be heard and understood. If a young person has reason to believe they will be heard and understood without judgment, their voices will choose to be heard. Like other parts of assessment, assessment of dissociative symptoms is ongoing throughout treatment. Assessment doesn't end after the first few sessions. Dissociation, like any other factor, is something we continue to assess, monitor and check in on as treatment evolves.

There are a number of symptoms to be alert for. Some may be witnessed during assessment and treatment; some may be reported by caregivers, school personnel, or the child or adolescent. Some can be witnessed and others are experiential.

- Unusual Forgetfulness—Everybody forgets things, and many of the children we work with have difficulty paying attention, and so information that people think gets in, does not. When kids dissociate they lose information that has been in their memory. They can talk about events some days, and have no memory for them another day. Sometimes they completely forget important events that happened recently, like a school trip or a birthday. When young people's forgetfulness does not seem to make sense, or if they or others comment on their memory being a big problem, it's worth getting a good understanding of what is happening.
- Lost Time—Lost time refers to blanks in memory or chunks of time that are missing. It can be hard to know about unless they tell you. I have had children confide in me that they are frightened because they have suddenly found themselves somewhere without knowing how they got there, or that they got home from school without remembering the school day. Sometimes this is mistaken for lying, because children don't remember something that they are in trouble for, like missing school, "running away," sexual behaviour or stealing. A good clue can be if lying doesn't make sense because the child should know that they have been seen doing what they are denying.
- Subtle or Obvious Shifts in Presentation—A child may suddenly seem younger or older; the inflection or tone of voice may change; or their relationship with someone suddenly seems different. Terra, thirteen, would sometimes hold her arms up to her grandmother like a toddler wanting to be picked up. Sophie, when woken, would appear frightened and run and hide under a table. When angry, she would look blankly at her parents and yell, "Who are you?" Her parents described episodes when she seemed to "not be there" while behaving oddly and being unresponsive. Anna would talk, laugh and share with her mother, and then suddenly say, "I don't like mom, she never talks to me!" and move away to a different chair.
- Eye Rolling—Often a child's eyes roll or flicker if they are experiencing a "switch" in parts. Some young people look away, or let their hair cover their face, to mask this.
- Sudden Disconnection or "Blankness"—Sometimes a young person will stop during a conversation and stare unresponsively. At times, they will not remember the conversation they were engaged in, or the question they were asked.
- Denial of Witnessed Behaviour or Conversations—A young person who is denies things that they have recently been seen doing or heard saying is

not likely lying. Children lie when they think it will help—not when it will cause more trouble.

- Found Items—A young person may find things they have no memory of getting or doing. This happens with artwork and journal entries, as well as objects.
- Apparent Unawareness of Pain—The ability to disconnect from pain can be dramatic. Daniel was in a fight at school, and his front tooth was broken off. He was seen at the hospital, and scheduled for dental surgery. The doctor was amazed, as Daniel's root was exposed, but he had no difficulty eating, drinking and speaking. We had a session the next day. Daniel, sitting calmly in my office drinking a cold soft drink, told me his pain was ten out of ten, but that he was not the one who felt it. He said he was aware of the pain, but another part was carrying it.
- Hearing Internal Voices—Dissociative parts often talk to the child, or different parts talk to each other. Different from most hallucinations, voices of dissociated parts are most often heard inside the child or adolescent's head.[2]
- Experiences of External Control—Sometimes kids feel that their actions are controlled by something or someone else.

There are a number of screening and assessment tools for dissociative symptoms and dissociative disorders. I use more than one tool, as well as careful interviewing. Each tool asks different questions and in different ways. The Child Dissociative Checklist[3] is a parent-report questionnaire developed by Frank Putnam to assess dissociative symptoms in young children. The Adolescent Dissociative Experiences Scale (A-DES),[4] based on the adult Dissociative Experiences Scale,[5] is a self-rated scale used with kids above the age of eleven. The Child Dissociative Experience Scale and Post-Traumatic Stress Inventory,[6] designed by Bradley Stolbach, is a useful tool that can be used with children or adolescents. The Trauma Symptom Checklist for Children (TSCC),[7] designed by John Briere, is a good tool for assessing PTSD symptoms in children and adolescents, but does not contain many specific dissociative symptoms. The Multi-Dimensional Inventory of Dissociation is an excellent tool designed by Paul Dell.[8] It comes on an Excel spreadsheet, has been well researched with the adult population, and is currently being researched with adolescents. Joyanna Silberg has also developed some very useful interview outlines and specific targeted checklists for exploring dissociation with children.[9]

Notes

1. Silberg, Joyanna. (2013). *The Child Survivor: Healing Developmental Trauma and Dissociation*. Routledge. New York.
2. Putnam, F. W. (1989). *Diagnosis and Treatment of Multiple Personality Disorder*. Guilford. New York.
3. Putnam, F. W., Helmers, K., & Trickett, P. K. (1993). Development, reliability and validity of a child dissociation scale. *Child Abuse and Neglect, 17*, 731–741.

4. Armstrong, J., Putnam, F. W., Carlson, E., Libero, D. & Smith, S. (1997). Development and validation of a measure of adolescent dissociation: The Adolescent Dissociative Experiences Scale. *Journal of Nervous and Mental Disease, 185*, 491–497.
5. Bernstein, E. M., Putnam, Frank W. (1986). Development, reliability, and validity of a dissociation scale. *Journal of Nervous and Mental Disease, 174*, 727–735.
6. Stolbach, B. (1997). The Children's Dissociative Experiences Scale and Post-Traumatic Inventory: Rationale, development and validation of a self-report measure. *Dissertation Abstracts International, 58*(3), 1548B.
7. Briere, J. (1996). *The Trauma Symptom Checklist for Children*. Psychological Assessment Resources. Lutz, FL.
8. Dell, P. F. (2006). The multi-dimensional inventory of dissociation (MID): a comprehensive measure of pathological dissociation. *Journal of Trauma and Dissociation, 7*(2), 77–106.
9. Silberg, Joyanna. (2013). *The Child Survivor: Healing Developmental Trauma and Dissociation*. Routledge. New York.

9 Phase One

Strategies and Interventions

Attachment

When building attachment security in children who have never experienced it, we use the experiences that build attachment for young children. We work to create safety, attunement, empathic responsiveness and joy between the child and their caregiver. We create these experiences in therapy, and work with adults and children to create them within the home and school environments.

The BASK Model

The BASK model of dissociation was developed by Bennet Braun,[1,2] and has continued to inform therapists working with dissociation. BASK stands for behaviour, affect, sensation and knowledge, and refers to the way these aspects of information, experience and memory can be dissociated from each other. Many traumatised children and adolescents experience disconnection between these aspects of experience. The information now available on brain development (Chapter 2) tells us that neurological integration is impacted by early trauma and disrupted attachment. This supports a biological basis for the BASK model of dissociation, and for the difficulties our young clients have in connecting the elements of their experiences and memories into a coherent whole. Interventions designed for work with these kids are most effective when they address the elements of the child's experiential information and work to create an integrated whole.

Window of Tolerance and Affect Regulation

The young people we work with have a narrow window of emotional tolerance. Within our window of tolerance we are best able to take in information, integrate it, and generalise the experience. We can learn and grow. Porgess's work on the polyvagal theory suggests that when we recognise the experience of safety, we enter our window of tolerance.[3] Safety allows us to shut down our defensive mechanisms and direct our energy towards growth, development, learning and connection. When we don't feel safe we enter one of two survival modes, the defensive fight or flight response (hyperarousal), or the

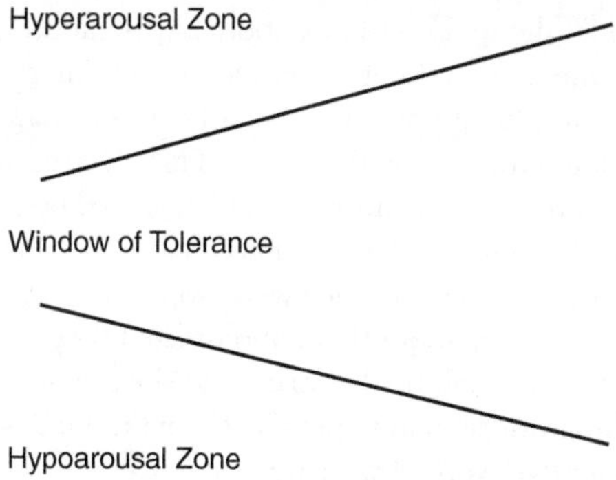

Figure 9.1 Widening the Window of Tolerance

defensive shut-down mode (hypoarousal). One of the goals of phase one work is to widen the window of tolerance (Figure 9.1) by gradually increasing our client's awareness of affective states and ability to regulate them. Because this is usually mastered early in the context of being soothed and then learning self-soothing within an attachment relationship, we want to use the attachment relationship as a resource while exploring and managing emotional experience.

Interventions

The interventions for phase one are designed to clarify the treatment frame, build treatment relationships, integrate experience, and help the child and their attachment figure coregulate and then regulate affect before addressing trauma in phase two. The interventions described here are developed to create connection and attunement between the child and caregiver and encourage neurological growth, development and integration that were missed in earlier stages.

Creative Use of Attachment Figures

Adult attachment figures aren't always available. Sometimes our clients are not ready for a real attachment relationship with a caregiver. This means that some therapy situations need more creativity than others.

When Rose, adopted from Liberia at the age of four, first came to see me, she was nine. She had limited awareness of emotion and little empathy. Engaging her in therapy was like working with a Barbie doll. She was always bright and cheerful. Her life was perfect and she denied negative emotions. When asked about an angry outburst or a problem at school, she would brightly say, "That's over. I don't talk about the past." When asked about how someone else may have experienced it, her response was, "I don't think about it. They know I didn't mean it." If others rejected her, her response was, "I don't care, I have lots of friends." She refused to talk about her preadoption history, saying, "That was a long time ago—I don't remember it, so I don't care about it." Any attempt to focus on a difficulty was brushed off as "boring," and would result in her cheerfully flouncing out of the room. This cheerfulness was broken at home by rageful and destructive tantrums and at school by impulsive, inappropriate and sexualised behaviour that had her labelled as odd and embarrassing. These events were over the second they were over. She remembered them; she was simply unwilling to talk about them and insisted they were "over."

Her family lived on a small hobby farm, and she seemed to care about and connect to the animals more than to people. I don't think this is unusual. Many of the young people I've worked with were able to care deeply for animals. I suspect it is because animals love in an uncomplicated and unquestioning way. She was able to talk about how she could sense what animals were feeling and that they understood how she felt, even when she couldn't put it into words. Her parents decided to buy her a small dog, who became our partner in therapy. The dog did not attend many sessions, but she was part of many conversations. She was able to talk about her dog's feelings and to extend this to how her dog *might* feel in certain difficult situations, like when left alone during a storm, or if she was not well cared for or fed. Her parents enrolled her and her dog in puppy training, and she did so well with the dogs that the kennel owner took her as a volunteer and later offered her a part-time job. Spontaneously she told me about an abused and neglected dog that she had connected with. She told me that a neglected dog who was not loved and given attention would not know how to get along with people. She said, "That dog's brain doesn't grow right, and it just doesn't know how to be a good dog—I understand it because that's kind of like what happened to me!"

Rose developed insight and improved attachment with her parents. She often says, "I'm so much better off than the other adopted kids I know because I have a great family and I got lots of help!" At eighteen she has a good relationship with her parents and a steady boyfriend, and is preparing to finish high school. Gradually, she has been able to talk about feeling very anxious, and how difficult it is to allow herself to feel bad or let others know how she feels. She knows her early life was traumatic and that this has affected her, but she struggled with doing trauma work. When asked what could make it possible, she asked to include her boyfriend in the sessions. It seemed appropriate at her age that she look to peers rather than parents for support, so I agreed to try if he was interested and willing. In the first session he attended, she was able to identify to him and me what in early life she felt had been traumatic, what she remembered and what she would like to work on. We talked about the options, and she decided to try EMDR.

When adults in a child's life are also struggling, they might not be able to tolerate the full extent of their child's trauma work. When this happens, it's possible to structure involvement, so that they can support the child and learn to be more attuned, participating as much as makes sense. Although this might not be ideal, it can improve the relationships, the quality of attachment, and the child's experience of being felt and understood. This can help the child work on the trauma with the therapist, providing feedback to the caregiver as we go.

Shaun's grandmother had dedicated herself to raising her grandchildren. She cared deeply for them, but was impacted by her own earlier traumas and the impact on her now adult children. This created limitations to what she could tolerate. We worked together in such a way that she was present and engaged for attachment work, and some of the trauma work which was not directly related to family dynamics. The rest of the work was individual. Shaun was an adolescent with fairly good ego strength. He was able to work with his grandmother during phase one, and she was able to understand that his depression, self-harm and suicide attempts were connected to loneliness and despair, rather than attempts to get attention or his own way. She could support him around his feelings of isolation, and worked with him to develop a plan should he need her help to deal with these feelings. Shaun's grandmother was also able to be with him and support him during some phase two EMDR work around bullying at school and a car accident when he was five. He could rely on her in ways he had not been able to in the past. Shaun then chose to continue with family-related trauma work in individual therapy. His grandmother drove him to sessions, picked him up, and they would often stop and spend special time together on the way home. Shaun and his grandmother were able to move from not being able to acknowledge or talk about negative feelings, to his being able to talk about his feelings and lean on her for support, but not to openly discuss their differences in experience around some family events.

Sometimes we work with young people who have limited or no adult support. Amie was sixteen. She was bouncing between parents who had been abusive and neglectful during her childhood, and who were more involved in their own lives than in parenting their daughter. Both came to a few sessions and did not continue. Shortly after beginning treatment Amie left home and lived in a series of shelters, group homes and friends' homes. Amie had no adults that she trusted, but she identified with Harry Potter. She owned all of the movies, the books, and the books on tape. When lonely, she would listen to parts of the books in which Harry was being nurtured or supported by teachers at his school. Using the ideas of the "Imaginary Support Circle"[4] we began to use her projections of these teachers as her attachment figures. We also worked to connect her to as many people in the community as possible. Again, this was not an ideal solution, but Amie made, and continues to make, many gains.

When I met Beth, she had left her abusive family and moved in with her boyfriend. She was dependent on him, and couldn't leave the house unless he was with her. He attended all of her sessions during her first six months of treatment. Although he was supportive, Chris presented with mental health and trauma issues of his own. I had reservations about including him, as he was not interested in his own therapy. Beth was too afraid to meet without him. We agreed he could attend until she was comfortable meeting alone. During those first six months, he was supportive, helpful and nurturing. He responded to her emotional states and alter personalities with empathy and understanding. I warned them both at the beginning, and many times, that when one member of a couple engages in therapy and the other does not, it can lead to changes that affect the relationship. Beth and Chris chose to continue as we had begun. Beth became stronger and began to come on her own. As she became less dependent Chris became resistant to the changes in her, and eventually to her therapy. After their relationship ended Beth told me that Chris had become first controlling, then cruelly critical, and eventually threatening. Beth and I have talked about this part of the journey many times. She feels that in the beginning, Chris was supportive. I would not choose to work this way within an abusive or controlling relationship, yet Beth has achieved what she has thanks in part to the initial support from Chris.

Dyadic Developmental Psychotherapy

Dyadic developmental psychotherapy is a model developed by Dan Hughes for incorporating attachment theory into the treatment of attachment-disordered and traumatised children.[5,6,7] Dr. Hughes outlines key principles and concepts for healing attachment relationships between children and adolescents and their caregivers. Key to this model is attunement and intersubjectivity. Attunement occurs when the child and caregiver are in sync or in tune with each other. Intersubjectivity creates shared meaning, shared understanding, and coregulation of the child's affect. Moments of intersubjectivity are the building blocks of secure attachment.[8] When working to create or repair attachment relationships, we work with the adult and child to create attunement and intersubjectivity. We want the child to experience that they are felt and understood in a genuine way. Although this type of connection often comes naturally when parenting an infant, it is less common in the parenting of children who have learned to avoid connection and experience. Several concepts developed by Dr. Hughes are important in the phase one work I do with young people and their caregivers.

Playfulness, Acceptance, Curiosity and Empathy (PACE)—In *Attachment Focused Family Therapy* Dr. Hughes uses the acronym PACE to describe the therapeutic stance of playfulness, acceptance, curiosity and empathy.[9] Approaching adult caregivers and children and adolescents from this position is invaluable. Genuinely caring about and connecting with adults and children from a playful, accepting, curious and empathic position minimises shame and creates enough safety to allow them to engage in difficult work.

Affective Reflective Dialogue—Dr. Hughes encourages dialogue between the child and adult that allows the adult to actively hear the child's experience and reflect it back to them, rather than attempting to reframe, change or alter their perceptions.[10] This expresses attunement between the adult and the child, allowing the child to be felt and understood, rather than minimised. It can be challenging for the child to express their experiences, and difficult for the adult to hear and respond without trying to reassure the child or correct their experience.

Break and Repair—I have found the idea of break and repair to be particularly helpful for parents and caregivers. Making mistakes in relationships is not only expected, but necessary. Understanding this is a great relief to parents and children. It isn't the goal to become perfect parents and perfect children. What strengthens relationships and creates security, particularly for young people who have not had empathic and attuned parents, is when there is conflict, anger, discordance, or an out-of-tune disconnection, that is then resolved. The experience of a break in attunement is necessary to allow repair to happen. It is break followed by repair that creates the experience of a relationship that can tolerate conflict and imperfections.[11]

Interventions

Some of the interventions in the early part of phase one are process-oriented, rather than specific. Many serve more than one purpose.

- **Setting the Treatment Frame**—This is covered in Chapters 7 and 8. The treatment frame is approached in a way that creates safety for the child and the caregiver, while drawing the focus towards the young person's affective experiences and away from behaviours.
- **Informed Consent to Treatment**—This is a necessary administrative task that, when done from a stance of PACE, clarifies roles and expectations, contributes to safety, and explores expectations of therapy and therapeutic roles.
- **Transparency and Use of Self**—I am a real person in a real relationship with the kids and adults I work with. I assume fear, mistrust, hidden realities and the felt need for manipulation and control, not in a negative way, but as a naturally learned survival tool that I accept, honor and understand.
- **Dialectical Stance**—I believe and accept that symptoms and behaviours have a meaning and a purpose,[12] while still knowing that they may not be helpful to the child. It may be worthwhile for the child to consider new ways of adapting to a world that is different and safer than the one they first experienced.
- **Voice**—Every person needs a voice. We work with young people who have had no voice. When young people have dissociated parts, those parts need voices. When a child or adolescent has overwhelming feelings that they have no words for, or that no one hears, their behaviours, symptoms and actions become their voice. Their voice will get as loud as needed to be heard. Terms like *manipulation* and *attention-seeking* negate the legitimacy of their voice. It's our job to help them find a voice, and to help their caregivers hear them.
- **Control**—I want kids to be in control of the course and process of therapy. I give them choices and options. I respect their wishes around timing of appointments as much as possible. If there's something I want them to

try, I explain why I think it makes sense and what I hope they will get out of it. I let them know that if an experiment doesn't work, we can change it. If there are activities they want in a session, I go with it if it's possible. Often what at first seems like a distraction turns into an effective tool (watching music videos, building with Legos, or playing games). When children don't want to talk, we come up with other ways, like writing answers on a whiteboard, using feeling cards or options lists, or scaling answers on a scale or wheel.

Allowing others to be in control requires trust. The children we work with only feel safe when they are in control. They will not give this up until they can rely on others to value their interests and needs. They will engage in therapy only voluntarily, and this will happen if it adds to their sense of control rather than taking away from it. Control has limits. We all have limits on our choices. Helping them know this is part of the process.

- **Shame**—Issues relating to shame permeate early phase one work. "Though terror speaks to life and death, and distress makes of the world a vale of tears, shame strikes deepest into the heart of man. While terror and distress hurt, they are wounds inflicted from the outside . . . but shame is felt as an inner torment, a sickness of the soul."[13] Shame is a common, normal experience in small amounts. Dr. Hughes suggests that shame interferes with events being integrated into a coherent narrative.[14] The need to defend against shameful material results in dissociation and gaps and fragmentation in the narrative. During early contact, every conversation needs to be framed as accepting, nonjudgmental, and as minimising of shame.
- **Emotional Truth**—Emotional truth is an idea I stumbled on trying to understand some of the complex "lies" told by the kids I work with. It's easy to understand why a child with a history of abuse lies to avoid consequences, or to get something. This goes back to trust and control. There are different types of lies that are more difficult to understand. Twelve-year-old Emily eats ice cream out of a soup bowl. Her foster father comments that she should have used a smaller bowl, and saved some of the ice cream for other people. Emily becomes hysterical and runs out of the house crying. She later gives a detailed description of a flashback of a time at home when she had been beaten for eating ice cream from a soup bowl. There is something about the description that is too detailed and too close to the recent experience, and the foster mother is sure the story is not true, but can't explain why Emily would make it up. As we slowly process the experience, Emily is able to acknowledge that something in the moment triggered terror and she could not explain the connection. Wanting us to understand that she was afraid, not willful, she filled the gap by describing a flashback of an incident that had not occurred, but that she thought would help her be understood. Emotional truth can be a type of

exaggeration. The children we work with are hyperalert and have a small window of emotional tolerance. Their reactions are out of proportion to the events they are reacting too, and adults see them as exaggerating or being dramatic. Wanting us to understand that the emotional reaction was real for them, they explain using words we will understand. For children who have dissociative experiences, they may come to believe the events are true. We need to focus on the emotion of the experience, and help the child understand that we hear the truth in their reaction.

- **Hope**—Many of the kids and caregivers feel hopeless about the future. Helping them know that what they're dealing with is manageable and that their future can be better than the past is a powerful engagement tool. Often being heard and understood creates hope.
- **Psychoeducation**—Helping adults and children understand and normalise their experiences, reactions and behaviours changes negative attributions and create safety and empathy. Specific educational interventions are described later in this chapter.
- **Scaling**—Scaling helps us get a sense of the degree of a child's reactions and feelings while helping them begin to think in shades of grey rather than black and white. Traumatised children get caught in absolutist thinking. Scaling helps them to move away from this.
- **A Whole Person**—The whole person idea is particularly relevant to kids with dissociative parts, but is applicable to all clients. The idea of working with a whole person refers to not picking and choosing which parts are good and worth keeping, and which parts need to be changed. We are all flawed, and treatment is not about getting rid of flaws to become perfect, it is about creating a cohesive whole.
- **Trauma Work**—Although processing and integrating traumatic memory isn't a good idea early in treatment, neither is ignoring it. Ignoring trauma sends the message that their experiences are too terrible to talk about or too dangerous to manage. Some children fear getting overwhelmed by talking about their experiences, and want to avoid them. Others have been told that talking about them will help, launch into it in the first session and get flooded. I tell kids that I know that bad things happened to them, and that it's part of the plan to talk about it, slowly and carefully, a bit at a time, as we learn to manage the feelings around it. I use the example of a dam, and we look up pictures, showing how they are engineered to let small amounts of water through at a time to prevent overflow or collapse.

Interventions for Neurological Integration

I create as many opportunities to support neurological integration as possible. Interpersonal neuropsychology supports that experiences involving attunement and coregulation encourage improved neurological integration. The BASK model of dissociation is based on the understanding that traumatic memories do not get organised as an integrated whole.[15,16] I focus on involving as many of the elements of experience as possible, while working to stay within the child and caregiver's window of tolerance. You will see as you go through these lists that there is overlap in interventions.

Psychoeducational Interventions for Neurological Integration

- I use a diagram of the brain which shows both left-right divisions and functional divisions (see Figures 2.1 and 2.2 in Chapter 2) to explain the impacts of trauma on development and integration. I tailor the explanation to the age and understanding of the child and parent. I want them to understand that some of their difficulties are caused by the way their experiences affected their development, and that this can be changed. (This is also an attachment-based intervention, in that it increases empathy and minimises negative attributions and behavioural focus.)
- I use a diagram to explain window of tolerance issues (see Figure 5.1 in Chapter 5) and to help children and their caregivers understand that to talk about something successfully, both the child and the adult need to find ways to be in their window of tolerance. (Again, this intervention is important for attachment purposes, and also is the beginning of teaching affect regulations skills.)
- I use scaling questions to help children and adolescents learn to think and experience in degrees rather than absolutes. (Understanding graded reactions is important in developing affect regulation skills.) I have a scaling wheel, as well as drawings of thermometers (see worksheets) that can be coloured, or use a line scale drawn on paper.
- I teach about body reactivity and emotional chemistry. I use a fingertip pulsometer to help them learn about their heart rate, and explain how it connects to emotional reactivity. We do breathing and relaxation exercises to explore the ways their heart rate and emotional and physical states change as a result. (This is also an affect regulation intervention.)

Experiential Interventions for Neurological Integration

- I involve as many aspects of experience as possible. I differentiate between thoughts and feelings. If I ask a child for a reaction and they tell me their thoughts, I will then say something like, "Good, those are your thoughts, can you tell me your feelings as well?" (If they give me their feelings, I ask about their thoughts.) I get them to pick feelings from a pack of "feelings cards."
    - I ask them to describe what those feelings feel like in their bodies. Often they don't know the answer, and so I then teach them how to do body scans.
    - I ask them to tell me how they can tell when their caregiver has that feeling, or ask the parent if they can tell by looking at the child what the child might be feeling.

- There are lots of available visual tools for learning to identify feelings. This type of sheet can be very useful. Figure 9.2 is an example of a useful tool for this purpose.
- I ask the child to choose colours that match their feelings, and then use those colours to write down their feelings or experience. (This is also an affect regulation intervention.)

- Balance—I use the Taoist symbol for balance, *taijitu* (yin and yang; see Figure 9.3), to teach about balance and the integration of darkness and light.

  The darkness contains some light, and the light contains some darkness. This image becomes a metaphor for acceptance of the whole person, the whole experience and all emotions. It also becomes a metaphor for acceptance and integration of parts of self. Christine Forner explains that "It's crucial to keep in mind that integration is not becoming blended or 'all one,' but rather involves the maintenance of differences while facilitating connection."[17]
- I introduce my clients to the ideas of relaxation and meditation. I use creative meditation, using meditations developed by Christine Forner,[18,19]

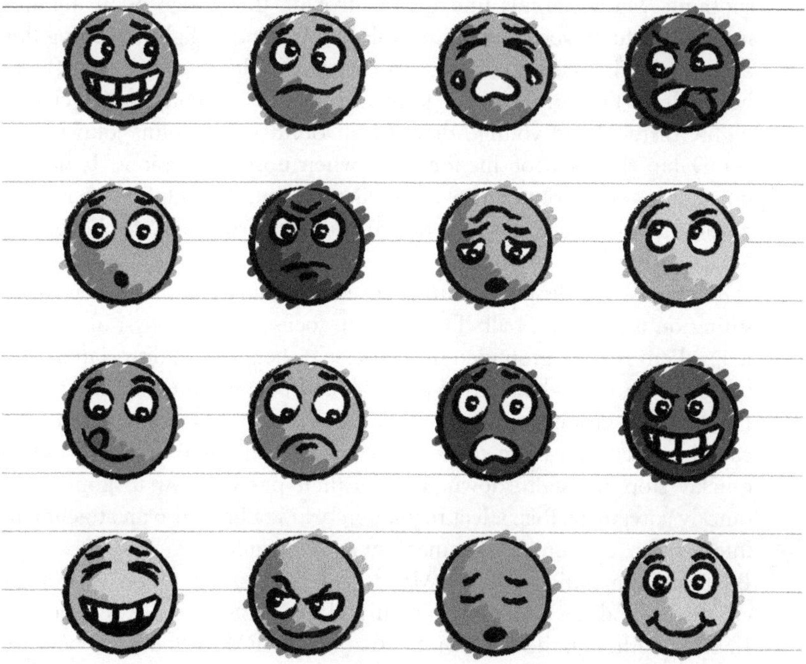

Figure 9.2 Feelings
Credit: iStockphoto

Figure 9.3 Taijitu

for individuals with post-traumatic and dissociative disorders. I do these meditations together with adults and children in the room, and encourage them to practice together at home. (This is also an affect regulation and an attachment intervention.)

- Also based on Christine Forner's work, I use front-brain processing techniques, asking my young clients to experiment with holding imagery in the front of their brain, encouraging frontal lobe development. The area above the nose, between the eyes, is a sensitive area for calming and soothing. Many parents find gently stroking the bridge of an infant's nose is helpful in soothing them to sleep. Stroking or lightly tapping this area can be helpful in calming overreactive children and is thought to help engage the frontal lobe.[20] John and Sophie, both highly dissociated, highly disregulated young adolescents, found this helpful. John would gently tap this area of his forehead when upset in sessions. It helped him not lose control to angry alters. Sophie found it helpful to have her mother gently stroke this part of her forehead when she was becoming anxious or upset.
- With clients who dissociate during sessions, I sometimes have them work sitting on an exercise ball. This need to focus on their physical balance helps them remain grounded in the present, helps avoid dissociation and trance states, and is believed to promote neurological integration.[21]
- I teach basic grounding and coregulation techniques to children and the caregivers. I teach them to notice when they are getting upset, and to quickly stop and calm down. I teach their parents how to notice and quickly coregulate. (See affect regulation below. This is also an attachment intervention, as it involves attunement and coregulation).
- Bilateral Stimulation (BLS)—My use of BLS is based on neurological theory and my experiences with EMDR. BLS is used extensively in EMDR. Although the mechanisms that lead to EMDR's effectiveness are not well understood, there is a wide acceptance based on a large body of research that EMDR is effective in the treatment of trauma.[22,23] My experience with EMDR is that it seems to improve connection between

cognitive and affective processes, so that feelings become more in tune with thoughts. Although there has not been research-supported connection between bilateral stimulation and the success of EMDR, there are certainly similarities between BLS and the eye movements of REM sleep. Dan Siegel describes the bilateral function of REM sleep as necessary to "encode episodic memory into a consolidated form."[24] I often use bilateral stimulation with young people when we are working on connecting their cognitive and affective experiences. I simply ask them to put the EMDR buzzers in their pockets or socks as we explore their emotional and physical reactions to whatever event we are talking about. This use of the buzzers also helps familiarise them with the concept of BLS and makes for an easier move to traditional EMDR when we begin to work on trauma in phase two.

Interventions for Developing Trust

Psychoeducational Interventions for Developing Trust

- I begin with an expression I hear often—"I trust everyone until they give me reason not to." I ask what they think about this idea, and whether they think it makes sense as a means of deciding who to trust. I suggest that this quickly leads to trusting no one, because everyone will give them reason. "All people are human. We are all imperfect. Everyone will let you down sometimes, and you will eventually let down yourself and others." I mention my many flaws, and the ways in which I can't be trusted—being on time, remembering to return phone calls at the right time, keeping my office tidy, etc. I make it clear that these difficulties are my own, and that they are not a reflection of how I value them. I talk about the ways in which I hope I can be trusted—respecting what is important to them, trying to understand their experience and point of view, not hurting them, and taking responsibility for my own mistakes.
- I tell a story from my own adolescence. I often tell it when parents or caregivers are caught between wanting to show their kids that they trust them and thinking they should not allow certain things because of past experience. The story goes something like this: "Teenagers have a way of trying use trust as a weapon. They try to equate trust with love, and will use the words 'You don't trust me!' to get their parents to let them do things that they aren't allowed to do. I remember using that accusation against my dad. He didn't always manage things well, but this time he got it right. His answer was, 'Of course I trust you—I trust you to be a sixteen-year-old girl—and I know exactly what that means!'" I like this story for a lot of reasons. It reflects humanity and fallibility in a way that's normalising. It suggests that trust is not the same as love, and that trust is not owed unconditionally. It also shows that being a kid is not a failing—it is an expectation.

- I mention that I suspect they also have parts of themselves and areas of life that they are not reliable in or good at, and that they likely have areas in which they can be trusted. I explore the idea of trust as being a complex and multilevel experience.

Experiential Interventions for Developing Trust

- Transparency—I do not try to manipulate. I explain step by step what I am doing and what I am trying to achieve as I move forward.
- I explain early and often that I neither expect nor assume trust, because I realise that they have had their trust betrayed.
- Trust Wheel—I developed this tool (Figure 9.4) to explore the complex nature of trust. I use the spokes of the wheel to represent different areas or issues of trust, with each spoke being a grade—from zero at the centre to ten at the outer rim. The way I use the wheel depends on when and how it comes up. I sometimes use myself as an example. If I am working with a young person who has a reasonably good relationship with a caregiver, I may ask them to use it to explore the differences in the ways they trust their

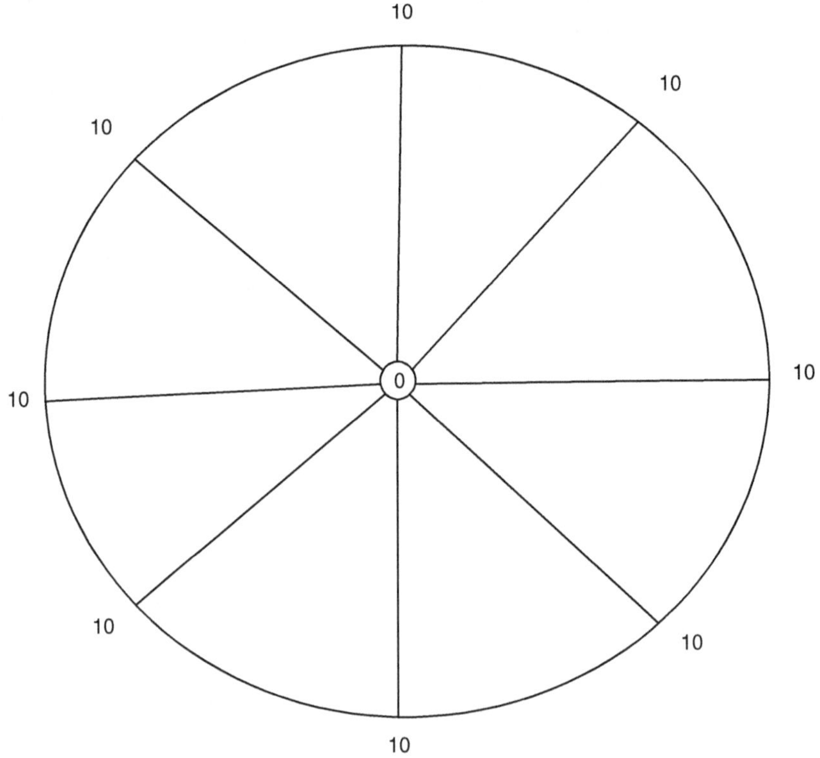

Figure 9.4 Trust Wheel

caregiver, or I use it to explore the ways they think they can be trusted. If the adult is well engaged, I may get them to use the wheel to explore areas they feel they can trust their child, and areas their child is not yet ready or able to manage. This is adaptable, and can be used as a specific tool that directly addresses issues of trust and safety in a relationship, or as a general tool to explain the concept, depending on need and readiness. (This intervention contributes to neurological integration by translating the experiential into the visual, and by increasing the focus on grey areas and multidimensional experience.) There is a full-page copy of the trust wheel in the worksheets section.

- PACE—Dan Hughes's stance of playfulness, acceptance, curiosity and empathy is an intervention that builds trust (Chapter 8). (This is also an intervention for building attachment.) In order to maintain this stance, we need to have good awareness and an ability to deal with our own countertransference experiences. We need to be able to like and empathise with both the adults and the children.
- Shared Direction—Often children and caregivers experience themselves on opposite sides of a battle for control. The reframing of behaviours as symptoms that make sense and the change of focus from behaviours to improved self-control, connection and well-being creates a shared direction instead of a conflict. We can't trust people who are working against us, but we can begin to trust people who are working together with us.

Interventions for Safety

Psychoeducational Interventions for Safety

- Questions around safety and perceived safety can lead to complications in treatment systems. At times, trauma survivors present a risk to themselves and others. Sometimes the perception of this risk leads to punitive and controlling measures; sometimes the underestimation of the danger leaves people at risk. Systems that work with children and adolescents are sometimes risk-avoidant.
- We need to take potential risk seriously, assess it seriously, and help the child or adolescent, their caregivers and their support systems develop realistic safety measures that do not strip the child of their humanity and privacy.
    - Self-Harm vs. Suicide—Many young people engage in self-harm. Many also have thoughts of, and are at risk for, suicide. These are not the same thing. We want to prevent self-harm, and the feeling of needing to self-harm, but we also need to assess whether their actions are intended to be lethal, as well as if they are potentially lethal, even accidentally. A person who is at risk for suicide should be hospitalised. A person who is not suicidal is better helped outside of the hospital. Some facilities take a young person to the hospital every time they

self-harm. Amie was taken to the hospital at least twice a week for several months for injuries that were not suicidal didn't need medical treatment. This is a misuse of the medical system. The result becomes resentment and labelling of traumatised patients, who are viewed as manipulative and treated as such. Another policy is that kids who self-harm can never be left alone with anything with which they can harm themselves. This makes sense on the surface, but the harm done by giving a traumatised girl the "choice" between not shaving her legs and armpits or being supervised while in the shower is greater than the harm done by superficial cutting. Self-harm is often a last refuge for those who feel they have no control over their bodies. Engaging in a power struggle over self-harm is an unwinnable battle.

- In order to effectively protect traumatised young people from harming themselves, we need to have a connection with them. It has to feel safe for them to let us, and their caregivers, know when they are struggling with overwhelming feelings.
- Education of parents and caregivers means helping them understand that self-harm is best prevented by creating a safe, caring, accepting environment, and developing realistic safety plans. Trying to prevent self-harm with control, shame, and punishment can make the self-harm more dangerous or drive it underground, or result in increased alienation.

- Emotion vs. Behaviours—Young trauma clients, their caregivers and the systems that support them need to know and be able to work around the difference between feelings and actions. Being angry is not being violent; getting angry does not make violence OK; expressing anger safely is not wrong, and should not be punished. Being sad, depressed or anxious also does not always lead to self-harm or suicide, and does not always necessitate hypervigilance. Having thoughts or feelings about wanting to lash out, get revenge, or die does not mean the child will harm themselves or someone else.
- Happiness vs. Healing—An understandable confusion for parents and caregivers who have had the experience of a child attempting suicide, or of some other disruptive symptom which has turned the child's and families life upside down. After such an experience, many adults respond by becoming over attentive to their child's emotional states, and becoming anxious, or even angry, when the child is upset. They check on their child, analyse their every response and invade their privacy. Although understandable, these responses increase the child's shame and tell them that their caregiver isn't strong enough to tolerate what they are going through. Young people become "protective" of the adults in their lives. They are protecting themselves from the added burden of caring for the adults feelings as well as their own.
- Communicating Desperation vs. Attention-Seeking—When a young person uses self-harm, suicidal behaviours, or violence and aggression to

communicate that they are desperate, this can lead to their being labelled as "just" attention-seeking. The risk here is in the word *just*. They are desperate to be heard and don't know how to have a voice. If the response becomes ignoring them to "not encourage the behaviour," it reinforces the message that they are not worth compassion, and increases their alienation and desperation, leading to more severe self-harm and aggression or suicide.

- We need to find ways to acknowledge and address the desperation, rather than over-responding to the injury or ignoring the communication altogether.
- When working with young people in these circumstances, we sometimes need to work with the school as well as the caregivers. Creating an alliance within the school system, so that there are some adults who understand the child's pain and can respond with caring and empathy before a situation escalates, can create added safety at school. The alternative of removing or restricting the young person's involvement with the school system should only happen if necessary.

- Dissociation—Helping children, caregivers, and if necessary school supports understand dissociation is critical to safety. A child or adolescent with dissociated alters may not experience themselves as at risk for suicide or for harming others. There may be no indication in therapy, or at home or school, that there is a risk inside. Kalli, my first client with a diagnosed dissociative disorder, once told me, "The outside never matches the inside." Most often, gentle exploration can uncover if such a risk exists. Therapists, parents, caregivers and others need to know it is not enough to check in on how a child is feeling, but that if you also ask, "And how about inside—how are you feeling on the inside? Is there any part of you that might be feeling angry, or frightened, or wanting to die or to hurt you?" the answer you receive can be startlingly different. This is a fairly safe way of asking, because it doesn't assume dissociation. Many children who don't present with dissociated parts have feelings inside that they don't choose to share. If asked in this way, they will usually be open.
  - See Beth and James in Chapter 3 for examples of dangerous dissociated states.

Experiential Interventions for Safety

- Open, nonjudgmental conversations about self-harm, suicidal thoughts and feelings, violence, and the place they hold in the young person's life allow for a new way for the child to communicate and be heard. It's worthwhile to check in individually with the child around safety, but when possible having these conversations with the child and caregiver together helps the child feel supported. The caregiver needs to understand how to listen and be helpful.

- Contracting against Suicide—Some therapists believe that contracting is a good idea, some don't. My experience is that depending on the child, the adult supports and the relationships involved, it can be a helpful part of safety planning, but it doesn't eliminate risk.
    - Contracting against suicide is a relational approach. If we choose to see ourselves as an outside consultant, or a detached and uninvolved professional, a contract between the client and therapist has little meaning. Given that the dynamic between the caregiver and the young person can be loaded and riddled with anger and mistrust at the beginning, a contract between them could backfire. A young person may be quite sincere around contracting, but their emotional state can change. Someone who truly wants to be dead may lie when asked to contract around safety, or when we are assessing for risk.
    - Because contracting is relational, when I do use contracting, I don't shy away from the relational aspect. If the child or adolescent is impacted by the new experience of being heard, felt and understood, then we may discuss the reasons why suicide is not an option. With clients who have an ability to engage and relate, I routinely ask for a commitment to stay alive as a part of the treatment frame. I clarify that the work we are doing involves entering into a relationship where we become connected to each other, and that relationships involve mutual responsibility for the impact of our actions on others. I find that only older adolescents have the ego strength for this type of conversation, but that for those who do, it can be helpful.
    - Related to contracting against risk is asking the young person to scale their commitment to stay alive. Again, this can be fallible, as they may not be honest, and their state of mind can change depending on what happens between sessions.
    - When contracting or scaling, we need to stay aware of possible dissociated parts or self-states, and ensure that their answers are included in conversations and agreements.

- Hope—Helping young clients have hope is a good defense against suicide. Once they have the experience that someone can hear and "get" them, that their caregiver may be able to find new ways to understand them, that they can have more control over their actions, and once they learn that their difficulties are symptoms that can be dealt with and changed, they find new hope and have less need for an escape plan from life. Hope can be given by hearing and understanding their pain, and by helping their caregivers do the same; by helping them see that relationships, connection and safety are possible. I want both the child and the adults to leave each session with something new, because this creates hope.
- Safety Planning—When there is a risk of self-harm, suicide or aggression, safety planning in the first few sessions helps. An ideal safety plan is based on the child's needs and abilities, as well as available resources.

- As developing a plan involves insight and trust, the plan will evolve over time. In the beginning it may include early identification of emotional escalation, basic grounding, coregulation and soothing techniques, and who to call in an emergency.
- Code Words—The child and parent can identify safe code words to use if the child or the adult notices that the child is getting overwhelmed or upset. This is useful in public situations such as family events, shopping or schools. The word can be used as a signal to the caregiver or a teacher that the child needs support or to be assisted in leaving the situation, or a signal from an adult that the child is beginning to look distressed and can rely on the adult for grounding and assistance.
- A particular code word or gesture can be identified for a young person to tell their caregiver or teacher that they are suicidal if they don't feel they can say so directly.
- The adult should plan with the child, and possibly rehearse, what response the child will feel is helpful. A child worried about a parent being angry might need a calm reaction, but a child worried about their distress being minimised or dismissed may feel invalidated by too much calm.
- Door number one, door number two, and door number three requests. A child can use this to identify the type of help they need, and the parent should try, within the limits of safety, to respect the child's wishes. A door number one request means listen reflectively so the child can express their feelings; a door number two request means listen and help by offering some ideas or suggestions; a door number three request means that the child is overwhelmed, and they need the adult to take over and solve the problem.
- Triggers—It's helpful to begin to identify triggers which may lead to a flashback or escalation.
- Planning—Adults and children can work together to plan for situations that might be challenging, such as a birthday, outing or first day of the new school year.
- Identified Safe People—The child and caregiver should identify who the child can turn to for help when they begin to get triggered or overwhelmed. There may be a variety of safe people in different situations. At home, it may be a caregiver. If they are looking only for support and a listening ear, it could be a peer or a sibling. In a dangerous situation they should be encouraged to talk to a supportive adult. Sometimes traumatised and alienated adolescents have been creative in developing their own support circles. James (see Chapter 3), although alienated from most of the adults in his life, was well-supported by a group of friends. He was rarely alone at school, and if difficult situations arose, his friends would surround him and help him feel safe. In this way, he managed for years to maintain control of his dissociative switching—a secret that his friends were aware of. Once he engaged

in therapy, James was able to identify staff at school who had been supportive. I met with this group to develop a plan that involved his friends and supportive teachers.

- Emergency Supports—Even with excellent planning, emergencies happen. Unexpected events may trigger a flashback or panic attack; a bad day for the child or caregiver could lead to conflict that escalates; bullying at school, rejection by a peer or partner, or unplanned contact with an abuser can lead to sudden suicidal ideation. Attachment difficulties inevitably mean that the young person will not always turn to their support people for help. Struggles over control, secrecy, peer conflict and many other issues will happen, and will lead to anger, shame and fear. If a situation becomes too risky, the caregiver needs to know who to contact and what to say. Crisis support services, emergency psychiatric services and the police can be called if a situation is out of control and dangerous. These services are not best designed to deal with traumatised children, and should be used only in emergencies. It's possible to build community supports through family, friends and neighbors if the relationships are close and the child or adolescent feels supported rather than shamed. I don't recommend that adults physically contain a child. This can lead to extreme escalations and dangerous situations. It can also retraumatise the child, who is out of their window of tolerance and not feeling safe.
- Coregulation Skills—I teach the parent and child basic grounding and coregulation skills in the first and second session. (See "Interventions for Affect Regulation" below.) These skills are important for managing risk of self-harm, suicide and aggression.
- Affect Regulation Skills (see below for more)—Most of our young clients will not always be with a parent, caregiver or support person. I also teach basic self-regulation skills in the first and second session.
- XYZ Strategies—I did not originate this technique, and unfortunately, I don't know who did. I haven't been able to identify an original source, and it seems not to have been published. This useful technique was shared with me years ago by a colleague who got it from a workshop at an ISST-D conference. An adapted version of the strategy sheet is included in the worksheets section.

    - The client agrees to engage in their choice of three activities, one from column X, one from column Y and one from column Z, *before* engaging in self-harm. (I have also used this for coping with urges to engage in other self-destructive behaviours such as substance abuse or online sex.) Column X involves **communicating** the overwhelming emotions or experiences with another person or through artwork or writing. Column Y includes an assortment of safe **endorphin-releasing activities**. Column Z activities are self-**soothing** or seeking soothing from a support person or pet. They must engage in one of each type of behaviour for a minimum of fifteen minutes each. They are not told not to self-harm. The control is theirs. Most often, these agreed-on behaviour techniques remove the felt need to self-harm and teach new ways of coping.

- Assessing and Understanding Risks Associated with Dissociation—When we are working with young people who want to connect and want to stay alive, the biggest risk to safety may come from dissociation. It's not unusual to have a few sessions with a committed, motivated young person who is willing to work hard, only to have their caregiver report back that the child suddenly became aggressive, suicidal or terrified, and refused to engage in or respond to any strategies. As mentioned earlier, first attempts at assessing for dissociation may not be successful. The young person may not be aware of dissociative symptoms, or they may not be ready to share them. When there are dissociated alters, there is often one or more part that is invested in maintaining secrecy, and doesn't want the child to talk about them. These are often parts that are identified as "bad," and they may threaten or harm the child for talking about them, or for talking to a therapist at all. These are also often parts that engage in self-harm, suicidal behaviours or aggression towards others.

    - When there are dissociated parts, we need to involve them in safety planning. Sometimes this is easy; sometimes it's vague and confusing. You may not be sure what you are dealing with, or if there are other parts, or how many, or what they are like. Sometimes the child's answers will change daily or even minute by minute. The child does not always know, and may not be sure how much to let you know. If there is a possibility of dissociation, it's better to be safe, and to phrase things to all inside parts, feelings or voices.
    - It's a good idea during early sessions to ask if there are any dangerous, bad or negative feelings or angry voices inside. The child can be asked to take a quiet moment and listen inside, to see what happens.
    - If this direct questioning gets a response, which it often does, it's possible to talk through the child to the other part or parts around what they need to maintain safety. Although the parts may not respond to the idea of safety, there's something that they will negotiate for. For dissociated self-states, it's often possible to set up an internal space where they can enjoy themselves, deal with frustration or anger, and feel better.

        - The kind of space chosen is a key to understanding the part better. Some parts choose a room with video games and climbing equipment, others choose an outside space with animals or dinosaurs. Some may choose a playroom and others may choose a weight room with a heavy punching bag.

- All parts are protective in function, even if they or the child aren't aware of it. It's necessary to build an alliance with the darkest or angriest parts early on. This doesn't have to involve direct conversation with parts—it can involve reassuring the young person, "talking through," and asking to make sure that all parts are listening—that you are not there to get rid of or make parts go away. All parts have an important voice; you are interested in what they have to say. Often the child will experience or hear a dismissing or minimising comment or feeling towards this, but don't be discouraged. This is a necessary part of negotiating. They may prefer not to appear interested.
- When the parts dismiss the therapist, it's a good idea to let the child or adolescent know that that's OK, or even good. They are there to protect the child. They are doing their job by not trusting you.

Interventions for Shame

Psychoeducational Interventions for Shame

- I always have the Compass of Shame (see Chapter 5) on a whiteboard in my office, and I explain it early and often. I explain that shame is a necessary emotion; we all have it, but that for children who experience early trauma and attachment issues, shame often becomes much bigger. I engage them and their caregivers in figuring out where on the compass their behaviours and avoidance strategies fit.

Experiential Interventions for Shame

- I often stop during sessions and ask if there is something from the board that is happening, or that explains what we are talking about. I might say something like, "Hey—you just changed the subject—do you think that fits somewhere on the compass?" or, "Hey—I suddenly feel like making an excuse to leave the room—do you think that fits on the compass?" or, "I noticed that as soon as your mom asked you that question you started acting mad, and you said something kind of mean—where does that go?"
- Reframing behaviours as symptoms and normalising trauma symptoms as an understandable and expected outcome of trauma helps kids feel less shame for their behaviours, and their caregivers feel less like they have failed.
- Acceptance and Dialectical Thinking—When we accept people for who they are and assume they've done the best they could in the situation they were in, we decrease shame. Attachment theory suggests that unconditional love in infancy is the beginning of a positive sense of self. The children we work with haven't had this. This creates shame. When we show,

and help the caregiver to show, joy over being with a child, and unconditional acceptance of who they are, we begin to correct this experience.

- As we work on building a more secure attachment, we are working towards helping the caregiver have increased empathy and more positive attributions towards the child or adolescent. This reduces the child's shame.
- When possible, it's helpful to provide insight to the school, so that teachers and staff have a better understanding and experience of the young person. As more people see them as hurt and frightened children rather than mean, manipulative or dishonest ones, the young people begin to have a different experience of themselves.

Interventions for Affect Regulation

Psychoeducational Interventions for Affect Regulation

- Development of Affective Language—I use a number of different child-friendly tools, such as feelings cards with pictures showing body language and facial expressions, feelings thermometers (included as a worksheet), charts (Figure 9.2, this chapter), lists and scaling exercises to assess and grow child's awareness and expression of emotional states.
- Emotional Education—It's important to teach young clients, and often also the adults in their lives, that emotions are important. There are no "bad" feelings. We need them all. Many people have the idea that anger is "bad" and that it isn't OK to feel or express it. Many of the kids we work with identify feeling or admitting fear as a weakness. Lots of people don't like to feel vulnerable. I talk about why our emotions developed and what we need them for. Fear and anger are emergency emotions. They help us respond in an emergency, and make us stronger and faster, although they also make us more impulsive and less clear-thinking. Sadness helps us value connection and relationships, and leads us to lean on others for closeness and support. Shame helps us learn right from wrong, and encourages us to repair damaged relationships.
- I go through a deck of feelings cards with a child and caregiver, and we talk about different feelings, what their purposes might be, and what kinds of situations they come up in. I ask questions about what emotions feel like in their bodies, to begin to get them thinking about the connections between emotions and feelings. (This is also a neurological integration intervention.)
- Education about the window of tolerance and the impact of "emergency" emotions on processing experience. We usually talk about how in an emergency, your body starts to work better and faster, but you don't think things through as much—when you are being chased by a tiger, you don't want to be stopping to think about the best response; you want to respond quickly. I also talk about the "freeze" effect and the reasons why it might be helpful for our bodies to shut down if we are not able to either fight or flee.

- While working with kids around affective education, I try to have their caregiver in the room. This allows everyone to have and share thoughts and ideas. Many adults are uncomfortable with children expressing anger, and this allows for conversations about the differences between feelings and actions, and ways of managing anger that are safe and acceptable. We come up with a list of ways that it is OK to express or process anger, fear, sadness or other feelings that are difficult.
- Emotion/Body Connection—I use many techniques to help children and adults to connect emotional experiences to physical reactions. Body scans can be done with or without hypnotic inductions. I often stop and ask, "What are you feeling in your body right now?" I reflect on body language, noticed tension, rigid postures, facial expressions, etc. I use a pulsometer to check heart rates, sometimes several times during a session, to help children and adults notice differences in how their body responds to emotional states, relaxation or meditation. A stress map can be a fun tool (see Figures 9.5a and 9.5b). The child can use stickers, or colour in areas, to identify the different places in their bodies they feel happiness, sadness, excitement, anger, fear, worry or any other emotion that is being talked about. (This intervention also promotes neurological connection, as it focuses on the connection between emotions and sensations.) The boys' and girls' stress maps are included in the worksheet section.

Experiential Interventions for Affect Regulation

- It's important to remember, and to remind parents and children, that some of these techniques take time to master, and some of them, in the beginning, may take a lot of time each time they are used. During periods of escalation, flashback, fear or anger, grounding and fractionated processing can require a lot of stopping, soothing and grounding, several times over. When talking about it the first time, parents sometimes object to how long it may take. I remind them that even if it takes a very long time to get anywhere the first few times, the meltdowns, tantrums and arguments take a very long time, and are more damaging. Escalations often happen when caregivers are stressed for time, and feel unable to stop and focus on the child. This happens for all parents. When it happens with our clients, it leads to a lot of stress and often no one is on time. This may be the choice between spending an hour slowing down and fractionating a response and being an hour late for work in the morning, or spending an hour dealing with a meltdown and being an hour late, distressed and exhausted.
- Grounding Techniques—Grounding techniques are emergency techniques for calming down when hyperaroused. For individuals with dissociative disorders or flashbacks, grounding is used to stay physically and emotionally connected to their bodies, in the room, in the present time. For those with anxiety disorders, grounding techniques are used to calm anxiety and panic attacks. Grounding techniques are a common facet of phase one

Figure 9.5a Stress Map—Boys
Credit: iStockphoto

Figure 9.5b Stress Map—Girls
Credit: iStockphoto

trauma treatment. In this model, I teach grounding techniques as coregulation when possible. The kids we work with have dealt with overwhelming experiences alone for too long. I work towards them accepting coregulation from a parent and caregiver, so that they can rely on someone to help them ground themselves and feel safer. I often teach grounding techniques to children and their parents in the first session. This is a useful tool that helps them feel immediately more in control. I remind them it will take practice and not work every time. One of the difficulties with using grounding as a coregulation process is that when angry, young people may react to suggestions as external control. Mentioning this in the session, when everyone is calm, helps avoid it. I say something like, "This is something you guys can try together at home. Remember, when you get upset, this is something you, Mom, are doing together to try and help Sandra be in control of herself. Sandra, a lot of kids at first feel like this is a trick to control them—it's normal to feel that, but if you get caught up in it, it'll get in your way. Remind yourself that you want to change this too. Let's try to think of it as a way your mom can hand you control of yourself. Mom—remember, don't try to force it—it might take a few tries, and it doesn't work if you're the one in control of it. It's OK if it doesn't work at first. It takes time."

- I want to keep grounding simple, guided and multisensory—the more parts of the brain involved the better!
- PACE—I encourage parents to work on maintaining a stance of playfulness, acceptance, curiosity and empathy[25] when their child escalates. This is tremendously difficult, but goes a long way when they can maintain it. Although playfulness is effective in grounding situations, I am cautious that the child or adolescent not feel laughed at or belittled. PACE is not sarcastic. Because remaining calm is difficult, I will sometimes meet with parents alone to teach them some basic affect regulation skills around grounding and self-control.
- Remaining calm does not mean dull or lacking in emotion. The caregiver needs to learn how to match the intensity of their child's emotional experience, without mirroring the same emotion. For instance, if the child is afraid, the caregiver does not want to be afraid, but they do want to match the intensity of their calming presence to their child's fear.[26] They can think of feeling intense love, or protection, or caring, as matching emotions. It is the energy and pace of the response that is matched.
- I guide caregivers through noticing early signs of reaction, so the child hasn't escalated or dissociated by the time they intervene.
- I ask the child and caregiver to start looking for "transition moments."[27] These are the moments before dissociation or loss of control. Identifying these moments helps identify triggers and the beginning of improved self-control.
- I teach body awareness about anger and fear responses, asking children, adolescents and adults to pay attention to breathing and heart

rate, muscle tension and restlessness. I use a basic pulsometer to experiment with heart rate while talking about experiences, and doing relaxation exercises.

- I teach deep breathing and progressive relaxation to slow the release of adrenaline.
- The first stage of coregulation with grounding exercises, when the parent or young person notices that they are getting activated, is to draw their attention to something sensory. I begin with something simple like having the parent say, "Quick—find five things in the room that are red, and name them out loud." Next, widen the sensory experience—"Focus on all of your senses—what can you feel, smell, taste, and hear?"
- If the child can tolerate it, the parent can direct them to make eye contact with them, and then guide them through some slow deep breathing to slow the release of adrenaline. If they can't tolerate eye contact, the parent can have them focus on the sound of their voice, and then guide them through breathing exercises.
- I improve the ability to tolerate eye contact and coregulation by having the parent and child do mirroring exercises in my office. At first I use these during moments of connection. Later I use them when the child is slightly activated or upset.
- I encourage children and their caregivers to have some squishy balls around and to play catch as part of grounding—I do this in my office as well. It's difficult to play catch and not be in your body and in the room.
- Sometimes holding something like a cold drink, focusing on the physical sensations, and then taking a sip and focusing on the taste is a good grounding technique.
- When young people are aware of dissociation, I teach them Jim Knipe's Back of the Head Scale.[28] The scale works like this: "If the back of your head is zero, and out here in the room is 10, where are you right now?" Obviously this is a pretty subjective scale, but each person can figure out what their best spot is for being connected to their body and in the room—most of the kids I work with settle on somewhere between 6 and 8. Once they know their number, they can use it as a way of gauging how connected or disconnected they feel.
- When children are already activated, escalated or dissociated, it can be harder to help them ground. If they are responding to a conflict, argument or control with their parent or caregiver, this can also make it more difficult to engage them. Once the child has reached "meltdown," the focus becomes on creating and maintaining safety, and regaining calm.
- A child in an escalated or dissociated state is outside their window of tolerance. They can't process information, think clearly, negotiate or problem solve. They may appear to be making decisions and choices, but the decisions aren't based in rational thought, they are based on

an emotional and physical response to the triggering of "emergency" states. This means that their primary goal is to remain in control of the situation in order to stay safe. It doesn't matter if there is no danger—they are in a state of hyperarousal, and will respond *as if* there was danger. Rage is as much of a protective response as terror.

- The only goals in this situation are to maintain safety and regain calm. This can't be done by reason, arguing or controlling the child. A battle for control, particularly a physical one, will heighten the experience of emergency and intensify their need to maintain control. The outcome will be for the child either to exhaust themselves or to enter a collapsed shut-down state. Both are the result of emotionally and neurologically overwhelming experiences, resulting in increased activation of traumatic neural pathways. In other words, they are retraumatising.

- There are times when physical safety takes priority. Using safe, planned strategies for calming the child is best whenever possible. If the situation isn't dangerous, the parent may have to attempt to soothe and wait it out. If it is dangerous I encourage caregivers to involve emergency services. Physically restraining an overwhelmed traumatised child is retraumatising and dangerous.
- It may seem that the child's outburst is related to some small difficulty, or a conflict around behaviour or rules. Adults see this as a strategic attempt to get their own way. The child may even agree or come across as boastful over being able to win their caregiver over. Even when the child reacts in this way, engaging in this type of attribution around the child's outbursts will lead to frustration and power struggles.
- A more likely and useful understanding is that the child experiences not getting their way, or getting consequences for behaviour as being powerless, which acts as a trigger for previous trauma memories.
- If these early memories are disconnected, disremembered or dissociated, the child is not sure what they are responding to.
- The result is a child who will fight literally or almost literally to the death over an issue that seems minor.
- Josh, seven, would fly into a rage when asked to come to the dinner table. Afterwards he would remember nothing, and be distressed, and confused by the damage he had caused. Prior to moving in with his mother six months earlier, Josh had lived with his father and his partner. Dad's partner had been controlling, harshly critical and physically abusive. While on visits, his mom had been the "fun weekend parent." They had few structures and routines, and his father had not needed to parent him around daily routines. They used to eat dinner in front of the TV, on the porch or in the park, or at McDonalds. As soon as Josh's mom was given emergency custody of Josh, she realised she would need to become the daily parent. Josh responded to limits

and expectations as triggers. He had only ever been told what to do by people who had hurt him.

- Responding with anger, hurt, fear or "firmness" will not de-escalate the child. Yelling, shouting or getting in the child's face may seem to de-escalate them. If the adult is bigger and the child is startled or frightened, their fight response may deactivate because their instincts tell them this is a fight they can't win. This doesn't mean they are calm, it means they have gone into a fear/flight response or a different dissociative state and shut down. Either way, they are outside of their window of tolerance and unable to process or make sense of what has happened. They are not soothed.
- I recommend caregivers try to engage their melting-down child calmly and lovingly, initially from a safe distance. There will not be a quick de-escalation, but it leads to fewer and milder meltdowns over time.
    - The adult needs to work to maintain PACE. They need to be calm, loving and empathic, while still matching the intensity of their response to the child's state.
    - The adult should not enter into the child's space—a person in a state of rage or fear will lash out if someone gets into their space. The adult needs to stay close enough to be heard and to try to engage the child visually. If they can, they can encourage the child to make eye contact.
    - If the child is raging, the adult should maintain a reasonably safe physical distance. If the child is frightened, the parent can get fairly close, get down to the child's eye level, and speak calmly.
    - The adult then needs to gently and slowly create grounding and safety. Identify that the child is angry, or frightened, or terrified, but that they are safe, and that the first job is to keep them and others safe.
    - Something like this might work: "You're mad. It feels like I'm pushing you around, and that freaks you out. First we need to calm down, and then we can find a solution. You're safe—nobody is going to hurt you. I'm going to stay here and keep you safe. I wish I could hug you but that might not be OK to you yet—so I'm going to hug you in my mind and my heart. When you want me to hold you, or just to come closer to you, let me know. Now, look around the room, see and feel where you are and who you are with. Take some deep breaths—take all the time you need—we can manage this together."
    - If the child says terrible things, or is mean or threatening, or even if the child is just really angry at the caregiver, they can try something like, "Wow—how horrible to be this mad at somebody who you sometimes need (or like). That must make it even harder!"
    - If the child is frightened, something like this might work: "You're really scared right now. Getting scared suddenly happens. Look

around you and notice where you are. Do you know who I am? Can you look at my eyes and hear my voice? I'm going to keep you safe. Nobody here is going to hurt you."

- Some children get very angry, without it being clear what the trigger is. If an adult doesn't know, they shouldn't assume. They can try something like, "You're really upset. Something happened that really set you off. Do you know who I am? Can you look at my eyes and hear my voice?" Let's work on getting a bit calmer, and maybe we can figure out what to do next."
- During meltdowns we need to be cautious with the playfulness in PACE. Playfulness can have a role in grounding, but it has to be well-understood and supportive. It depends on the nature of the relationships, but also on the child's trauma history. It's important that the child not feel like the adult is talking down to, belittling or making fun of them—the caregiver needs to try to connect to how hard it really must be for the child to feel what they are feeling.
- If possible, the caregiver could try to involve some kind of calming ritual, like music. Sam's grandmother once sat outside Sam's door, singing the songs she sang when Sam was a little boy. At first, Sam would close the door and go back to throwing things around, but his grandmother kept singing, slowly nudging the door with her foot. Sam calmed, and eventually came and laid his head in his grandmother's lap. This took about an hour. Sam did continue to struggle with traumatic memories and internal conflicts, but he had no more explosive meltdowns. They had been happening weekly for a year.
- Fractionated Processing—Rick Kluft has developed the concept of fractionated abreaction as a means of processing and integrating overwhelming memories of traumatic experiences.[29] The idea of fractionating any experience which could lead to emotional overwhelm is useful. Although working through traumatic memories can be challenging for children and adolescents, I find that in the beginning, it is the experience of being "parented" that can be the greatest trigger.
- Fractionated processing is slow at first, but it pays off. The goal is to help the child stay within their window of tolerance and to stop and regain calm and grounding as soon as anger or fear start to happen. A pattern that many caregivers share is that they ask their child to do something, such as brush their teeth or do their homework. The child delays, and eventually, there is an argument. The argument escalates and the child becomes explosive. A variation is that the child explodes as soon as they are told to do something. The same can happen when trying to address a problem. Part of the difficulty is that the parent tries to push through

the child's resistance. In fractionated processing, as soon as there is resistance or escalation they stop and coregulate before moving on. It goes something like this:

- Dad—"I'm just letting you know the school called today and told us you've been skipping third period. We're going to have to talk about it—would you feel better talking about it now or in twenty minutes"?
- Kid—"I haven't been skipping—they screwed up." (already getting angry)
- Dad—"Sometimes that happens. We're not going to freak out, let's take a bit to calm down, and we can talk in a bit."
- Dad—(twenty minutes later) "OK, this kind of thing gets everyone pretty stressed out—are you feeling tense in your body or butterflies in your stomach or anything?"
- Kid—"I feel kind of sick."
- Dad— "I hate feeling that way too—let's take a few deep breaths, and we can start—we don't have to finish right away if we get upset. Third period is math, isn't it?"
- Kid—"Yeah, my math teacher hates me. She talks to me like I'm stupid."
- Dad—"Hmm—I might not want to go either."
- Kid—"I told you—I wasn't skipping—she's just picking on me."
- Dad—(after a break to reground) Now—how do we solve this—are you saying you've never skipped? Should we go in and talk to her about it together?"
- Kid—"Well, I've probably missed a few, but I went yesterday and today, I swear!"
- Dad—"OK, well, how about if we take a break for a bit, watch a half hour of TV together, and then we come up with a plan?. . . . . . .

- This kind of approach has worked with many kids who have struggled with addressing issues or talking about problems.
- Collaborative Problem Solving—Going along with fractionated processing is collaborative problem solving. It is more effective, at least in the beginning, if done in sessions. Kids are more likely to resist the conversation at home. They may also think that their parents won't follow through, and so they like having the therapist as witness. When kids are resistant to rules, chores, curfews or consequences, I ask them how they would solve the problem. First I check with the parents if it's OK if I get involved in the conversation. I'm not getting involved in the rules; I'm getting involved in solving an argument. The rules have nothing to do with me, and I don't set or enforce them. I then start the conversation alone with the child or teenager. I ask them what

they think makes sense around rules or chores. They often come up with ideas that are not that far off from their parents, and they almost never suggest anything unreasonable. Then I bring the parents in and we negotiate a plan. The plan is agreed on in session, and they go home to try it out. It's rarely smooth, and I point out that the young person is still likely to get angry or resistant, but if they work on calming down anytime getting upset *starts*, things will go better.

- Hypnosis—For therapists trained in hypnosis, it is an invaluable tool for affect regulation. Some clients are afraid of hypnosis, but most often this is a misunderstanding of what it is and how it works. I explain that all hypnosis is self-hypnosis, and that I will be teaching them how to hypnotise themselves. I also tell them that I include, early and repeatedly through the induction, that they remain completely in control of their actions and responses. There are many scripts for affect regulation. Carolyn Daitch has written a useful book, *Affect Regulation Toolbox*,[30] that has many techniques to pick and choose from and to tailor to your individual clients' needs. I use hypnosis for teaching affect regulation skills both to kids and to caregivers. I sometimes put these scripts on a recording that young people and their parents can use at home for relaxation. Some of the scripts I use are:
    - Body Scan—I teach all my young people and most of their caregivers how to do a body scan in order to identify areas of tension in their body and to begin to identify when they are beginning to feel stress.
    - Safe Place—The creation of a safe internal place which someone can use as a resource for staying calm when frightened or angry. For those who can't conceive of safety, a calm or soothing place is an option. I usually include the suggestion "This is your own place, inside of you, where nothing bad has ever happened and nothing bad can ever happen because it is yours and yours alone!"
    - Dialing Down Reactivity[31]—The creation of an internal imaginary dial for changing the degree of stress or anxiety they are feeling.
    - The Tight Fist[32]—I combine this with the body scan—once they have identified areas of stress in their body, I have them imagine that the stress is a coloured gas. They then make a fist, and as they make the fist, they begin to notice the gas moving through their body towards their fist, as their fist gets tighter and tighter. Once all the gas has reached their fist and arm, they can release their fist and allow all of the stress to pour out of their hand and through the floor.
    - Cleansing Breathing—This is a variation on "Breathing in the Light"[33]—again combined with the body scan and similar to the tight fist, after they have identified the areas of stress and imagined them as a coloured gas, they then imagine that the air around them is a cool, cleansing blue colour. With each focused, deep breath in, they

imagine the cool blue air entering their body, entering their blood, flowing through their body, and washing it clean of all the stress. With each breath out, more of the stress leaves their body.

    - Hypnotic Eye Roll—Usually used as the beginning of a standard hypnotic induction, the eye roll and deep breath quickly decreases reactivity and induces a sense of calm.

- Anger Outlets—

    - Anger has a purpose. During phase two, it will be important to work on connecting anger to experiences. Before this can happen, our clients and caregivers need to find ways to cope with anger. Controlling it and calming down help, but anger leads to the release of adrenaline in our bodies, creating physical stress. Many people believe that anger is "bad" or that expressing anger is "bad." A lot of abuse victims equate anger with violence. They've been hurt by people who have been angry, they've been hurt for getting angry, and they've hurt people when they were angry. There is a gender difference in what we are taught about anger. Some girls and women struggle more with anger. Suppressed anger is connected to headaches, stomach and digestive difficulties such as irritable bowel syndrome, muscle and joint difficulties, body pain, high blood pressure and heart disease. Working with anger in dyadic therapy is complex, and involves helping adults and the children understand dialectical thinking. The experience of anger is not, and does not need to be, connected to right and wrong. The child does not need to be "in the right" to have the right to be angry. This applies whether the child is angry at the caregiver, someone else, or the situation. The caregiver can hear, understand, empathise with and support the child's feelings, even if they do not agree with their point of view. A child will sometimes struggle with feeling they don't have the "right" to be angry. Some parents hope that therapy will help the child understand that the parent was not at fault, so that they won't be angry at them anymore. This may happen, but first, the parent needs to be able to hear the child's anger, and support their entitlement to their feelings. This is part of the division between left and right brain. What we feel does not always match what we know or think, and we need to experience and explore the feelings before we can connect them to what we know. Seven-year-old Jim insightfully announced, "I know that my dad is here for me and won't ever leave me again. I just can't believe it." His dad has no intention of leaving, but was able to understand how angry Jim was that he hadn't been there to protect him, and how hard it now is to trust him.
    - There are ways to release anger that aren't violent. Not every way works for everyone. Some people need a physical release, some people need an emotional release, and some need to make noise or break

something. Experiment with different techniques to find a few that work. We are working with anger, not violence. We want to help the child release anger, but we want to ensure containment and safety. It's important to try to be aware of dissociated angry parts, because releasing these parts without a safety plan can leave the child out of control and frightened. It can also result in someone getting hurt.

- During the expression of anger, it's helpful if the caregiver can be present to support. Much of the child's anger is directed towards caregivers. This may be because a caregiver has had some role in the child's trauma, or it may be that this is the way the child perceived their experiences. It may be because the child holds the caregiver responsible for not having kept them safe. It may simply be because the child, mistrusting adults, does not acknowledge the adult's right to authority over them. If the anger being expressed is towards the caregivers, their ability to hear, experience and support their child's expression of anger, and even to join in, validates the child's experiences. If the anger is directed elsewhere, the caregivers may share the anger and support their child by showing this.
- A number of years ago I worked with a family from South America. Nada and Juan had had to leave their home suddenly, in the middle of the night. They left their daughter with grandparents, planning to send for them in a few weeks. Several years had passed before they could get their daughter to Canada, by which time they had had two more children. The long-dreamed-of reunion was not what they had imagined. Maria had been sexually abused by a neighbor and physically abused by her grandparents following her parents' disappearance. She was traumatised, enraged at her parents for having left her, and jealous and resentful of her younger siblings. One day, while doing dishes, Maria dropped a coffee cup in the sink and it shattered. One by one, she picked up the cups and glasses, smashing them in the sink. When her parents came to the kitchen, Maria stood crying and terrified in front of a sink of broken dishes, expecting to be beaten. When her mother asked her what happened, Maria responded, "I broke all the cups." Her mother answered with "Why didn't you call us—we would have helped you!" This unexpected playful, attuned, curious and empathetic response broke down a barrier and led to a solution. Maria and her parents laughed together for the first time, and then created a ritual just for the three of them. They began to buy used dishes at junk stores and flea markets. Once a week they would meet in the basement, and tape newspaper to the cement wall and floor. Then safely, but loudly, they would take turns smashing dishes and yelling the many things that they were all angry about that had happened in their lives. Maria's anger towards her parents, and their anger towards her mistreatment of her siblings, was transformed into a shared anger at the war their government, and her abusers, which they expressed together

as a family. Maria's anger towards her parents was also expressed, but they were able to hear it. They were angry at themselves for having left their daughter, even though they all knew they had had no choice.

- Obviously this is not the release for everyone, but for children and families who have space and some ability to regulate; it can be helpful. What makes this example so wonderful is that it was organic. It arose spontaneously out of Maria's momentary loss of control. Instead of responding with negative attributions around bad behaviour, or with anger and punishment, her parents were able to respond with PACE. This story occurred long before I had ever heard of PACE. These caring, loving and attuned parents who were able to respond in the moment in a way that was helpful to them and to their daughter.
- Other types of physical release exercises that can be helpful involve tearing up old towels and sheets, freezing trays of ice and smashing the ice, using a punching bag, punching a pillow or bed, and physical exercise. One family renovating their home involved their child in the demolition of several walls, which they tore down together. This involved her in the rebuilding of the home the family shared together.
- Some young people find release in sports or athletic activities. If they are able to do so safely, and don't get involved in fights on the field or excessive aggression during sparring, these are excellent outlets that teach containment and self-control while providing mastery and achievement.
- Several families I've worked with who have outdoor space have trampolines. The safe use of a trampoline is an excellent release of adrenaline, can be playful and can help build physical mastery.
- Releasing adrenaline and anger does not need to take the form of breaking, smashing or tearing. For many clients, this is helpful. For others, there are other ways that help. Imagery, writing, artwork and use of voice all have a role. In all of these, there can be a role for the adult as supportive witness, listener and empathic sharer. When working on anger in sessions, I find it helpful to support the child in using as many different neurological capacities as possible. For example, encouraging a child to write down all the angry words that seem to fit how they are feeling, but to do so using different colours that they choose, and then to read their list out loud. I ask them to pay attention to how their body feels before, during and after expressing anger.
- Many children have angry, violent images in their heads that frighten their caregivers. I've been called to many school meetings about children who draw violent pictures or write violent stories. Sometimes they've use names of peers who have bullied them or teachers who have misunderstood them. These situations could be reason for alarm, and need to be followed up, but they could also be an outlet for the child to express their anger and alienation safely. There is a difference between fantasizing revenge and planning it.

In these circumstances we need to check what the child's intent is, without judging the anger. Was this a private expression that was found accidentally or intrusively, or was there intent to frighten or intimidate? Does the child plan to harm someone, or were they expressing anger after feeling harmed or excluded? This is another situation in which dissociation should be explored. Does the child remember writing the story and why? Are there parts inside the child that have different intentions than the part you are speaking to? If there are dissociated parts that are angry and considering acting on their anger, what measures can be taken to ensure safety? (See interventions for safety, above.) Once safety is established, if the child has a clear understanding about the difference between imagining and doing, this use of fantasy can be an outlet for anger. Again I encourage the use of voice, colour, imagery, written or drawn expression, and body awareness in order to create as integrated an experience as possible.

- Music—Listening to music or writing, creating or playing music forms a good outlet for many. Music, particularly when played, is an integrative experience.[34]
- As important as anger outlets are, timing is important. Nobody can control when anger happens. Because of fear and control issues around bedtimes, nightmares and night-related traumas, power struggles and escalations at bedtime are common. It's important to try to avoid this (see below for sleep issues), and not to plan activities around releasing anger too close to bedtime. Leftover adrenaline in the system makes sleep more difficult, creates more fear responses and interferes with nighttime routines.
- Hypnosis—Many scripts can be adapted for connecting to and releasing anger.

Interventions for Attachment

Most of what I have already discussed contributes to building attachment relationships. Supporting the parents in using PACE (playfulness, acceptance, curiosity and empathy) in their interactions with their child, building trust, minimising shame, focusing on experiences rather than behaviour and developing shared goals rather than conflict over control all help the young person to experience their caregivers as sources of support rather than sources of rejection and pain.

Psychoeducational Interventions for Attachment

- Attachment-focused ideas can be counterintuitive. We need to help caregivers understand the principles of attachment work with attachment-disordered and traumatized children.

- There are a number of excellent books, articles and videos on the subject that interested parents can read or view. Dan Hughes has a number of videos, as well as books for parents and foster parents.
- Some agencies and organisations offer information nights and training programs for caregivers and foster parents on raising children with attachment disorders.
- If a group is not available, it is possible to put together a package of information for caregivers. Both Dan Hughes and the Association for Treatment and Training in the Attachment of Children (ATTACh) have websites with available resources.
- It is helpful to have at least one or two sessions alone with caregivers in order to gain an understanding of their views, expectations and experiences on both parenting and treatment, and if needed, to help them widen their experience to include an understanding of why their child may need a slightly modified approach.

• Young people will also need help in understanding attachment-focused work. Since they are coming from a position of being hurt, let down, rejected and moved around, the idea of relying on their parent or caregiver does not make much sense to them. They are much more likely to prefer the idea of independence over interdependence.

- When children lean towards independence, I ask them to imagine what "real" independence would be like—if each person had to rely only on themselves for everything: food, clothing, shelter, warmth and protection. Even the most independent people can survive only for a short time without resources created by others. We have evolved, as a species, to need each other for survival.
- I talk to kids realistically about their brains and how they develop. I show them how we need other people, even if we might get hurt, to grow the parts of our brain that we need to get by.
- "The Fable of the Porcupine" is a story that traces its origins to German Philosopher Arthur Schopenhauer.[35]

> It was the coldest winter ever. Many animals died because of the cold.
>
> The porcupines, realising the situation, decided to group together to keep warm. This way they covered and protected themselves; but the quills of each one wounded their closest companions.
>
> After a while, they decided to distance themselves one from the other and they began to die, alone and frozen. So they had to make a choice: either accept the quills of their companions or disappear from the Earth.
>
> Wisely, they decided to go back to being together. They learned to live with the little wounds caused by the close relationship with

their companions in order to receive the heat that came from the others. This way they were able to survive.

The best relationship is not the one that brings together perfect people, but when each individual learns to live with the imperfections of others and can admire the other person's good qualities.

- Figure 9.6 shows a picture of a Lego activity done with parents and children together, challenged to build towers. The tower with the most solid, broadest base is the strongest and can withstand the most pressure. The tower with no base can stand on its own, but the slightest breeze will cause it to topple.

Experiential Interventions for Attachment

Early attachment relationships usually begin their development preverbally, and are at first experiential and right-brain-driven. When working to develop attachment relationships I try to find means of achieving similar experiences. This doesn't mean that the adults engage with the child as if they were an infant. Many of the young people I work with experience dissociative age regression. I try to avoid triggering dissociative experiences so as not to strengthen the neural pathways involved. I try to create experiences that connect right brain to right brain, and that use as many neurological functions as possible, including

Figure 9.6 Secure Attachment Base Lego Activity

those that are used when infants are first in an attuned relationship with an adult.

- Affective Reflective Dialogue—This is a term used by Dan Hughes to describe a dialogue in which the experience of the child heard, felt, understood and reflected back in a caring, empathetic way without trying to alter, shift or "fix" it. This sounds easy, but it is in fact difficult for both the therapist and the parent. It is hard to reach the point where the child can do this, and it's hard to hear painful, angry, alienated emotions and not try to help them feel better. It goes against our instincts as healers and parents. I often remind parents, and myself, that when we are convinced of something terrible, having someone tell us it isn't true is never helpful. In fact, the experience is more one of having our feelings minimised and feeling that the other person doesn't understand. The adult's ability to hear their child's pain and stay attuned to their experience in this way really is essential, and does a great deal to help the child feel connected. An example of an affective reflective dialogue goes like this:
    - Child—"I don't want to go to school because I have no friends. All the kids and teachers hate me. I'm ugly and stupid!"
    - Parent—(desperately wanting to remind the child that they have two close friends, their teacher likes them and that they are beautiful and smart) "Oh my God—now I get why you don't want to go to school. It must be so hard to go to school when you feel that way and feel so alone there! I feel terrible that it feels that way for you!"
    - I do believe that no matter how well you prep parents for this, it's going to get messed up at times, because it is so hard for a parent to not try to make their child feel better. I have found these mistakes not to be disastrous. I work with the parent around being open to gentle reminders in sessions. If they try to change or argue with their child's experience, I simply say something like, "It is hard to hear her say those things, isn't it—do you really think you can change her mind?" The parent then knows to say something to the child like, "I'm sorry I was trying to talk you out of that. It's hard for me to hear that you feel so sad and alone, and it makes me want to try to make you feel better."
- Nonverbal Sharing of Affective Experiences—There are lots of reasons why children and adolescents don't talk. They don't always have the language, and they don't always have the concepts. Being vulnerable can be frightening. I use the tools described for developing affective language to help them communicate feelings. They can choose many feelings at once. This allows them to understand how complicated and conflicted their feelings can be. This helps caregivers, because the child is able to show them how they feel, and they see how overwhelming it can be. Some young people choose to write feelings on paper or on a whiteboard—this uses both left and right brain functions, by bridging the gap between language

and feelings. I have a basket of river stones that have different positive and negative self-thoughts written on them. Clients can pick as many as they like in a session. Then they can get a sense of the "weight" of carrying these around. Eight-year-old Jake insisted they weren't heavy, but after holding the basket out for a few minutes, he struggled—his father spontaneously stepped in to help him carry them.

- Experimental Empathy—This involves a simple question that I have gotten in the habit of asking in many sessions. I will ask a parent, "What do you think it's like to be your daughter right now?" I will ask the child, "What do you think it's like to be your mother (or father, or sister)?" I've found that even with families who don't usually talk about what others are feeling; they stop and think about it, and reflect with insight. They are often surprised by the experience.
- Mirroring—Mothers and infants spend long periods gazing at each other. The young people we work with rarely make eye contact. I encourage caregiver and child to face each other, palms outwards, and take turns copying each other's movements. Sometimes I do this with the child on an exercise ball, sometimes not.

    - Sophie and her adoptive mother had had a difficult session, after which Sophie needed to go to school and her mother needed to go to work. I asked them to sit on the couch facing each other, and touch the palms of their hands together. After about thirty seconds, the mother scratched her nose, and put her hand back against Sophie's—Sophie exclaimed, "A booger connection!" They burst out laughing, and fell into each other's arms. Together they agreed that any time during the day if either one of them was feeling stressed, they would remember their "booger connection" and know that the other one was remembering it too. It was a perfect attunement moment. "Booger Connection" is now one of their code words, and has taken the edge off of many difficult moments.

- Soothing—I encourage parents to soothe their child during sessions. For many families, it's not part of their routine. At first it can seem awkward and weird to them. They often start with the child or teen on the couch and the parent in a chair. When the child becomes upset, I ask the child if their parent can sit with them. Almost always they agree. If they don't, I encourage the parent to reach out and touch their child's shoulder. Eventually, the child does allow the adult to move beside them. After a few sessions, it's common that the young person tells their caregiver to move beside them. Even parents who struggle with connection seem to appreciate the chance to hold their child, stroke their hair or hand them Kleenex. For some, the barriers have been built over years, and they don't know how to approach each other. Once the door has been opened, it becomes easier.
- Musical Connections—Many parents share music with very young children. They sing to them, or play lullabies. Older children and teens

often identify with music, and feel that certain songs reflect their feelings. I use music in different ways. Jake often wants to end sessions with his dad by choosing a song to listen to together. We look them up on YouTube and watch the video and listen to the song on my computer. He has chosen many songs that speak to connection, loyalty and being there for each other. Anna was separated from her mother when she was young. On visits her mother sang her traditional native songs. Christine was surprised that Anna had many of these songs on her iPod. We often end sessions by listening to one of them. Anna's mother will sing along, while Anna either sits facing her, or lies with her head in her mother's lap. Sometimes young people with dissociated alters will identify that different parts like different songs. Each part will choose a song that represents them.

- Attributions—A colleague of mine developed the worksheet shown in Figure 9.7 to help parents understand their children's symptoms. This is useful in helping to change negative attributions.

Interventions for Sleep

Sleep can be one of the biggest challenges for our clients. Disrupted sleep patterns, nighttime fears, fear of the dark and nightmares lead to poor sleep quality, resistance to sleep, resistance to bedtime routines and conflict at bedtime. The result is that many of our clients don't get enough sleep. Lack of sleep can increase the intensity of other difficulties. Mood, anxiety, relationships, concentration, ability to learn, problem solving and cooperation are negatively

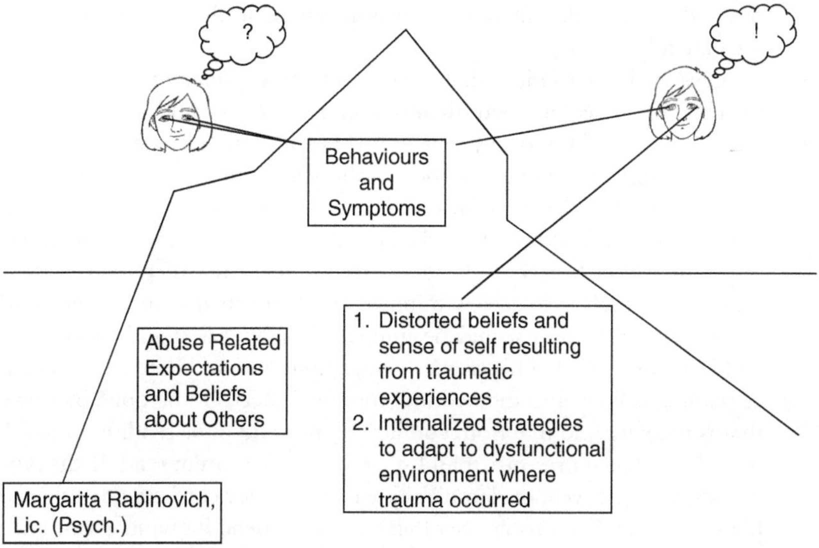

Figure 9.7 The Iceberg Experience

affected by sleep deprivation. Older children get into the habit of staying up all night on the computer, watching TV or listening to music. Sometimes they do this secretly; sometimes their parents are unable to control it. This is hard for parents to control, because there is no good answer for "I just can't sleep."

There are strong opinions in our society about independence and bedtime routines that I don't see as geared towards children's needs. Most parents believe that independence is important, and that children should be able to go to sleep by themselves from an early age. We take it for granted, because that is what we are taught. Most children are trained to go to sleep by themselves from infancy, and parenting discussions are filled with advice on the best way to achieve this. For some, this is considered evidence of good parenting.

Young children are dependent on their parents for soothing and coregulation. Among the more intense feelings of early childhood is the fear of being alone in the dark. The idea of independent sleep leaves children on their own to deal with these fears, and suggests that responding to them reflects weakness as a parent. For most children, this becomes manageable. They learn to self-soothe, and are able to manage their fears on their own. I'm not aware of any evidence that suggests that they grow up to be less afraid.

For children whose early attachment histories have left them with more fears and fewer skills for self-soothing, this expectation of going to bed at night, staying calm and relaxed, and going to sleep is beyond their abilities. Yet both they and their adult caregivers are caught in believing that they "should" be able to.

- I suggest other ideas about bedtime routines. The idea of parenting to sleep is a new idea in many families, but for these young people, it can be helpful. If the parent and young person are willing, I suggest quiet activities and routines that involve the parent staying in the child's room until they are asleep.
- I suggest bedtime routines that involve calm and relaxation, and that help the child or adolescent focus their thoughts on comfortable topics.
- Because many of the young people I work with have had difficulties with school, I suggest reading together, in the young person's room in a way that is stress-free. For some kids it's more comfortable if the adult sits in a chair beside the bed, which works well. If the young person has an interest in any subject or type of story, I recommend that they read to their parent or caregiver for a few minutes; the adult then reads to the child a book that the child would be interested in, that is slightly above the child's reading level. This creates connections and an interest in reading. If reading is built into the bedtime routine, it needs to be done in a way that is relaxing and free from conflict. If the child finds reading stressful, or feels too much pressure, than I suggest only the parent read. If the parent doesn't read well, or doesn't enjoy reading, they can listen together to books on tape. Even teens are often willing to spend individual time with a caregiver at bedtime once the "shoulds" are removed. It's freeing for kids to realise that their fears are normal and that they don't need to be ashamed.

- Another option is that the parent and young person engage in meditation or a guided imagery that involves progressive muscle relaxation. Progressive muscle relaxation involves tensing and releasing muscle groups. There are many good breath meditations and progressive relaxation exercises available, and one can be made by the therapist or parent into a digital recording that can be used together at bedtime.
- Dan Hughes suggests that for children who rock at night, the caregiver sit beside them and rhythmically pat their back in sync with their rocking until the child is asleep. I have suggested this to many families who have used it successfully.
- One young teen I worked with years ago lived with her grandparents. Their beds were on the opposite side of the same wall. The grandparents would go to bed at the same time as the granddaughter. She and her grandfather would tap Morse code messages through the wall until she fell asleep.
- Good sleep hygiene is important. This means no caffeinated drinks, no exercise, no scary movies or TV and limited screen time close to bedtime. This last one can be challenging. If it becomes a struggle, the young person needs to keep the brightness turned low, as there is some suggestion that exposure to bright screens interferes with the development of sleep hormones.
- I recommend children get adequate exercise during the day, but that this ends at least an hour to ninety minutes before bedtime for adrenaline to dissipate. For kids who have a trampoline, a punching bag, or some other physical activity as part of their anger release, timing this to end ninety minutes before bedtime works well. Getting regular exercise is difficult for kids who are depressed or often overtired.
- It's a good idea to avoid naps during the day, no matter how tired they are from not sleeping.
- These recommendations often take time to be effective, and I suggest that families give them a good try. If sleep continues to be a problem I suggest talking to their doctor. Many doctors will recommend natural or medical sleep aids when sleep is a serious issue and other things have been tried.

Interventions for Dissociation

Dissociation needs to be addressed directly, in order to avoid having parts of experience or parts of the self excluded from therapy. When parts of either experience or the self are left out of therapy, at best they remain hidden, the child continues using dissociation to avoid contact with these parts, and dissociation remains an issue to arise later, causing sometimes serious harm. At other times parts that are not identified can actively resist and undermine treatment.

Psychoeducational Interventions for Dissociation

It's important for children, adolescents and their caregivers to understand dissociation in a way that is helpful and demystifying. I explain that dissociation happens when kids have a lot of stress when they are little, and that it helps them to manage stress that would be too much for them. I explain that if this happens too much, kids can start dissociating without realising it and it can get in their way. I help adults and kids to understand that even though it might not seem like it at first, that all parts, even the ones that are scary or cause trouble, started to help them, and that it is our job to figure out how they were helpful and what needs to happen so that they can find ways to continue to be helpful. Just like the parts of an engine, all parts are necessary, even if we don't know what they are for.

- I often use the book *United We Stand*, by Eliana Gil, to help kids and adults understand dissociative identity disorders. It is an accessible book written for people who have DID, and provides a lot of reassuring information and knowledge.[36]
- There are many examples in popular culture and literature of adventures in which individuals of very different types work together as a team in a way that creates strength and resilience that they did not have on their own. I look for examples of this that are age-appropriate and likely to appeal to the child to use as a metaphor for the benefits of their parts working together. Examples of this are the Harry Potter series and the game Dungeons and Dragons. In Harry Potter, the students at the school of Hogwarts are grouped into four houses with very different characteristics. Gryffindor represents strength and courage, Ravenclaw represents wisdom and learning, Hufflepuff represents kindness, gentleness and healing and Slytherin represents darkness and power. It becomes necessary for members of all four houses to work together in order to achieve their survival. Dungeons and Dragons is a role-playing game where players develop complex characters and engage in quests as a team. Experienced players learn that the wider the range of characters, the wider the skill base and the greater the chance of success.

Experiential Interventions for Dissociation

- I connect with and begin to understand dissociative parts. When working with kids I often ask them to listen inside or to pay attention to inside feelings to see if they are any that are different from the ones that are being expressed. I ask often about internal voices. I notice and become curious about changes in presentation, age regression, or the appearance of being distracted by something internal. I repeat often that all voices and feelings are important and have something to say.
- If parts begin to be identified, I continue to talk through the child and encourage listening in. I prefer not to encourage dissociation by asking for direct contact with parts, but I don't refuse to speak with them if they make their presence known.
- If switching does happen, I ask if it's possible for the child or adolescent to remain aware and to listen and observe, rather than to "go inside" or "go away."

- I use the examples discussed above from popular culture to explore the roles of the different parts. I can work with a child to figure out which Hogwarts house each part belongs to, for example.
- There are a number of resources and quizzes on the internet that can help kids identify which Hogwarts house, or what type of character from multiple other popular culture examples, each part is. Kids find these quizzes fun and they help them identify which ways their parts can work together to support each other.

Working with Caregivers

Attachment and trauma work are challenging for the adults in a child's life. Different caregivers have different needs, but they all need support. Caregivers willing to engage in their child's treatment face a range of tasks from learning new and different approaches to parenting, through tolerating their child's emotional experiences and memories, to managing their own triggers and reactions to their own histories and their real or perceived role in their child's trauma history. As difficult as this is, they need to be able to manage their own experiences while focusing on their child's needs in the moment.

There is a line between working with caregivers and becoming their therapist. Throughout treatment I do a lot of supportive work with caregivers, but my role and alliance is with the child or adolescent. Many parents and caregivers have their own trauma histories or have been traumatised by their experiences with their child. When I work with them, it is focused on their role as caregiver or on enabling their role in the child's therapy. If a parent or caregiver wants and needs a therapist, I help them find one. Even if they are in their own therapy I continue to work with them around the child's therapy. I will, with their permission, collaborate with their therapist.

The first challenge is to engage caregivers in a role in their child's treatment that was unexpected when they referred, or agreed to a referral. I approach adults from the same stance that I approach kids with. I use the stance of PACE, although slightly differently.

Playfulness—I keep playfulness in my stance with adults, but I'm cautious that playfulness stays respectful, and doesn't seem to minimise their struggles. There is room for humour. It's important to build the relationship and develop a sense of what the adult is comfortable with. In the beginning, I try to keep humour focused on generalities around the experiences of parenting. I will, if it fits, use anecdotes from my experiences as a parent and stepparent, as well as those of friends and colleagues. This contributes to an equal balance of power between me and the parent or caregiver, making collaboration easier.

Acceptance—Just like the kids we work with, adults make mistakes, and sometimes they make pretty big ones. When we are allied with their children, sometimes their mistakes seem unreasonable. Often the child is angry at them, and they are angry at their child. I'm aware that I've made unreasonable mistakes, and I can't imagine how big they might have become if I was dealing with the circumstances that my clients have dealt with. I stay in a dialectical stance—the mistakes or lapses in judgment make sense somehow, or they wouldn't have happened. Whether they were made out of anger, or protectiveness, or anxiety, or fear of judgment, or terror for their own lives, they made sense. We can now make something different happen together.

Curiosity—This is a great tool for getting to know people. If we are able to show genuine, open-minded curiosity about people's experiences, their point of view, and what they need now, they will be able to tell us. Curiosity allows us to interview in-depth without judgment.

Empathy—Empathy comes naturally with acceptance. Even if we can never really know what it has been like to be someone else, if we are able to accept that everything somehow makes sense, than we can care about and feel something of their experiences.

Other than engagement, it's necessary to see parents individually now and then, in order to support and guide them through work with their child. How often this happens depends on how difficult the child's treatment is for them, and on how complex the child's needs are. Anna's mother has a severe trauma history of her own, and has had difficulty connecting emotionally. Anna has a dissociative identity disorder. Some parts of her are connected to her mother; other parts are angry, distant and rejecting. Christine was often hurt in sessions by Anna's sudden anger and rejection, appearing at times as if from out of nowhere. Although Christine had a good understanding of Anna's anger, and was most comfortable staying there and shutting down her own feelings, in order for her to be able to be emotionally available for Anna, she needed the chance to safely talk about these experiences. During our first few months, I often met with Christine to debrief therapy sessions.

A different example comes from the Stock family. Both parents had been severely impacted by their trip to Liberia to adopt their children. Marco struggled with anger outbursts, and Angela experienced numbing and depression. With both parents I used both hypnosis and EMDR to support them to manage their affect and cope with the impact of the memories and the changes in their lives.

Caregivers often need help with affect regulation. If staying calm as a parent was as easy as knowing we are supposed to, most parents would never lose their temper. Raising attachment-disordered traumatised children is likely to take most adults outside of their window of tolerance. The less often this happens, the more effective phase one work will be. This doesn't mean that parents can never get angry. As a matter of fact, "break and repair" suggests that some anger, well managed and responsibly handled, is helpful. With most parents I do at least one or two sessions around basic grounding and regulating techniques. If they are interested I do some hypnotic work with them around body scans and stress release, some guided imagery around safe and calm places, and some relaxation techniques.

Sometimes the events that traumatised the child also impacted on the parent. Michael's depression was triggered by the suicide of his best friend followed closely by the accidental death of family member. Michael's mother, Linda, had her own therapist, and had done a lot of work on her depression. Linda had known the friend who had killed himself since he and Michael were very young. His suicide, followed by Michael's attempt, was very painful for her. She was committed to supporting Michael through his trauma work, but was afraid that her feelings would be distressing for him. With the support of Linda's therapist I provided Linda with two EMDR sessions to help her prepare for Michael's trauma work. This was helpful, and she was able to stay present and connected when Michael worked on this issue.

Sometimes parents are not aware of how they come across to their children. If they appear critical or harsh, but seem to have caring, nurturing intentions, it can be helpful to discuss this privately and then videotape a session or part of a session so that they can observe themselves in action. When I have done this, I always explain the "why" to the children after having talked to the adult. "Sometimes people don't realise what they sound like when they talk—I want to tape a session with you and your nan, so that she can see why you sometimes think she's angry or upset when she doesn't think she is."

There are many ways to support parents. The goal is to remain focused on the child's needs, and to meet with the parents when and if necessary, to help them be emotionally available for their child's treatment.

Systems Work

There are almost always larger systems involved when we are working with children and adolescents. Schools, group homes and child welfare agencies often have a role. Sometimes the parent is also involved in their own therapy. The child and family often benefit from our involvement with larger systems. Open communication is important, in order to gain as much support for the child as possible, while avoiding the systemic splitting that comes naturally for children who struggle with trust (see Chapter 12).

If a child really struggles at school, then they, and sometimes the family, are viewed in a negative light by the teachers and school system. Writing letters, advocating and attending school meetings can help the school have a different understanding. When working with a child with a dissociative disorder, I often arrange a meeting with the school in order to explain what this means, what they might expect, and how they can respond supportively.

When a child or adolescent is in a group home, I encourage the staff to attend the first session and often ongoing sessions as well. If the child doesn't have an available parent or foster parent, I ask the group home to choose a staff person the child is comfortable with as my contact person and encourage them to join sessions as an attachment figure. If a child is in child welfare care I encourage the child's worker to be involved in the first session and update sessions.

If a parent has their own therapist, and the issues they are working on impact on their work with the child, or vice versa, I suggest that their therapist be informed about the work we are doing together. I also ask that I be informed if issues arise in the individual work that may impact on the child's work.

There are many layers to phase one work. This does not always end as we move towards trauma processing. We often return to these tasks as needed through phase two.

Notes

1. Braun, B. G. (1988). The BASK model of dissociation: Part I. *Dissociation, 1*(1), 4–23.
2. Braun, B. G. (1988). The BASK model of dissociation: Part II. *Dissociation, 1*(2), 16–23.
3. Porgess, Stephen W. (2011). *The Polyvagal Theory: Neurophysiological Foundations of Emotions, Attachment, Communication, Self-Regulation.* W. W. Norton and Company. New York.
4. Daitch, Carolyn. (2007). *Affect Regulation Toolbox; Practical and Effective Hypnotic Interventions.* W. W. Norton & Company. New York. p 98.
5. Hughes, Daniel A. (2004). An attachment-based treatment of maltreated children and young people. *Attachment and Human Development, 6*, 263–78.
6. Hughes, Daniel A. (2006). *Building the Bonds of Attachment* (2nd ed.). Jason Aronson. New York.
7. Hughes, Daniel A. (2007). *Attachment Focused Family Therapy*. W. W. Norton & Company. New York.
8. Hughes, Daniel A. (2007). *Attachment Focused Family Therapy*. W. W. Norton & Company. New York. p 14.
9. Hughes, Daniel A. (2007). *Attachment Focused Family Therapy*. W. W. Norton & Company. New York. pp 61–94.
10. Hughes, Daniel A. (2007). *Attachment Focused Family Therapy*. W. W. Norton & Company. New York. pp 95–120.
11. Hughes, Daniel A. (2007). *Attachment Focused Family Therapy*. W. W. Norton & Company. New York. pp 191–214.
12. Silberg, Joyanna. (2013). *The Child Survivor: Healing Developmental Trauma and Dissociation.* Routledge. New York. p 29.
13. Tomkins, S. S. (1963). *Affect/Imagery/Consciousness. Vol. 2: The Negative Affects.* Springer. New York. p 118.
14. Hughes, Daniel A. (2007). *Attachment Focused Family Therapy*. W. W. Norton & Company. New York. p 55.
15. Braun, B. G. (1988). The BASK model of dissociation: Part I. *Dissociation, 1*(1) 4–2.
16. Braun, B. G. (1988b). The BASK model of dissociation: Part II. *Dissociation, 1*(2) 16–23.
17. Siegel, Daniel J. (2013). *The Developing Mind: How Relationships and the Brain Interact to Shape Who We Are.* Guilford. New York. p 19.
18. Forner, Christine. (2012, October). *Creative Meditations and Medial Prefrontal Cortex Processing for Traumatic Dissociation.* Workshop presented at the annual conference of the International Society for the Study of Trauma and Dissociation, Long Beach, CA.
19. Forner, Christine. (In development). *Creative Meditations for Complex Trauma and Dissociation: Fostering Mindfulness and Facilitating Growth.* Routledge. New York.
20. Forner, Christine. (2011, November). *Creative Meditations and Medial Prefrontal Cortex Processing for Traumatic Dissociation.* Workshop presented at the annual conference of the International Society for the Study of Trauma and Dissociation. Montreal, QC, Canada.
21. Warner, E., Koomar, J., Lary, B., & Cook, A. (2013, October). Can the Body change the score? Application of sensory modulation principles in the treatment of traumatized adolescents in residential settings. *Journal of Family Violence, 28*(7), 729–773.
22. Chambles, D. L., Baker, M. J., Baucom, D. H., Beutler, L. E., Calhoun, K. S., Crits-Cristoph, P., Daiuto, A., DeRubeis, R., Detweiler, J., Haaga, D.A.F., Bennett Johnson, S., McMurry, S., Mueser, K. T., Pope, K. S., Snaderson, W. C., Shoham, V., Stickle, T., Williams, D. A. & Woody, S. R. (1998). Update on empirically validated therapies. *The Clinical Psychologist, 51*, 3–16.

23. Chemtob, C. M., Tolin, D. F., van der Kolk, B. A., & Pitman, R. K. (2000). Eye movement desensitization and reprocessing. In E. B. Foa, T. M. Keane, & M. J. Friedman (Eds.), *Effective Treatments for PTSD: Practice Guidelines from the International Society for Traumatic Stress Studies*. Guilford. New York.
24. Siegel, Daniel J. (2013). *The Developing Mind: How Relationships and the Brain Interact to Shape Who We Are*. Guilford. New York. p 77–78.
25. Hughes, Daniel A. (2007). *Attachment Focused Family Therapy*. W. W. Norton & Company. New York. pp 61–94.
26. Hughes, Daniel A. (2007). *Attachment Focused Family Therapy*. W. W. Norton & Company. New York. pp 51–52.
27. Silberg, Joyanna. (2013). *The Child Survivor: Healing Developmental Trauma and Dissociation*. Routledge. New York. pp 26–27.
28. Knipe, J. (2012, October). *EMDR with Complex Trauma and Dissociation*. Workshop presented at the annual conference of the International Society for the Study of Trauma and Dissociation, Long Beach, CA.
29. Kluft, R. P. (2013). *Shelter from the Storm: Processing the Traumatic Memories of DID / DDNOS Patients with the Fractionated Abreaction Technique*. R. P. Kluft. North Charleston, SC.
30. Daitch, Carolyn. (2007). *Affect Regulation Toolbox; Practical and Effective Hypnotic Interventions.* W. W. Norton & Company. New York.
31. Daitch, Carolyn. (2007). *Affect Regulation Toolbox; Practical and Effective Hypnotic Interventions.* W. W. Norton & Company. New York. p 91.
32. Daitch, Carolyn. (2007). *Affect Regulation Toolbox; Practical and Effective Hypnotic Interventions.* W. W. Norton & Company. New York. p 88.
33. Daitch, Carolyn. (2007). *Affect Regulation Toolbox; Practical and Effective Hypnotic Interventions.* W. W. Norton & Company. New York. p 84.
34. Siegel, Daniel J. (2013). *The Developing Mind: How Relationships and the Brain Interact to Shape Who We Are*. Guilford. New York. p 253.
35. Schopenhauer, A. (2000). *Parerga und Paralipomena* (Vol. 2, Ch. 31, Sec. 396). E.F.J. Payne (Trans.). Oxford University Press. Oxford.
36. Gil, Eliana. (1990). *United We Stand: A Book for People with Multiple Personalities*. Launch Press. Walnut Creek, CA.

10 Phase Two

Trauma Processing and Integration

Phase one work covers a lot of bases. The amount of phase one work is individual, and needs to be assessed on a case-by-case basis. A young person with self-regulation skills, a stable, caring living situation and few or no dissociative symptoms may be ready to work on trauma after a few sessions. Children who have experienced multiple early traumas and disruption to their attachment relationships, whose experience was fragmented and dissociated, and who have ongoing destabilising events may require months or more than a year. Michael, who had good support from his mother, and had had a stable first eight years, was able to start trauma processing within a few sessions. This contrasts with Terra, who had no stability in her earlier years, was abused by her first caregiver, had alter personality states, fragmented memories, and dissociative shutdowns, experienced the sudden death of two caregivers, and was being raised by an elderly grandparent with life-threatening health problems. Terra and her grandmother spent two and a half years engaged in phase one work. Some of this was spent restabilising after her grandmother's near fatal heart attack.

By the time a client is ready to work on trauma, their symptoms are under control, and the intrusions that brought them to treatment are reduced or gone. When they are stable and coping at home, school and the community, many therapists wonder if it makes sense to do trauma work. It seems counterintuitive to open up painful, triggering experiences with a child who is coping well, possibly for the first time in years. There are more reasons than not to move on to phase two. In my experience if therapy stops when the young person becomes stable, the unresolved trauma makes itself known eventually, sometimes with tragic impact. Arianne Struik[1] comments that many therapists are reluctant to address trauma with children for fear of causing further disregulation and greater traumatic impact. This runs counter to trauma research. Trauma-focused therapies stress that addressing, processing and integrating traumatic memory is important in treatment.[2,3,4,5,6,7] Judith Hermann describes trauma work as when "the therapist plays the role of witness and ally, in whose presence the survivor can speak the unspeakable."[8] In attachment-focused, phase-oriented treatment, it is the adult caregiver who acts as the "witness and ally." This places the parent or caregiver back in the role of protector and soother, filling the space that parents generally fill in the lives of their children. It is this space that was left empty when the child experienced trauma, alone and afraid with no one to protect and soothe them.

Traumatic experiences are overwhelming; the memories are not integrated into experiential narrative. This narrative, the life story, creates meaning, understanding, identity and experiential learning. Traumatic memories remain fragmented, stored as intrusive sensory, affective and visual pieces, able to be triggered to overwhelm the child repeatedly, without being fully understood and built on. The goal of phase two work is to integrate these memories into a coherent narrative; they become just another aspect of the child's experiences.

The phase two interventions in this model are designed to rely when possible on the support of the adult caregivers while exploring traumatic experience within the child or adolescent's window of tolerance, using multiple neurological processes. The description of phase two is less involved than the description of phase one, and based on similar principles. Phase one lays the groundwork, developing new ways of relating and coping. Phase two uses the same ideas and skills to address traumatic experience. Phase two may take significantly less time than phase one, and if negotiated carefully, should be free of the type of crisis and deterioration common to early phase one work. Many years ago, before being familiar with phase-oriented trauma work, I worked with Krista, thirteen, who had been the victim of a violent sexual assault. She experienced terror and suffered serious injuries requiring surgery. Krista suffered from post-traumatic symptoms including anxiety, fear of men, nightmares, shame and intrusive flashbacks. She was depressed, suicidal and refused to go to school. Krista engaged well, but was unable to talk about what had happened. She was able to talk about her symptoms and intrusions, but not about the actual assault. She had not disclosed this to anyone. Talking about her symptoms did nothing to relieve them. I asked Krista to tell me all the negative thoughts, worries and anxieties she had about telling me what had happened. She produced a long list of worries about my possible reactions and hers, fears that a man would accidentally enter my office while she was feeling vulnerable, concerns about how involved her mother should be, how I would handle a flashback or panic attack, what would happen if she became suicidal, and many other anxieties. We spent weeks systematically addressing each worry and coming up with a plan for each one. We scheduled a date, made a plan for her mother to be available in the waiting room and made warning signs for my door. We talked in detail about every possible reaction either of us could imagine either one of us having during the conversation. Finally, all the plans were in place and the scheduled day arrived. Krista arrived in my office, we sat down and matter-of-factly she shared the details of the assault. She started at the beginning, worked her way through, sharing her fear, her pain, her anger and her shame. The whole narrative took less than half an hour. When it was over, she looked at me in amazement and said, "That was so easy—all the other things we talked about were much harder!" The next day, Krista returned to school for the first time in months, on her own accord. She told her mother a less detailed account of what had happened to her, and her mother was able to be present and supportive. Krista experienced no more fears, nightmares or flashbacks. Over the years I have heard from her occasionally, and she has continued to do very well, with no further depression, suicidal thoughts or anxieties. Although I had not heard of phase-oriented therapy at the time, this demonstrates it at its most effective. I have no doubt that if Krista had tried to tell me about her experiences without being able to create an environment in which she felt safe, supported, heard and in control, she would have become overwhelmed and had a traumatic flashback, rather than a full integration of her experience.

Assessing Readiness

The goal of phase one is to help the child and their caretaker create enough stability to talk about trauma without getting overwhelmed or pulled into traumatic reexperiencing. When they are able to achieve this they can process their experiences, bringing together and integrating the fragmented memory, and create a coherent narrative which becomes part of the narrative of their life experience. It is this lifetime narrative, not just their trauma and attachment history, on which they build their identity, their concepts of themselves and others, and of their place in their world.

It's realistic to expect that when trauma work begins, the young person will experience distress,and some of their previous difficulties may return. They should not decompensate and become unable to cope or function.[9,10] If the child begins to get very distressed, it's important to slow down and restabilise.[11] Significant deterioration or increased safety concerns that are not easily resolved suggest that more phase one work is needed before trauma processing.[12] Sometimes, this may occur if dissociation or one or more dissociated parts have remained hidden. At other times it may be that phase one work is not complete, or that something is causing the child or adolescent to feel unsafe. Readiness for trauma work means having the internal and external resources to manage strong, painful emotional experiences. This involves a reasonable sense of safety within the therapeutic relationship, stable external relationships and supports, and the ability to regulate responses to their traumatic experience. When clients experience dissociative symptoms, safety and attachment need to be achieved among and between the parts, and all parts need to participate and cooperate. Given that overwhelming experiences which take us out of our window of tolerance result in fragmentation of experiential memory, it seems reasonable that to integrate them, the memories need to be worked on within the window of tolerance. Memory work that leads to flooding and overwhelming emotion can be retraumatising. The child, the therapist and the caregiver's ability to monitor the child's affective arousal and help keep them within their window of tolerance is an indication of the readiness for trauma work.

Interventions

Fractionated Abreaction

Rick Kluft and Catherine Fine have developed sophisticated and detailed protocols for achieving safe, contained abreaction work with adults with dissociative disorders who become overwhelmed and destabilised by trauma work.[13,14] This technique involves extensive preparation and containment through the use of hypnotic interventions in order to process trauma in incremental pieces. Kluft's caveat, "the slower you go, the faster you get there"[15] applies well to fractionated abreaction, and is a good guide for trauma work. Although this is a useful tool with some very dissociated and disregulated adolescents, I have found that most children and adolescents don't have the solidity of dissociative barriers to make the full process necessary or workable. The idea itself, however, is important in managing the work. When working on traumatic memories, I work with the child and their caregiver to process each memory slowly and in small amounts, stopping frequently to ground, regulate, and allow the child or adolescent to connect emotionally with their caregiver or with me. Their caregiver's role is empathic witnessing, soothing and coregulating the young person. Once the memory has been processed, the child, the caregiver and I work to develop a new understanding, a "cocreated meaning" which contributes to the development of a coherent narrative of the events and their place in the child and familiy's life.

Eye Movement Desensitisation and Reprocessing (EMDR)

EMDR is a strongly supported, effective method for processing and integrating traumatic memory. I use EMDR in many ways in attachment-focused practice. As mentioned in the previous chapter, I use EMDR to assist caregivers in becoming ready to be available and present for their child or adolescent. With older children and adolescents I use traditional EMDR protocols to process memories, while their parent or caregiver is in the room with them, witnessing, hearing and providing soothing and comfort as necessary. With several young people who were stable but struggled with distress or shutting down during trauma work and traditional EMDR, I have done EMDR while they sat on an exercise ball, again with their adult or caregiver in the room with them. This added external focus keeps them grounded and present. For some teens, the idea of doing all of their work with their parent or caregiver in the room isn't comfortable or practical. I sometimes do individual EMDR, and then meet with the caregiver afterwards to share the experience. Some adolescents choose to videotape sessions and view parts that they want shared with their caregiver.

Both for engaging children, and also to use as many neurological functions as possible, I use different mediums to plan sessions and set up EMDR targets. I use the game "The EMDR Journey"[16] when working with children and young teens. I use several resources such as feelings cards, feelings charts, stones with positive and negative emotions or cognitions on them, feelings thermometers, a rating wheel, and a "Core Belief Checklist" (included in worksheets)

For some children, the EMDR protocol feels formal, or too much like schoolwork. With these kids, I engage in conversations, sometimes with them, sometimes with their caregiver, about their experiences, while they hold the EMDR buzzers or keep them in their socks or pockets. Often they will draw during this process, or I ask them to choose colours for their experiences and write down words that fit how they are feeling. When children don't have words or ideas connected to their traumatic experiences, if their parents do, I use Joan Lovett's story technique.[17] The caregiver composes a story about the child's experience, and then either they or I read the story to the child, who is holding the buzzers, while sitting on the parent's lap or beside them on the couch.

When using EMDR I focus as much as possible on the integrative properties of the experience. Although the exact processes by which EMDR works are not well understood, I am convinced that at least one of those processes involves the connection of information between the left and right side of the brain. Bessel van der Kolk[18] believes that EMDR facilitates the movement of information from one hemisphere to the other through the corpus callosum. Dan Siegel, discussing the integrative functions of REM sleep, states:

> Looking to the left activates the right prefrontal cortex, looking to the right activates the left. The left is involved in retrieval, the right in encoding. During REM sleep both are alternately activated. REM sleep is an important part of memory re-organization and consolidation. The essential feature of such a process is the synchronous activation of right and left hemispheres to synthetically retrieve and encode episodic memory into a consolidated form.[19]

Having experienced EMDR both myself in training, and as a therapist, this seems to describe the experiential process of EMDR. Memories are retrieved, reorganised, and the initially disparate emotional and cognitive components seem to form together to create a coherent whole.

I don't rely only on bilateral stimulation for integrative experience. I incorporate as many neurological processes into therapy as possible. I draw the young person's attention to body memories, current body sensations, posture, emotional experiences, visual descriptions and sensory experiences. I encourage them to draw pictures of their memories or write about their feelings and experiences using different colours. I use grounding techniques during EMDR which physically engage them, such as sitting on an exercise ball or stopping to play catch. I use Jim Knipe's Back of the Head Scale (see previous chapter) to orient them to the room and their bodies. During and after EMDR I encourage attachment-focused exchanges such as soothing, eye contact, mirroring, experimental empathy and affective-reflective exchanges (both verbal and non-verbal). I begin or end sessions with creative meditations.

Preverbal Trauma—Preverbal trauma, or trauma which occurs before language development is sophisticated enough to organise experience, has long been a complication in the area of trauma treatment. For most people, "memory" refers to explicit or narrative memory, that which we are aware of as memories. There is a common belief that we don't remember events that occurred in infancy and early toddlerhood, with the exceptions of brief images of the age at which we began to use language more fluently. Those few people who report remembering being in their crib, being born or other events from early childhood are viewed sceptically. There is a related belief that events that happened before we "remember" don't affect us. Often, when talking to caregivers about their child or adolescent's early childhood experiences, I've been told about terrifying events which the parent qualifies by saying, "But they were much too young to remember it." Many parents who adopt toddlers are of the belief that their child will be unaffected by their preadoption histories, once they settle in, as long as they are physically healthy. This is understandable. What is less so is that for many families I've worked with, the adoption agencies not only did not advise them otherwise, they encouraged the belief. One family was told that children adopted before the age of three (from poor and overcrowded orphanages in third-world Africa) could be expected to make a completely normal adjustment. Another family was explicitly told that their child did not have a trauma history. When their child began to exhibit terrified and terrifying reactions, the agency appeared mystified. When the family demanded more detailed information, it became clear that through infanthood and early toddlerhood their child had been exposed to an overwhelming amount of chaos, disorganisation, neglect, multiple transitions and disruptions. As there had been no verification of abuse and she had "lived" in a stable foster home during her nearly daily and often multiple-night visits with her chaotic, addicted biological parents, she was identified as having no trauma history and no attachment disruption.

Because of these beliefs about memory, many children with trauma histories are not identified. John's mother asked me, "Why wasn't John's sister affected by the violence? I had thought that he was too young to remember, but if that isn't true, why does she seem to be OK?" (At the time that Shelley left her husband, John had been two and his sister had been eleven months.) I responded that I didn't know his sister, so I couldn't be sure, but that if she had been affected, the effect would look different from John's, because of their different developmental stages at the time. An infant would experience sensations and emotions, but would not have much ability to interpret them. A toddler has already begun to experience themselves as having an identity that is different from others. As a result, the infant would be triggered by sensory experiences connected to the events, which would then trigger the emotions they experienced at the time. The toddler would be more likely to internalise experiences in terms of identity, relationships, cause and effect, and the world as a whole. An infant who had witnessed violence and terrorising behaviour would be more likely to be afraid of loud noises, unexpected movements, and have an exaggerated startle reaction. John's mother looked at me with shock evident in her expression. "You just described my daughter. She can't tolerate loud noises. She is instantly terrified. We tease her about being a scaredy-cat. She called 911, in the middle of the day, when we were all home, when a door blew shut!"

Parents are often mystified as to what is bothering their children, and search for biological answers. Sometimes the abuse has been a terrible secret the parent wanted to protect their child from. Parents who have left abusive partners when their children were young sometimes bring their child to therapy believing that their child has "inherited" abusive characteristics from their other biological parent. This becomes a fear for the nonabusing parent and the child, who worry that the child is "destined" to become like the other parent. This can become a threat and self-fulfilling prophecy. The child may be raised hearing "you are just like your father" or "if you don't smarten up, you're going to end up just like your mother." These are shaming messages. Even for parents who don't want their children growing up with a negative view of their other parent, and who are careful not to label their child's behaviour as bad, there can be secret and not-so-secret fears transmitted to their child, that they have inherited the illness or problem that caused so much pain. This belief that the child "couldn't remember" what happened can lead to secondary trauma, in the form of negative attributions and unspoken fears about mental illness and inherited traits.

Infants and toddlers clearly learn. They respond to the familiar vs. the unfamiliar. They try a new action, and if they like the outcome, they do it again. They learn to understand, and later to use language. They remember. Before they can use language to organise and store memories, their experiences are processed, organised and stored in the emotional and sensory parts of their brains. This is preverbal memory. Preverbal memories form an important part of our implicit memory system, because so much of what we learn in infancy creates our working models of ourselves, our world and our place in it. Trauma, neglect, abandonment and deficits in a parent's abilities to respond to and care for an infant or toddler are events that are remembered, but they are remembered in the child's emotional and sensory brains. These are critical memories; they form the beginning of identity, worldview and relationships. These memories can be recalled, but without a narrative structure, the memories are experienced on an emotional and sensory level. We are not aware that they are memories at all.[20,21,22]

Considering how much therapy has been based on talking, the difficulty created by preverbal memory is obvious. It has been suggested that directly addressing preverbal trauma in treatment isn't possible. Efforts have focused on dealing with symptoms, working models and relationships. John Briere initially felt that preverbal memories could not be targeted directly, but that they would be activated by the therapy relationship, and could then be addressed through the relational process.[23] Other modalities of therapy have been, and continue to be, used, including play therapy, art therapy, music therapy and sensorimotor therapy.[24] These methods are better suited than talk therapy to address preverbal and implicit memory, although they vary in their intentionality and in their focus on integrating more than one aspect of neurological process.

As we become more aware of the role of implicit and preverbal memory, and the ways in which experiences are absorbed, integrated, processed and stored, we have an opportunity to incorporate this into our work with trauma victims of all ages. As we encounter young people who have been derailed in their development by experiences that occurred when they were infants and toddlers, we need to find ways to access these memories, and to create as much of a coherent narrative as possible. This is not the same as a search for truth. In many cases, we will never know what "happened" in the early lives of these children, but that doesn't mean that they can't find ways to understand their experiences.

Mark was adopted from Liberia at the age of two. When his parents first arrived in the country, he was in the hospital in traction, having suffered a broken femur. His parents were forced to leave him at the hospital and return to Canada to make legal arrangements, before returning to get him. They were refused permission to have one of them stay with him. As a toddler Mark was independent and distant. He did not turn to his parents for soothing or connection. As a school-age child he underachieved, becoming frustrated and giving up easily. As he was intelligent and athletically gifted, these issues did not get in his way much. He did, however, have difficulties with his temper and was not close to anyone. He was popular but had no close friends. Teachers and coaches initially liked him, but eventually felt he was manipulative and underachieving. Neither he nor his parents felt he had formed an attachment. He did not misbehave in big ways, but he was rarely honest or straightforward. Mark was not very interested in therapy, but as I was also working with his sister and family, I had the opportunity to work with him as the occasion called for, and this approach worked well for him. At a time when Mark was experiencing a lot of anger and was in conflict with his father, he agreed to try some EMDR. To my surprise, he chose as his target the experience of being in the hospital in Liberia. Mark had no explicit memory of this event, but had heard about it from his parents. Mark chose as a negative cognition "I'm not good enough—nobody wants me." As his positive cognition he chose "I am good enough." Mark imagined the possible sights, sounds, sensations and emotions he thought he might have felt all alone in a crowded, understaffed hospital. He rated his initial Subjective Units of Distress Scale (SUDS) at 9 out of 10. That EMDR session was unlike any I had experienced at that point (although there have been many since). Mark's EMDR experience was dark, abstract and sensory. There were no thoughts, words or cognitions. When we stopped between sessions of bilateral stimulation he had to work to find words to describe what was happening. He described falling into a dark pit; crawling cold and wet on stony hard ground at the bottom; he felt aloneness and waves of terrible anger and fear. Within an hour and a half, he began to see light. His SUDS reached a zero and stayed there. When asked if the positive thought of "I am good enough" worked for him, he brightly responded—"No, I've changed it. I'm better than good enough. I am as good as anybody and everybody. I am amazing!" Mark found the experience rewarding. He also chose not to continue. He felt he had achieved a lot, but it had been painful and intense. He didn't think he needed more. He agreed that if he did, he would come back. Over the next year, Mark changed in subtle ways. He worked harder, he planned more, he built close and lasting relationships, and he connected more with his family. About a year later, he experienced a catastrophic personal loss, the suicide of a very close friend. He came to see me and talked about his feelings, his experiences and how supportive his parents had been for him. He again chose not to do EMDR—the emotions were too raw and he was not ready. Mark negotiated the next many months using his supports, making decisions to balance his own needs, and relying on his peers and family. Mark has an avoidant style as a result of his early trauma. He is not in a hurry to experience intense emotions, but he has been increasingly able to when necessary. He seems to have coped, grown and moved forward. Mark has a long-term girlfriend, and he has attached to his parents and sister. This year he started university.

Mark did not involve his parents in his EMDR experience directly. He has had a number of attachment-focused sessions before and since. He did tell his parents about the experience, and has felt that EMDR has done a lot to improve his feelings of connection to them.

There are other ways of processing preverbal trauma. Using imagination to create images and experiences, and then exploring those using sensory experiences, visualisations, and adding narrative descriptions can be helpful. With Mark's sister Rose, we initially connected through her dog and then her work with abused and neglected dogs. She was able to talk about the experience of neglect and abuse on the development of a dog's personality and its ability to relate to people. She was then able to relate that to herself. We have also used family pictures of the orphanage in Liberia and have used the internet to search for images and stories of orphans and orphanages in Africa. Rose's parents have been involved in many of these sessions, including sessions where we have discussed her preadoption and early postadoption history.

For both Lilly and Terra, their caregivers wrote stories about what was known of their children's earlier lives. The children drew pictures to go with the stories, and we used EMDR while reading the stories aloud. Terra has done much of her EMDR either sitting on her grandmother's lap, or sitting on an exercise ball with her grandmother in physical contact with her. Lilly did her EMDR session sitting on the floor, drawing, leaning against her adoptive mother (in a chair) while her mother stroked her hair.

Cocreation of Meaning

Events become part of our narrative, influencing our experience of self and other, not only as events, but as meanings. Children develop their understanding based on shared meanings of events developed with others. The meanings children give to traumatic experiences are based on their isolated experiences, or on meanings shared with those who harmed them. Because these experiences are not integrated, they do not shift, evolve and grow with the child's understanding. Phase-oriented attachment-focused therapy allows for the child, caregiver and therapist to cocreate meanings for the early events in the child's life.

Young children see adults as powerful and knowledgeable. The toddler John would have assumed his mother knew what was happening when she left him with his father, and that she was making a choice. Exploring this as a young teen, he and his mother were able to cocreate a new meaning—of a trapped and frightened mother who thought she was protecting her son, and who rescued him as soon as she understood that he was being hurt. John was a loved child for whom she risked everything.

Notes

1. Struik, A. (2014). *Treating Chronically Traumatized Children: Don't Let Sleeping Dogs Lie!* Routledge. New York.
2. Struik, A. (2014). *Treating Chronically Traumatized Children: Don't Let Sleeping Dogs Lie!* Routledge. New York.
3. American Academy of Child and Adolescent Psychiatry. (2010). Practice parameters for the assessment and treatment of children and adolescents with post traumatic stress disorder. *Journal of the American Academy of Child and Adolescent Psychiatry, 49*, 414–430.
4. Gill, E. (2006). *Helping Abused and Traumatized Children: Integrating Directive and Nondirective Approaches*. Guilford. New York.
5. Chu, J. A. (2011). *Rebuilding Shattered Lives: Treating Complex PTSD and Dissociative Disorders*. John Wiley and Sons. New York. pp 109–128.
6. Struik, A. (2014). *Treating Chronically Traumatized Children: Don't Let Sleeping Dogs Lie!* Routledge. New York.
7. International Society for the Study of Trauma and Dissociation. (2011). [Chu, J. A., Dell, P. F., Van der Hart, O., Cardeña, E., Barach, P. M., Somer, E., Loewenstein, R. J., Brand, B., Golston, J. C., Courtois, C. A., Bowman, E. S., Classen, C., Dorahy, M., Sar, V., Gelinas, D. J., Fine, C. G., Paulsen, S., Kluft, R. P., Dalenberg, C. J., Jacobson-Levy, M., Nijenhuis, E.R.S., Boon, S., Chefetz, R. A., Middleton, W., Ross, C. A., Howell, E., Goodwin, G., Coons, P. M., Frankel, A. S., Steele, K., Gold, S. N., Gast, U., Young, L. M., & Twombly, J.]. Guidelines for treating dissociative identity disorder in adults, third revision. *Journal of Trauma and Dissociation, 12*, 115–187.
8. Hermann, J. (1992). *Trauma and Recovery: The Aftermath of Violence from Domestic Abuse to Political Terror*. Basic Books. New York. p 175.
9. Chu, J. A. (2011). The therapeutic roller coaster: Phase oriented treatment for complex PTSD. In *Rebuilding Shattered Lives: Treating Complex PTSD and Dissociative Disorders* (pp 109–128). John Wiley and Sons. New York.
10. Brand, B. (2001). Establishing safety with patients with dissociative identity disorder. *Journal of Trauma and Dissociation, 2*(4), 133–155.
11. American Academy of Child and Adolescent Psychiatry. (2010). Practice parameters for the assessment and treatment of children and adolescents with post traumatic stress disorder. *Journal of the American Academy of Child and Adolescent Psychiatry, 49*, 414–430.
12. Brand, B. (2001). Establishing safety with patients with dissociative identity disorder. *Journal of Trauma and Dissociation, 2*(4), 146.
13. Kluft, R. P. (2013). *Shelter from the Storm: Processing the Traumatic Memories of DID/DDNOS Patients with the Fractionated Abreaction Technique*. R. P. Kluft. North Charleston, SC.
14. Fine, C. G. (1993). A tactical integrationalist perspective on the treatment of multiple personality disorder. In R. P. Kluft & C. G. Fine (Eds.), *Clinical Perspectives on Multiple Personality Disorder* (pp 135–153). American Psychiatric Press. Washington, DC.

15. Kluft, R. P. (2013). *Shelter from the Storm: Processing the Traumatic Memories of DID/DDNOS Patients with the Fractionated Abreaction Technique*. R. P. Kluft. North Charleston, SC. p 53.
16. Courtney, D. M. (2010). The EMDR Journey [Board game].
17. Lovett, J. (1999). *Small Wonders: Healing Childhood Trauma with EMDR*. Free Press. New York.
18. Lovett, J. (1999). *Small Wonders: Healing Childhood Trauma with EMDR*. Free Press. New York. p 8.
19. Siegel, Daniel J. (2013). *The Developing Mind: How Relationships and the Brain Interact to Shape Who We Are*. Guilford. New York. pp 77–78.
20. van der Kolk, B. A., McFarlane, A. C., & Weisaeth, L. (Eds.). (1996). *Traumatic Stress: The Effects of Overwhelming Experience on Mind, Body and Society*. Guilford. New York. p 290.
21. Ogden, P., Minton, K., & Pain, C. (2006). *Trauma and the Body: A Sensorimotor Approach to Psychotherapy*. W. W. Norton & Company. New York. p 6.
22. Briere, J. N. (1992). *Child Abuse Trauma: Theory and Treatment of the Lasting Effects* (Interpersonal Violence: The Practice Series). Sage Publications. New York. pp 2–4.
23. Briere, J. N. (1992). *Child Abuse Trauma: Theory and Treatment of the Lasting Effects* (Interpersonal Violence: The Practice Series). Sage Publications. New York. p 17.
24. Ogden, P., Minton, K., & Pain, C. (2006). *Trauma and the Body: A Sensorimotor Approach to Psychotherapy*. W. W. Norton & Company. New York.

11 Phase Three

Moving Forward

Phase three is about moving forward, creating an identity and a future.[1] For children and adolescents this means that they are joining a developmental trajectory. When adults enter into phase three, they are connecting with an adult world, with adult expectations. Children and adolescents who haven't struggled with trauma and attachment do not have fully solidified identities or social life skills. We need to be cautious about not expecting more from our clients than we would from their peers. A certain amount of immature behaviour, defiance, conflict, and peer and relationship difficulties are expected. It's easy to view these as symptoms rather than normal parts of development.

Ideally, by the time we've reached phase three, the child or teen has connected with adult caregivers and has the opportunity to grow and develop in a family environment. We hope they can be children or adolescents, not little adults. For some of our clients, particularly those in the transition to adulthood, a family environment may not be available. They may be living independently, semi-independently or in a group home. We hope they can have the type of supports that make sense for someone their age. Many kids will choose to maintain relationships within troubled and struggling families. This may make sense when the alternative is to have no family. If they have a realistic understanding of their experiences, and realistic boundaries for themselves, this can be a good choice. Sometimes this means living with family members while also having other supports and caring people in their lives. Sometimes this means that they will be living outside of their families but maintain connected and caring relationships. These are decisions that each person makes for themselves, when they are old enough. Our role is to support and guide them, and to help them understand and negotiate their roles within their worlds.

Young clients also need to have friends, interests and activities. School is important, and often the experiences of trauma, loss and healing have interfered with their meeting their potential. Supporting kids in negotiating the school system, and supporting their caregiver in advocating for them effectively, is part of our role. Young people who have made good use of phase one and two are often able to do better in school than they initially believed possible. School is not the only priority. Our society, at least on the surface, seems to identify "good functioning" by academic and employment measurements. It can be easy for young people who have felt alienated and disconnected to focus on these areas to show themselves and others that they are "better." Amie's early life was so trauma-involved that keeping secrets and trying to fit in and look like other kids took all of her energy and focus. Dissociation, lost time and several alter personalities made learning in school nearly impossible. At home, her parents showed no interest in her education and ignored the school's recommendations around homework, while telling the school that they were putting in many hours without success. Teachers who showed her kindness became the closest she had to attachment figures, and she desperately wanted to learn in order to please them. As she grew older, entered into high school and then therapy, she connected to some of her teachers who cared and were committed to her. She also connected with me. Amie struggled to understand what people who cared about her wanted. The idea of happiness or wholeness seemed unrealistic to her, but she knew these people wanted her to "get better" and she wanted them to be proud of her. She knew that people were proud when other students did well in school, and she knew that these caring people wanted her to go to school, get her education and even go to college. This became a focus for Amie of identifying success, doing well and getting "better." It also posed some real hardships. Amie struggled, and still struggles, with an internal sense of who she is. What matters to her is maintaining the few relationships she feels safe with, and to her that means being whoever she thinks those people want her to be. Without knowing who she is, it's hard for her to think in terms of what she is "interested in" or even what she likes. She finds it hard to have opinions, ideas, or to take chances with expressing herself. She has worked hard at school, and often gets good marks, but still feels that she is failing and that she doesn't understand what she is learning; it has no intrinsic meaning to her. It seems like a cruel joke that the only thing these strange caring people "want" from her is something she doesn't know how to find—herself.

For young people traumatised in very early childhood, without healthy relationships and an ability to rely on adults for support and guidance, the lives of other children are a strange and alien world. I remember Tom—removed at nine from a home where he had been isolated from other children, "home-schooled" without being taught much about the world around him (see Chapter 5). When he came into care, he was a stranger in a strange land. It was difficult to tell whether he was delayed, autistic, psychotic or simply unusual. He did not know how to behave with other children. He didn't understand ideas like dinnertime, bedtime or family time. The idea of voluntarily having a conversation with another person, in which you shared information about yourself, seemed odd and dangerous. Play was something he did himself, when no one was looking, not something you did with others. Tom is an extreme example of a dilemma many young complex trauma victims face. The common experiences on which identities, interests, values and friendships are based are different from their own. The idea of interests and values can be challenging, when survival and then recovery have been the focus of their lives.

There's a boy I know, who is not a child I work with, and who is not in therapy. He has experienced many traumatic events in his life similar to those experienced by my young clients. He does not have PTSD, a dissociative disorder, or an attachment disorder. He has people in his life who, for the most part, listened, believed, heard, cared, protected and responded. He has had safety and connection. He is not a perfect child, but he is a whole child, who in spite of his experiences, has not had his resources overwhelmed by having to cope alone and afraid. His parents are not perfect. They make mistakes and get stressed, but they try to stay aware of his needs and when things go wrong they regroup, plan and work towards what is best for him. He knows who he is, where he belongs and what he wants. I suspect that this is the mystery of what has been called "resilience."

Phase three is about finding that self. It is about helping our young clients, with the support of their parents or caregivers, find a way in the world. It is about the child and family moving forward into life, defined by the regular day-to-day expectations and struggles of children and families. Healing from trauma does not mean that the future becomes easy and uncomplicated. It doesn't mean that the past never happened, or doesn't matter, and it doesn't mean that there will never be other traumatic events. Even the most effective therapy is not a magic solution to life's troubles. Phase three involves helping place the child on their developmental trajectory, with the skills, capacities and supports that they need to negotiate the future. The developmental stage of the child or adolescent determines what phase three looks like, as it determines where on their developmental pathway they belong. Phase three work began in phase one and two, and is consolidated in this latter part of treatment. The interventions listed are more of a series of ideas to be explored as appropriate to the child, their developmental level and their need.

Interventions

Balance

I incorporate the idea of balance throughout therapy. Many of the young people we work with have fixed ideas about what is "normal" or "healthy" or "success." They have the idea of good and bad. They believe that "getting better" means getting rid of the "bad" and "being good." Phase three work often involves expanding on the idea of "grey areas" and gradual shifts. From phase one I reinforce that anger, sadness, grief and pain are parts of a healthy life, but that they are balanced with acceptance, joy, love and pleasure. I use the image of *taijitu* (yin and yang) to symbolise both balance and integration (see Chapter 9). This is an idea that needs to be not just known, but felt and experienced. The concepts of balance, grey areas, knowing, feeling and experiencing are concepts that require integrative brain functioning.

Who Am I and Who Do I Want to Be?

Questions around identity and values are part of healthy development. Like Amie and Tom, some of the young people we have worked with haven't had the opportunity to think outside of themselves. They are more "self-involved" than their peers. This does not mean that they are selfish, although they are socially "immature." This is not a value statement; it refers to their not having opportunity to develop social skills adapted to an interdependent society. They haven't had the chance to think of anything beyond their own pressing needs. Sometimes they give too much of themselves, not out of caring so much as out of needing to connect. I was once told (regarding social agency funding issues), "It's hard to think about partnerships when the person next to you is looking at you like you might be dinner!" This is comparable to the world in which they have grown up.

While doing attachment work, we focus on empathy. In Chapter 9 I talk about "experimental empathy," or having the child imagine what they think it's like to be someone else in their family. I usually do this after the caregiver has been able to talk about what they think it might be like to be the child, so that the child gets both the experience of being understood and the experience of mutual understanding. During later therapy I encourage parents and caregivers to talk about values with their child, and to help their child explore their own values. There is a "values exercise" I use, which is included in the worksheets. This exercise lists lifestyle values that kids can number in order of importance to them. There is a third column to number in terms of where they place their energies. It's a good way to open a dialogue. Throughout the first phases of treatment we have been working on safety and acceptance. By this time it's hoped that exploring values can be a safe topic of discussion, not a way for caregivers to find out about and "mold" their child's views. This doesn't mean that it's not OK for parents to teach values, but that's not a job for therapy. Values adapt and change over time, and children are not likely to be selfless or noble. The ways this conversation evolves will depend on the age of the child. Children may need more discussion and open questions than adolescents in order to explore values. The goal is just to begin a conversation.

What Do I Like?

Similar to values, the kids we work with may not pay attention to their own interests and likes. They may be eager to please others, and willing to subjugate their own interests or enjoyments in order to be liked. They may have some interests or activities. If they have, these can be encouraged and supported. Many schools have groups, clubs and extracurricular activities. Some communities may have subsidized recreation or cultural programs for young people or families with low incomes. Children in care often have access to recreational or cultural funding. Finding and encouraging interests and strengths help young people to connect to others who they share interests with, and protects them from becoming involved in negative peer experiences to create connections that they are missing.

What Do I Want?

The experience of wanting is a complicated question for young people who have little sense of identity and belonging. Sometimes their "wants" seem endless, and yet it can be hard for them to identify wanting something for themselves. Children and adolescents can be helped to come up with realistic lists of the things that they want, and goals for how to achieve them. Their caregivers can be enlisted in helping them figure out steps towards the things they want. These things can be short-term, like "I want to make a friend" or "I want to paint my room green," or longer term, like "I want to go to college" or "I want to be able to live independently by the time I'm eighteen."

Who Do I Have?

This involves helping kids identify who the people in their lives are in a realistic way. An understanding of who those people are and what roles they play can be helpful once kids have a better grasp of trust and relationships. Beginning to understand that relationships are not all or nothing helps young people connect to real people in their lives. This can allow for a sense of connection without a continuous experience of being let down. A parent who has a mental health or addiction problem may love them unconditionally and be supportive, but may not be able to provide consistent parenting. A foster parent may not be their "real" family, but may truly care, love them and want to be there for them. An older sibling may be supportive, but too young to give them everything they need. Exercises like support maps (included in worksheet section) help young people explore who is in their world. This can be a good time to revisit the "Fable of the Porcupine" from Chapter 9. A central challenge for all of us, and particularly for traumatised children and adolescents, is finding the line between the normal challenges and conflicts of connected relationships, and when those challenges become too much and overwhelm the relationship. How does the young person decide what realistic expectations are?

What Are Friends and How Do I Get Them?

Without being aware of it, most of us begin to explore the meaning of friendships, with the help of the adults around us, very early on. Very young children's first connections are with caregivers. Through these relationships they develop the ideas of connection, safety, trust and being cared for. As toddlers, when children begin to be interested in other children, their interests are mostly selfish. Young children show signs of empathy, responding with distress when others are sad or crying, but when their own needs are involved, it's hard for them to be aware of the needs of others. Toddlers want to be with other children.

When that doesn't go well, they get upset and angry. Usually an adult helps them to regulate and then to reconnect with their friend. Slowly they start to realise that other children want to be with them when they are kind and caring, and don't want to be with them when they are mean or selfish. The idea of mutuality arises from these early explorations.

This experience is often missing or distorted for kids who have poor attachment relationships and early trauma. They may have no idea how to respond to peers, and may not have had adults help them negotiate this. Some children will still be driven to find connection, but not knowing what this means, will view "friends" as someone who will meet their needs or as someone who will tolerate their presence. Some of these children find ways to exploit or control other children, and others will allow themselves to be exploited or controlled. By nine, Amie had connected with a group of neighborhood boys who thought of themselves as a "gang." She was proud of being the gang leader's girlfriend, a position that meant she was important. For this she tolerated having to be sexually available not just for him, but also his friends. Other young people find themselves isolated and labelled as odd. They don't know how to make friends, and the idea scares them. Seventeen-year-old Anna attended an art group where she met peers her age with similar interests. She loved attending, and the other girls were always happy to see her. They walked out laughing and talking together at the end of every group. When I asked if she saw them between groups she said that she didn't have their contact information. In this age of social media, I was surprised. I asked why, and she quickly regressed to a childlike state; curled up in a ball, she whimpered, "Noooo—close is scary!"

These stories are not about kids in phase three, but they outline the challenges these young people face in relationships. They have missed the beginnings of understanding connection, safety and mutuality. Some of them have mastered social relationships based on being together, having fun or doing things, but few know how to build a deeper connection. I am often surprised by how few of the young people I work with talk to their friends about anything meaningful.

I've developed a friendship list for talking about friends. It's included in the worksheets. It can be adapted depending on the age of the child. It includes ideas around mutuality and connection that may be new. Items can be checked off or scored from 0–10. It also includes the possibility of doing a "trust wheel" to look in more detail at the strengths and weaknesses of the friendship. This explores the idea that no friendship is perfect, and no friendship will get a perfect score in all areas.

Depending on the age of the young person, caregivers can be instrumental in helping children build relationships. Parents can talk to teachers to find out about other children who may be a good match or an appropriate friend, and then create activities in which to include the child. If a young person has moved to a new area, and seems to have reasonably good social skills, their caregiver could have a small party for children in the child's class with fun activities. The beginning or end of the school year, Halloween, and other occasions are good choices, as they don't involve the same pressure as birthdays. They don't make one child the centre, and there is no expectation of presents. For a child who might not do well in a group, an activity like going to a movie with an adult and one friend, or going bowling, may be a better choice. Older children and young teens may need some ideas on how to start a conversation or what they can invite a friend to do. If they are comfortable with it, it's still OK for the adult in their life to arrange something, but they may need to be a little bit more hands-off. Teenagers will likely want and need more privacy and independence. For those with reasonable boundaries and limits, remaining available for conversations and questions and providing an open enough environment for friends to drop by may be enough. Other young people may need more support and supervision, even if they are resistant to it.

Sex and Sexuality

We know that young people who have been sexually abused may have distorted views around sex and sexuality. What is less understood is that other types of trauma or attachment issues impact on sexuality. The development of healthy sexuality involves identity, self-esteem, empathy, understanding of relationships and mutuality, respect for self and others, the ability to connect emotionally, body image, self-efficacy, and the ability to regulate emotions and behaviours. In the early years of my practice, sexual acting out, sexualised behaviour, and "promiscuity" were thought of as "footprints" of sexual abuse.[2,3,4] Children and adolescents who engaged in sexual behaviour were assumed to be victims of sexual abuse. Sexuality is a complex area of development. It is confusing for most young people. Few adults are comfortable talking about it, and many children and teens are taught only the mechanics. Many of the young people I've worked with who hadn't been sexually abused but did have histories involving poor attachment relationships, domestic violence, physical abuse and medical trauma engaged with peers and adults in ways that left them vulnerable to sexual exploitation, and were retraumatised as a result. These girls and boys were lonely, with poor self-esteem. They wanted connection and affection, and so entered into situations where they were at risk. When this went wrong, they felt both responsible and victimized. These experiences reinforced their negative beliefs about themselves and others.

Young people are often more comfortable talking to their therapists than to other adults about sex and their sexual relationships. As awkward as this can be, sexuality is an important part of identity and development, and not something we can safely ignore. As much as possible I support and encourage the involvement of adult caregivers in these conversations. For the adult partners in attachment work, as for any parent, this is difficult. These aren't conversations about the mechanics of sex. It's more important to talk about the relationship aspects of sex, mutuality, responsibility and "enthusiastic consent." This term describes consent that is not simply not saying "no," but wanting to engage in sexual activity. Talking about values is important, but the adults need to know that they might not be successful in enforcing their values on the young person.

The age of the child is an important factor. If sexual abuse, exposure to pornography or witnessing sexual behaviour has led to an awareness beyond the child's age, then they will need help understanding what has happened, and fitting it into what they know about relationships. If this is not the case, then the focus for younger children will be on catching up their knowledge around friendships, relationships, safety, boundaries and connection to others. Developing self-esteem, a healthy body image and the ability to assert their needs in relationships is the groundwork to later healthy sexual development. As with any child, caregivers are encouraged to answer questions as they are asked and to keep communication open. For latency-age and teenaged clients, their developing sexual awareness and hormonal development needs to be part of an ongoing dialogue, with sensitivity to the added vulnerability created by issues with self-image, identity and desire for connection.

What Resources Are Available?

As therapy begins to come to an end, we think about what other resources may be available. Supports and resources vary from country to country, jurisdiction to jurisdiction, and city to city. We may need to do some searching and make phone calls, or point the young person and their family towards likely starting places. Supports around education, medical and physical rehabilitation, financial assistance and further therapy are some of the needs our clients may have.

Many of the kids we work with have fallen behind academically, or have learning disabilities, but have potential for ongoing education. Students with learning disabilities or mental health diagnoses are often eligible for added support in high school, college and university. If a young person has been diagnosed with a dissociative disorder or with complex post-traumatic stress disorder, this may allow them to access academic supports that will help them be successful. High school students can sometimes be allowed to complete some of their coursework at home if anxiety interferes with them attending during difficult periods. They can also often receive extra learning resources and supports to accommodate difficulties. In my part of Canada, a young person who is determined to be "disabled," even if the disability is temporary, can attend postsecondary education taking sixty percent of a full caseload while still being considered a "full time" student. This is helpful in accessing student funding. I have also helped students negotiate longer exam times, extended time frames for assignments, audio texts, and added computer technologies. Many young people who are wards of the child welfare system may be eligible for funding for postsecondary education. In Canada they can also remain wards until twenty-one if they are in school or disabled. This means that their living and medical expenses are supported.

The word *disabled* can have negative meanings, and the label of disability can contribute negative beliefs to a young person's identity. I am concerned about labels, but I am also concerned about helping our young clients receive whatever assistance is necessary and available. Many young people with complex trauma disorders are disabled in ways that impact on their ability to cope in regular school settings or the workplace. Often these disabilities are temporary—the developmental trajectory has been set back by their need to focus first on survival and then on healing. For many older adolescents heading into adulthood, being found to be disabled can provide them with financial and medical benefits that can give them the chance to catch up on their education and move towards a rewarding future. James struggled with severe learning disabilities as well as a dissociative disorder during his school years. Being identified as a disabled student allowed him to access academic supports, computer technologies and financial assistance which contributed to his being able to attend college and university.

Some of the young people we work with are disabled physically as well as emotionally as a result of their trauma experiences. Beth was diagnosed with cervical cancer at the age of twelve, as a result of having contracted human papilloma virus through childhood abuse. She has experienced chronic damage to her muscles, tendons and joints and requires orthodontic work resulting from physical abuse. Intelligent, motivated and increasingly resilient, Beth has been able to access a number of supports for disabled youth and for victims of violence which have helped her receive the medical and dental treatment and financial supports necessary to improve her life and attend postsecondary education.

The end of therapy with us may not be the end of therapy. Some children enter in and out of therapy with the same or different therapists many times. It is sometimes necessary for young people to have long-term therapy. Other times, it's helpful for them to have briefer periods of treatment as needed. This may help them not incorporate "client" into their identity. Some young people will age out of the children's mental health system and need to transition into adult therapy. Identifying other resources for treatment, and the potential for return or moving on, is part of planning for the future.

Termination

Termination is important in the therapeutic process. For clients whose early relationships have been a source of trauma or anxiety, termination can either be a healing experience or a reenactment of traumatic loss. The end of therapy is triggering and potentially overwhelming. When termination occurs abruptly and without appropriate processing, the experience can undermine the gains made in treatment. In individual therapy the therapist is cast in the role of the primary attachment figure. When ending attachment-focused phase-oriented therapy the caregiver has been recast in the primary attachment role and remains available to the child or adolescent. This can make the ending of treatment less difficult, but still presents the opportunity of creating a healing experience through a positive, resolved separation. Although the involvement of an attachment figure is protective, it's still necessary to address the end of therapy in a planned, sensitive manner.

The termination process begins with the beginning of therapy. From the outset there is an understanding that therapy is a process with a beginning, middle and end which is expressed throughout treatment by contracting and reviewing goals and progress. This understanding may not be obvious to children and adolescents unless it is made explicit early and repeatedly. The ending of therapy should not come as a surprise to the child, the caregiver or the therapist. Early questions such as "how will you know when you don't need to come to therapy anymore," asked in first and second sessions, help to set the stage for an understanding of therapy as a time limited process. Even when this is discussed at the beginning, it should be revisited throughout treatment. A periodic review of the progress of therapy and what still needs to be achieved can be helpful to keep treatment focused and on track, and to keep the future endpoint visible.

Connection, relationships and separations can be painful for all of us, and can be more difficult for those with attachment-related difficulties. When young people begin to feel connected they may distance themselves by missing appointments, becoming disconnected during sessions or ending treatment altogether. I have found it helpful to label this possibility early on during treatment. I say something like, "We've talked about how it can be hard for you to trust people. I've noticed for some kids, when they start to feel like they're getting connected, or maybe that they've let me know too much about themselves, they start feeling uncomfortable about coming and think about ways to not come. Sometimes they notice this themselves, sometimes they don't. That's a really normal thing to have happen, and if it starts to happen for you, we should probably talk about it and see if we can find a way to make it easier."

Towards the end of treatment, it's not uncommon for young people to take sometimes drastic actions to take control of the process. I have found this particularly true in a children's mental health setting, when sometimes the ending arrives because of the child's age, and not because they've reached the end point of treatment. I had been working with Joe for about eight months. He knew that treatment would need to end before his nineteenth birthday. One day, shortly after his eighteenth birthday, I called him to him to reschedule an appointment by one day due to a clinical emergency on another case. I spoke to him directly, and he appeared fine with the change. He called that night, after hours, and left a message stating, "I've decided not to come to our appointment. You obviously have more important things to do, and I don't think I can work with a liar." This was not the first time an appointment had been rescheduled, and prior to this we had worked together in a warm and collaborative way. I contacted him and encouraged him to come in and meet with me to discuss his feelings, but he refused. He stated, "I'm an adult now, and you don't work with adults, so you obviously just want to get rid of me." He refused to talk about it any further. Another young man, Gary, simply stopped showing up on his eighteenth birthday. I would call him to reschedule, and he would be very apologetic, claim to have forgotten, and schedule a new appointment that he would then also not attend. Prior to his birthday he had attended every scheduled session on time, like clockwork. These situations do happen, and I haven't found a way to completely prevent them. They can often be worked with and resolved. Such absolute impasses have been rare, particularly when working with an adult caregiver who supports the process. It should be noted that both the young men mentioned above were in individual therapy, not having a caregiver who was available to participate. Even in individual treatment, however, it is usually the case that when their concerns and anxieties are listened to with caring and empathy, the adolescent will return to treatment.

Greenberg describes eight principles to ending therapy.[5] These principles provide a useful guide to ensure that termination is a helpful, healing end point to the relationship. They are:

1. ending, like therapy, is a collaboration;
2. ending is a "choice point" that is reached in reviewing the process, not a predetermined time frame or set of met goals;
3. a therapeutic ending needs a process of separation;
4. the ending reflects client empowerment;
5. ending is a time to consolidate new meanings arrived at in treatment;
6. ending is a time to create realistic as opposed to idealised expectations about change;
7. endings should involve the tapering down of treatment rather than a sudden ending;
8. endings should include the discussion of the possibility for future treatment.

Jay Lebow describes a similar process involving ten steps.[6] His process involves:

1. tracking progress in therapy to determine the appropriateness of termination;
2. reviewing the course of treatment;
3. emphasising the gains made and the client's role in these gains;
4. abstracting what has been learned from the treatment and how it may be applied later;
5. internalising the therapist;
6. considering the ending through the lens of other endings in life;
7. saying good-bye with an opportunity to express gratitude and exchange feelings;
8. discussing the conditions for returning;
9. referring (when necessary);
10. defining post-treatment availability.

What is reflected in these discussions is the understanding that a therapeutic relationship is a real relationship, which involves depth, connection and emotional involvement, not just for our clients, but for us as well. It would be a disservice to ourselves and to our clients to imagine that we could engage in a process as intense and intimate as trauma therapy, sometimes for a period of years, and then walk away as if it shouldn't matter to us. This does not mean that therapy is a personal, social or familial relationship. Therapy is a unique relationship with its own set of purposes and boundaries. This does not stop it from being a real relationship that has meaning to everyone involved.

Nancy McWilliams discusses love as an aspect of the therapeutic relationship.[7] Not just the love of clients for their therapists, but the love of therapists for their clients. The use of words such as *love* and *intimacy* stress the humanity inherent in a relationship of this type. When we process the ending of our therapeutic relationships, it's important that we are able to stay real, present and genuine. We need to be able to explore with our clients the meaning of the work and the relationship for us, not just for them. It is this mutuality that can help move the termination into an exploration of the real ending of a real relationship. It is also because of the reality of the relationship that I stress agreement with both Greenberg and Lebow about a discussion around the possibility of future contacts or the return for further therapy. Many young people need to know that they can call, or book a time to come for a coffee and an update now and then. I generally leave this option open, particularly with those for whom therapy has been long or intense. I haven't had this option misused, nor have I felt that my previous clients have unrealistic demands or expectations. I'm open about the limitations of time and scheduling. I frequently receive enjoyable updates and warm messages from young people who remember the work we've done together as they move forward into the future.

The completion of phase three is the end of the termination process. The concept of therapy being "complete" is somewhat like the concept of education being "complete." We will never know everything, nor will we ever resolve everything. Life is a lifelong process. We look instead for the choice point referred to by Greenberg. I tell the young people I work with that no one should be in therapy forever, that therapy should not be the focus of their lives or part of their identity. Trauma therapy is a process (one of many) by which we explore and heal what has been hurt. Often, when school, friends and activities become more important that coming to talk to me, it's a sign that this part of the journey is ready to end.

Notes

1. Chu, J. A. (2011). The therapeutic roller coaster: Phase oriented treatment for complex PTSD. In *Rebuilding Shattered Lives: Treating Complex PTSD and Dissociative Disorders*. John Wiley and Sons. New York.
2. Browne, A., & Finkelhor, D. (1986, January). Impact of child sexual abuse: A review of the research. *Psychological Bulletin, 99*(1), 66–77.
3. Yates, A. (1982). Children eroticized by incest. *American Journal of Psychiatry, 139*, 482–485.
4. Friedrich, W. N. (1993). Sexual victimization and sexual behaviour in children: A review of the recent literature. *Child Abuse and Neglect, 17*, 59–66.

5. Greenberg, L. (2002). Termination of experiential psychotherapy. *Journal of Psychotherapy Integration, 12*, 358–363.
6. Lebow, J. L. (1987). Developing a personal integration in family therapy: Principles for Model Construction and Practice. *Journal of Marital and Family Therapy, 13*(1), 1–14.
7. McWilliams, N. (2004). *Psychoanalytic Psychotherapy: A Practitioner's Guide*. Guilford. New York. pp 70–71.

12 External Systems

In child and adolescent therapy there are often larger systems involved. Group homes, child welfare organisations, hospitals and schools become part of the team. A community team that works well together can provide a holistic approach that supports the child or adolescent through recovery. This can be remarkably difficult to achieve. The team members are there to help and support the child. This does not mean the same thing to each system. Beyond helping the child, each part of the team is focused on their role, the needs of their organisation and the needs of other children they serve. For example, the school's focus is education, not mental health. The school needs to consider the needs of other children in the class and school and the needs of the teachers and support staff. Each person on the team has their own background, histories, training, relative experience or inexperience, and their own beliefs and understandings of what the child needs. It can be a struggle to pull together a team from different agencies that can cooperate and work well together. Young people with complex trauma or dissociative disorders present challenges to this already difficult process.

Transference and countertransference have a significant impact on the process and outcome of therapy. "Survivors of childhood trauma bring the abuse related interpersonal assumptions of their childhood trauma into their (adult) relationships, including the therapeutic relationship."[1] Our clients have different worldviews than we do, and this plays itself out repeatedly in the ways they experience us—ways which are different from the ways we see ourselves. Chu reminds us that

> despite therapists' efforts to be helpful and benign, they will not always be regarded as such. Therapists must recognize that no matter how kind, tolerant or skilled they may be, they will find themselves as the objects of "traumatic transferences," being regarded as abusers and being the object of patients' anger, suspicion and even sadism.[2]

Putnam discusses transference and countertransference with clients with dissociative identity disorders in *Diagnosis and Treatment of Multiple Personality Disorder.*[3] Transference and countertransference refer to the unconscious dynamics of previous relationships which are repeatedly played out within the therapeutic relationship. These dynamics are both a complication and a tool as we help the kids we work with understand the impact of their earlier relationships. Clients with dissociative identity disorders have more than one reaction simultaneously to each situation and relationship, and so form multiple transference relationships with their therapist and with others in positions of authority or support. Putnam's discussion refers specifically to clients with dissociative identity disorders; in my experience this generalises to all traumatised clients. One does not have to have a dissociative identity disorder to experience complex and confusing ambivalence. It is this ambivalence combined with internalisation of lack of safety in relationships which leads to what is referred to as "splitting" in clinical environments.

When I first entered the field and learned about "splitting," it was viewed as intentionally manipulative behaviour that kept the individual in a position of power or control. Over the years I've come to experience it differently. I am sure that there are people who engage in intentionally controlling and manipulative behaviours. I suspect that even among those who are intentional and aware in their actions deep fears and anxieties are factors. Mostly I've experienced young people (and adults) responding in the ways that feel safest to them in the moment, while still attempting to get support and connection. Because being direct about conflict has never been safe, the result is splitting.

Consider Elizabeth, who I worked with years ago. Elizabeth was fourteen and a half on entering therapy. She was one of a group of sisters in the care of a local child welfare agency because of physical, sexual, and emotional abuse and family violence. All of the girls were referred to my agency for treatment, with me seeing the older two and a coworker seeing the younger three. All five had serious emotional difficulties. Several had dissociative symptoms. My initial interview with Elizabeth and her caseworker revealed an engaging, open and insightful girl, eager to engage in therapy. She seemed verbal and bright, but immature and vulnerable.

As treatment with the girls progressed, there was a continuous shifting and changing in the information regarding what had happened to them. It's difficult to manage placement issues in a sibling group, and there are many considerations. This was twenty years ago, and none of us had an understanding of the complexities we were dealing with. The situation was chaotic and confusing. We attempted to take a team approach, with planning conferences between the child welfare agencies, placement agencies and therapists. This was a good start. As happens, competing needs arose early, along with disagreements between agencies, group homes and foster parents over which needs took priority. My agency began to feel we were not being heard, and that the children's mental health needs were not understood. In retrospect I can see that we were equally unable to hear the complexity of the child protection, case management and placement needs that the other players were attempting to manage. As therapists the mental health needs were our priority. For the other team members, they were one consideration among many.

Things became strained between our agency and the other players. There were upheavals in the family, and these took an emotional toll on Elizabeth and her siblings. Elizabeth moved from our residential treatment into a foster home, at about the same time that she and her sisters became permanent wards. There were hints that she was acting out at school and in the foster home in ways that seemed out of character, but these were vague. I went on vacation, and while I was away her placement broke down. Neither she, her new placement staff nor her social worker were able to explain what had gone wrong. It seemed clear to me that her new placement did not "get her." (Of course I didn't quite get her either.) She came to therapy sessions devastated about being taunted and bullied by peers, and not listened to by staff. She told me how she had talked to her social worker about the problem, and that her social worker had witnessed staff treating her unfairly and disrespectfully, and ignored it. When I attempted to problem solve with the staff, it was like they were talking about a different person—not just different from the one I knew, but different from the one that her social workers, foster parents and previous placements knew. They talked about her as a manipulative and disruptive force. They came across as closed and nonresponsive to my efforts at creating a team, in spite of our having worked well together in the past. What I did not know is that there were parts of Elizabeth who did not like me. Elizabeth was enraged at her biological mother for not protecting her and her sisters from their abusive father. She talked about this anger in therapy, and I supported her feelings. A different part of Elizabeth was allied with her mother, and angry at my support of Elizabeth. This part saw me as being allied with Elizabeth against her family. She talked to her staff about not trusting me because I "bad-mouthed" her mother and wanted to undermine her wishes to maintain this relationship. This part had nothing good to say about me, and so the staff in her group home and her social worker began to see me as not supporting her well. During those several months, I met only the Elizabeth that was fully engaged in treatment, but felt vulnerable and unsafe in her group home. The staff and her social worker met only the Elizabeth that was not at all engaged in treatment, distrusted me and resisted coming to see me. Whenever Elizabeth began to struggle, she would talk in therapy about feeling unsafe in her group home. In her placement, she was angry and hostile. She talked about the things that I was stirring up in therapy sessions. Both were somewhat true. There were large amounts of her negative experiences in the group home, with her social worker, and with me in therapy, that were unheard and being unprocessed. We were unaware that we weren't being caring and responsive. We each, however, thought the others were being uncaring and unresponsive. In these situations, as the mistrust grows, so does the countertransference experience of being the "only safe person who can understand and protect the child."

Eventually, the other Elizabeth, "Justine," attended a therapy session and let me have it for supporting Elizabeth's anger at her mother. She announced that I was simply stupid to believe childish Elizabeth, and that I had been completely sucked in by her. Shortly afterwards Elizabeth was diagnosed with a dissociative identity disorder, and some of the conflict was smoothed over.

The diagnosis did not completely clear things up, although it temporarily helped to determine treatment directions. At that time, DID was an unusual diagnosis. Mistrust had developed between the involved agencies, and the new diagnosis did nothing to help with that. As long as treatment was going well, relationships were smooth, but as soon as there was trouble, the old suspicions returned. Teenagers can respond pretty quickly to treatment, and it was only a few months before Elizabeth was mostly coconscious and using therapy to resolve some of her trauma and take control of her life. We worked well together for about another year, and then there was a crisis in her family. She began to struggle emotionally and behaviourally.

The guarded atmosphere of distrust became more open. Elizabeth's guardian attempted to take control of the therapy, asking that I stop working on dissociation, and work instead on behaviour. I felt defensive and attacked, as well as concerned for what would happen to the therapy. I stood my ground, and backed my recommendations up with as much documentation as possible. Defensiveness, of course, didn't help. We didn't trust each other, and Elizabeth was good at sensing this. Remember that young people with complex trauma histories are expert at recognising when the adults in their lives are focused on their own needs and issues, and on surviving in conflict situations. No matter how clear the position in the conflict seems at the time, it creates an atmosphere lacking in child focus and safety for the young person. Not surprisingly, Elizabeth's choice was to end therapy and to leave care. She was then sixteen, and legally able to make that decision for herself.

It's possible to look back on this case and see mistrust between agencies played out against the backdrop of an early misunderstanding of dissociative disorders. The dynamic was more complex by far, and there was a lot to be learned from Elizabeth and the ways in which she responded to the system and the system responded to her. Although it's true that the groups involved do not always trust each other, and that the discomfort around a dissociative disorder diagnosis fed this mistrust, the degree of conflict that arose had many more levels. Unfortunately, the mistrust between the agencies lasted for several years after Elizabeth left the system.

This kind of splitting is the result of both transference and countertransference. All of us played varying roles throughout this reenactment. At different times we played different roles with different parts of Elizabeth. Twenty years later, with more experience and wisdom, I have seen variations of this many times. It still isn't that much easier to see, avoid, negotiate and manage it.

Davies and Frawley describe eight transference/countertransference positions within four relational matrices which are enacted in the therapy of sexual abuse survivors.[4] The positions they describe are: the unseeing, uninvolved parent and the unseen, neglected child; the sadistic abuser and the helpless, impotently enraged victim; the idealised, omnipotent rescuer and the entitled child; and the seducer and the seduced. Each of these positions is complex and played out with varying degrees of unawareness within the individual therapy relationship. When working with children within larger and complex systems, where many different individuals are in positions of power, authority, guidance, nurturing and control with the child, there are many more than four possible matrices and the possible combinations are seemingly endless. Table 12.1 outlines only some of the different combinations which arose during Elizabeth's time in treatment. For the sake of simplicity, I have included only key players. Other roles were simultaneously being filled by Elizabeth's mother, her teachers in various schools she attended, hospital staff during several hospitalisations, consulting psychiatrists and various child welfare authorities. Again, for simplicity's sake, I also included Elizabeth as a whole person, when the experience of the situation was much more fragmented, and her positions were being taken simultaneously be at least two other alters with varying amounts of coconsciousness. The full picture is by far more complex.

The case of Elizabeth is not an unusual one. Complex trauma treatment, with its many layers of trust, shame, fear, anger, righteous indignation, protection, self-protection and competing loyalties on the part of both the client and the therapist, is an intensely complicated endeavor. When working with children and adolescents we must then add parents, caregivers and guardians, foster homes, group homes, child welfare agencies, schools, teachers and teacher's aids, police, courts, lawyers, hospitals, psychiatrists and pediatricians. Overlaying the need for therapy is the need for safety and protection from further harm, education, family, attachment and connection, social justice, legal issues, and physical, emotional and cognitive development. Given that there have been many decades of confusion and misunderstanding over these issues, it isn't surprising that all these players do not always trust and respect each other.

In describing therapy with adult trauma survivors, James Chu writes that "difficulties occur frequently, repeatedly, and with remarkable predictability" and that "an understanding of the traps does not prevent them from occurring. However, an understanding prevents therapists from becoming enmeshed in traps, and helps therapists tolerate them with less anxiety."[5] This is even more accurate when describing working with child and adolescent trauma survivors in conjunction with larger systems. Our best defence is to do our best to build supportive systems with open communication and shared understanding of the issues involved. When I become involved with a child or adolescent who has multisystemic involvement, I attempt to arrange systems meetings with the many players early and often. I am open with the child, adolescent and adults about the limits and obligations around confidentiality. I reassure the young person that the details of their information are safe, and that I won't share information without their consent or knowledge, but I also ask permission to be able to have open conversations and ongoing dialogues around important issues when they arise. I want to be able to share process, rather than content. When possible I try to set up an "email chain" that the young person is a part of, so that information can be shared. When this happens, the information needs to be protected, nondetailed and nonidentifying, but can alert teachers

Table 12.1 Possible Transference/Countertransference Positions for Elizabeth

	Elizabeth	*Myself*	*Child Welfare*	*Residential Staff*
The uninvolved nonabusing parent and the neglected child	Neglected child	Uninvolved nonabusing parent	Uninvolved nonabusing parent	Sadistic abuser
The uninvolved nonabusing parent and the neglected child	Neglected child	Sadistic abuser	Uninvolved nonabusing parent	Uninvolved nonabusing parent
The sadistic abuser and the helpless, impotently enraged victim	Impotently enraged victim	Sadistic abuser	Uninvolved nonabusing parent	Uninvolved nonabusing parent
The sadistic abuser and the helpless, impotently enraged victim	Impotently enraged victim	Uninvolved nonabusing parent	Sadistic abuser	Uninvolved nonabusing parent
The sadistic abuser and the helpless, impotently enraged victim	Impotently enraged victim	Uninvolved nonabusing parent	Uninvolved nonabusing parent	Sadistic abuser
The sadistic abuser and the helpless, impotently enraged victim	Sadistic abuser	Impotently enraged victim	Uninvolved nonabusing parent	Uninvolved nonabusing parent
The sadistic abuser and the helpless, impotently enraged victim	Uninvolved nonabusing parent	Impotently enraged victim	Sadistic abuser	Uninvolved nonabusing parent
The idealised omnipotent rescuer and the entitled child who demands to be rescued	Entitled child who demands to be rescued	Idealised omnipotent rescuer	Sadistic abuser	Uninvolved nonabusing parent
The idealised omnipotent rescuer and the entitled child who demands to be rescued	Entitled child who demands to be rescued	Sadistic abuser	Idealised omnipotent rescuer	Idealised omnipotent rescuer
The seducer and the seduced	Seducer	Seduced	Uninvolved nonabusing parent	Uninvolved nonabusing parent
The seducer and the seduced	Seduced	Seducer	Uninvolved nonabusing parent	Uninvolved nonabusing parent
The seducer and the seduced	Seducer	Uninvolved nonabusing parent	Seduced	Uninvolved nonabusing parent
The seducer and the seduced	Seduced	Uninvolved nonabusing parent	Uninvolved nonabusing parent	Seducer

and staff, for instance, when a young person has had a difficult session, or can alert the therapist when a young person has had a conflict at school. The involvement of a primary caregiver in many of the sessions has the benefit of circumventing some of the hidden communications that can lead to system splitting and team conflicts.

I try to arrange a meeting between adult team members early on, before conflict and confusion arises. Many of the young people have been in adult roles, and hold more responsibility and worry than is helpful around issues such as court, financial considerations, legal difficulties and planning. I always involve my child and adolescent clients in treatment directions, and ensure they have control over issues like pacing, treatment activities and a voice in planning that has a direct impact on them. I do maintain that there are adult jobs and information that they are not responsible for, and that they should not be directly involved in. This is the purpose of meetings of the adult system. Sometimes young people aren't comfortable having me meet with their staff or school to talk about them, but are open to my meeting with them to advise them of issues involved in supporting children with complex trauma disorders. I am open with the child or adolescent about the purpose of the meeting and what will be discussed. Usually when they understand that the meeting is going to help other adults understand that their behaviours and problems make sense, and that this might improve the way these adults see and support them, they are willing to give it a try. I've attended many group home and school meetings to make presentations on complex trauma or dissociative disorders when working with such a child in their system. My presentations are not one-sided. Schools and group homes work with the children in situations where I do not. They will always have information, insights, ideas and questions that I have not thought of. My approach is to ask what they need from me, and what insights they have, that can help us work together as a team. When this is arranged early, when the therapist is a new member of the support system, other team members are eager for ideas and information. Creating a working team is smoother. Once conflict starts it becomes more difficult. It's far better to prevent splitting than to do damage control. I've found that perhaps the easiest way to minimise future difficulties in a child's team is to explain the process of splitting, how behaviour that appears intentional and manipulative is about fear, safety and self-protection, and to talk about the impact that this has on teams. James Chu of course is right. Awareness does not completely avoid traps. At times, it may become impossible not to be pulled into them. These are vulnerable young people whose needs and internal conflicts are very real. There are times when one needs to choose between the child's safety and the integrity of the therapy or the functioning of the treatment team. These are difficult and painful choices. Judith Hermann comments that "They remind us also that moral neutrality in the conflict between victim and perpetrator is not an option. Like all other bystanders, therapists are sometimes forced to take sides."[6]

Consider John (Chapter 7). John was a young man with a dissociative identity disorder resulting from severe early trauma and disrupted attachment. He had had eleven placements in the previous two years. John was at times a sensitive, caring, insightful young man. This was the part that came to therapy. John also never felt safe when in the presence of more than one or two other people. When triggered, he presented with an angry, hostile part that enjoyed starting conflict between others, and felt powerful when others were hurt as a result. He gloated and laughed over others' pain. When this part retreated, John had no memory or awareness of what had transpired, and was devastated and hurt by others' reactions to him. This happened multiple times a day. The result was a young man who was likeable one on one, motivated and determined to change his life, but who was nearly impossible to find a safe placement for. When I met John, he was being abused daily by peers in his group home. He was often bruised and bleeding. He had received emergency medical care several times. He had begged and pleaded to be moved, including launching a formal appeal of his placement with a government review board. He won the appeal, but was not moved because it was impossible to find another placement that would accept him. The staff in his group home were not protecting him. Not because they were bad people, or uncaring, but because in spite of their best efforts, he continuously and seemingly intentionally baited everyone around him, and then denied responsibility. He also baited the staff, setting up cruel and painful pranks, or undermining them to the degree that their jobs were at risk. His social worker was helpless to help him, because attempts to find a new placement had failed repeatedly. This was not a question of who was right and who was wrong. There was no good answer in a system with limitations and imperfections. It was impossible to do therapy with John while he was being retraumatised. It was impossible to work with a system that did not have the resources to protect him. It was impossible not to advocate for him, and to help him find a voice, even knowing that doing this would be experienced by every other part of the system as undermining. John is not one child. John could as easily be Julia or Miguel. John is hundreds of children in impossible situations, whose trauma impact has become more than the system designed to protect them can respond to. I have known many Johns and Julias and Miguels, and I will know more. The best hope for them is to begin to build a system that can identify early the impacts of severe trauma, and build in supports before eleven placements break down. This involves teamwork, compromise and breaking down barriers of mistrust that have developed over decades.

When involvement happens early, and we respond to young people in a unified, caring and supportive way, other outcomes happen. Sophie's foster parents and school have worked hard to create a responsive, attuned environment, and her meltdowns and dramatic dissociative episodes have decreased. Amie's group home and school were open to communication and teamwork from the start, and she has made incredible gains in the years since I met her. James's school responded from the start, working together with him and with me to meet his needs. He has integrated, graduated from high school and done well in college. Tony's social worker and group home worked hard to understand how his rages were connected to his mistrust and rejection. He has since moved into a long-term foster home and is doing well. What these young people have in common, beyond their own resilience and willingness to keep working at healing, is that those involved in their care were able to come together, talk, share, compromise and learn from each other. This has never been smooth and easy, but it is always necessary.

Notes

1. Chu, J. A. (2011). *Rebuilding Shattered Lives: Treating Complex PTSD and Dissociative Disorders*. John Wiley and Sons. New York. p 120.
2. Chu, J. A. (2011). The therapeutic roller coaster: Phase oriented treatment for complex PTSD. In *Rebuilding Shattered Lives: Treating Complex PTSD and Dissociative Disorders*. John Wiley and Sons. New York. p 122.
3. Putnam, F. W. (1989). *Diagnosis and Treatment of Multiple Personality Disorder*. Guilford. New York. pp 183–196.
4. Davies, Jody M., & Frawley, Mary G. (1994). *Treating the Adult Survivor of Childhood Sexual Abuse*. New York. Basic Books. pp 167–185.
5. Chu, J. A. (1988). Ten traps for therapists in the treatment of trauma survivors. *Dissociation, 1*(4), 24–32.
6. Hermann, J. (1992). *Trauma and Recovery: The Aftermath of Violence from Domestic Abuse to Political Terror*. Basic Books. New York. pp 246–247.

Appendix

List of Worksheets

Phase One

Phase Two

Phase Three

The Brain

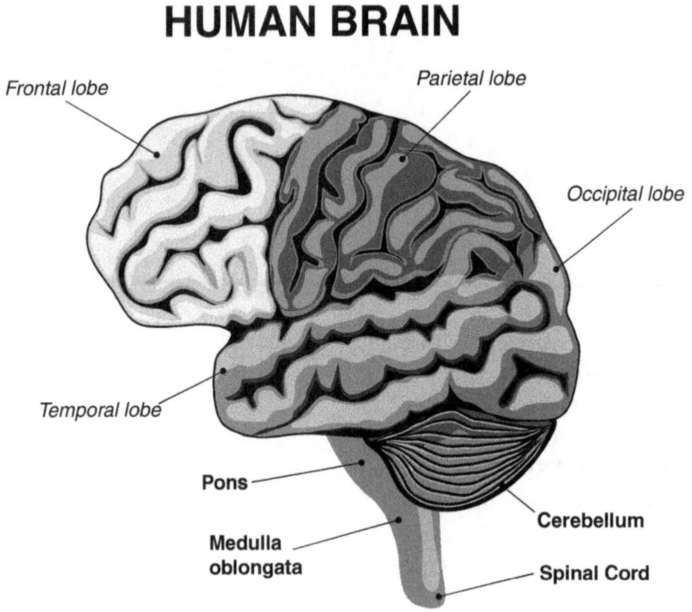

Pictures from Istockphoto

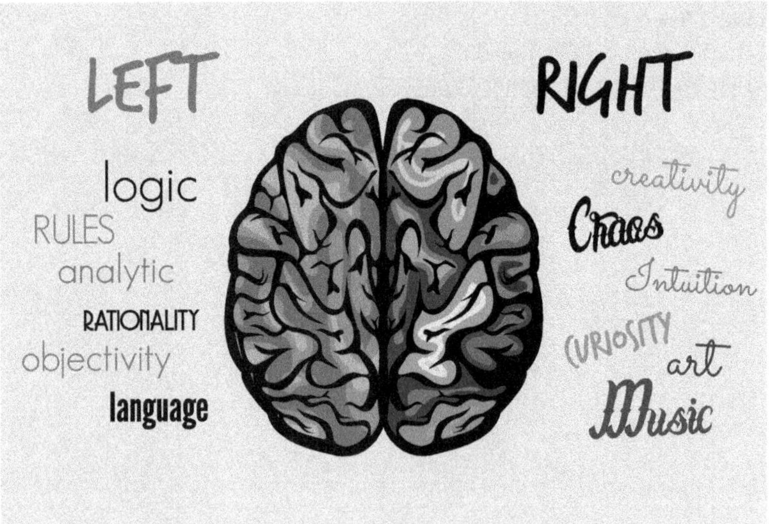

Pictures from Istockphoto

Feelings Thermometers

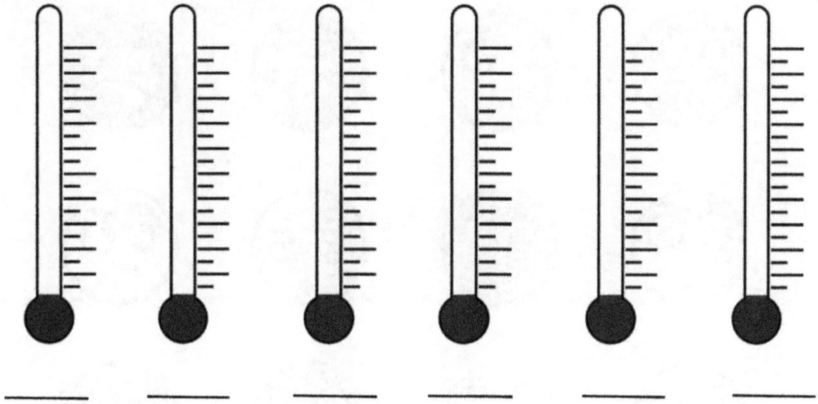

Feelings Chart

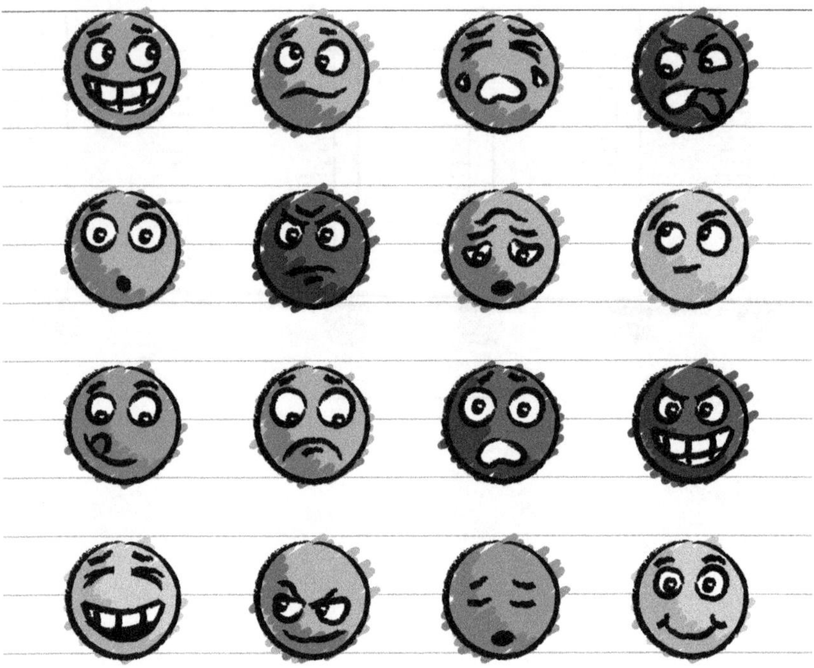

From Istockphoto

Trust Wheel

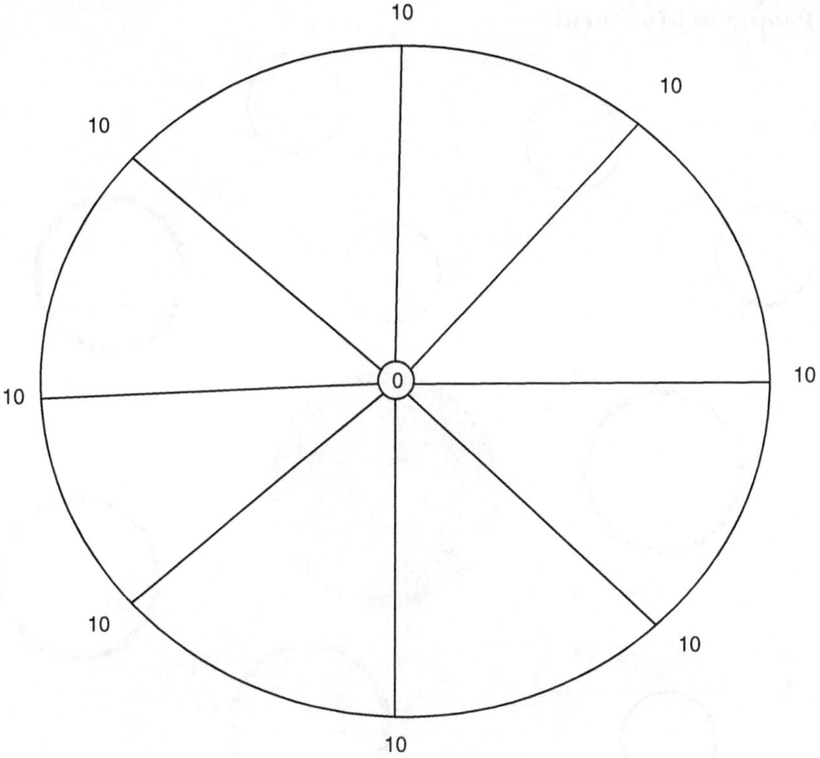

Support Map
People in My World

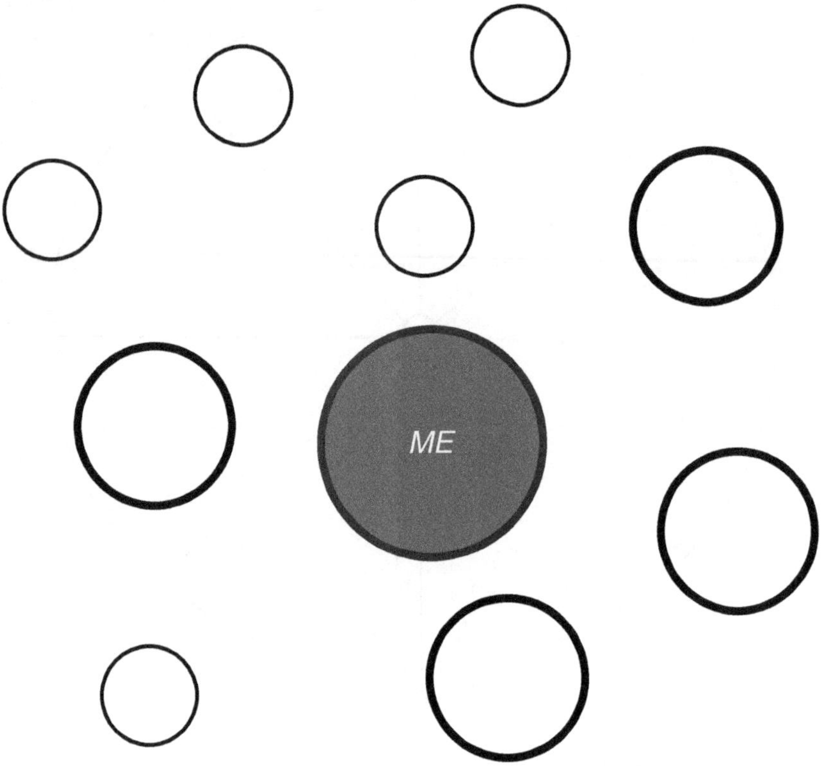

The X, Y and Z Strategies of Coping with Urges

Before you give in to the urge to do something that could be harmful to you, it is recommended that you complete the following sequences of events to reduce this urge. It is important to develop tools to address these urges as most people feel a profound sense of shame after they have given in to the urges that are harmful. Using these tools will eventually provide a sense of mastery over feelings of excruciating pain.

X. Communication

Set a timer for 15 minutes. Use this time to communicate your feelings of pain. This can take the form of:

- Writing in a journal
- Expressing your feelings through artwork (drawing, painting)
- Talking to a friend (in person, by phone, via text or email)
- Calling a crisis line for support

Y. Trigger Endorphins

Set your timer for another 15 minutes. Use this time to trigger your endorphins (your natural physical way of combating stress). Types of activities that fit under this category include:

- hugging a friend
- holding and stroking something soft
- petting a cat or dog
- engaging in laughter
- running or jogging
- speed-walking or swimming
- holding some ice in your hands

Z. Engage in Self-Soothing Behaviours

Set your timer for another 15 minutes. Use this time to engage in self-soothing behaviour. This is a time to be gentle to yourself. Some activities in this category include:

- listening to music
- listening to running water
- enjoying a stroll in your garden or near park
- meditation
- reading (often reflective or inspirational readings help)
- going to a safe place either in your mind or a specific location
- taking a bath or long shower

Stress Map—Boys

Stress Map—Girls

The Iceberg Experience

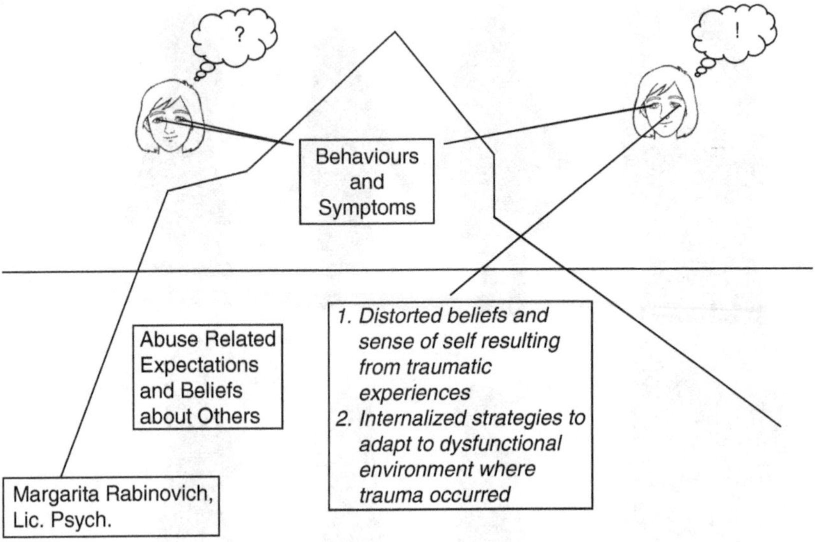

Core Belief Checklist

Belief	I never feel I am	I sometimes feel I am	I always feel I am	True—1–10
Helpless				
Strong				
Not good enough				
Powerless				
Trapped				
Inferior				
As good as others				
Better than others				
Stupid				
Smart				
Lazy				
Damaged				
Weak				
A failure				
A loser				
Needy				
Out of control				
Unlovable				
Lovable				
Unattractive				
Ugly				
Attractive				
Fun to be around				
Weird				
A nerd				
Unwanted				
Unloved				
Cared about				
Important				
Helpful				
A burden				
Boring				
Useless				
Bad				
Dangerous				
Evil				
Disgusting				
Good				

Niki Gomez-Perales, MSW, RSW, 2014

Values Exercise

Importance		Energy
	A comfortable life (money to have enough)	
	An exciting life	
	A sense of accomplishment	
	World peace (free of war and conflict)	
	Protecting the environment	
	Protecting animals	
	Safety	
	Human rights	
	A world of beauty	
	Equality	
	Family	
	Freedom	
	Happiness	
	Inner harmony or inner peace	
	Finding or keeping true love	
	National security (the safety of our country)	
	Pleasure—enjoyment	
	Fun	
	Salvation—religion—spiritual connectedness	
	Popularity	
	Friendship	
	Wisdom	

Friendship Checklist

1. Do you like them?
2. Do you like doing the same things?
3. Do you have fun together?
4. Do you share values?
5. Could you talk to them about a problem?
6. Would you listen to a problem they had?
7. Do you think they care how you feel?
8. Do you ever care how they feel?
9. Do they try to push you around?
10. Do you try to push them around?
11. Do you get into trouble together?
12. Can you do a trust wheel?

Index